P9-CDX-066

BELMONT UNIVERSITY LIBRARY
BELMONT UNIVERSITY
1900 BELMONT BLVD.
NASHVILLE, TN 37212

The World and the West

This book is a study of the interaction of the Western societies of Europe and America with others around the world in the past two centuries – the age of European empire. It deals with the European threat and the non-Western response, but the focus is on the ways in which people in Asia, Africa, and Indian America have tried to adapt their ways of life to the overwhelming European power that existed in this period. The challenge and the response are presented through a series of selected and widely scattered case studies. They vary from those of the Maya and Yaqui of Mexico, to millennial responses as varied as the Ghost Dance or the cargo cults of Melanesia, as well as those of major players like the Ottoman Empire and Meiji Japan.

Philip D. Curtin, the Herbert Baxter Adams Professor of History at the Johns Hopkins University and a fellow of the American Academy of Arts and Sciences, is the author of many books, including *The Image of Africa, The Atlantic Slave Trade: A Census,* and *Death by Migration.*

The World and the West

The European Challenge and the Overseas Response in the Age of Empire

Philip D. Curtin

CAMBRIDGE
UNIVERSITY PRESS

PUBLISHED BY THE PRESS SYNDICATE OF THE UNIVERSITY OF CAMBRIDGE
The Pitt Building, Trumpington Street, Cambridge, United Kingdom

CAMBRIDGE UNIVERSITY PRESS
The Edinburgh Building, Cambridge CB2 2RU, UK   http://www.cup.cam.ac.uk
40 West 20th Street, New York, NY 10011-4211, USA   http://www.cup.org
10 Stamford Road, Oakleigh, Melbourne 3166, Australia
Ruiz de Alarcón 13, 28014 Madrid, Spain

© Philip D. Curtin 2000

This book is in copyright. Subject to statutory exception
and to the provisions of relevant collective licensing agreements,
no reproduction of any part may take place without
the written permission of Cambridge University Press.

First published 2000

Printed in the United States of America

Typeface Caslon 224 10/13.5pt   *System* QuarkXPress™   [HT]

A catalog record for this book is available from the British Library

Library of Congress Cataloging-in-Publication Data

Curtin Philip D.
    The World and the West: the European challenge and the overseas response in the
Age of Empire / by Philip D. Curtin.
        p.   cm.
    ISBN 0 521 77135 8
    1. Civilization, Modern – European influences.   2. Civilization, Modern –
European influences – Case studies.   3. Social change – History.   4. Social change –
History – Case studies.   5. Culture conflict – History.   6. Culture conflict – History
– Case studies.   7. Europe – Territorial expansion.   8. Europe – Territorial
expansion – Case studies.   I. Title.
CB417.C87   2000
909.82 – dc21   99-040254

ISBN 0 521 77135 8 hardback

215577
BELMONT UNIVERSITY LIBRARY

CB
417
. C87
2000

ABF–8609

Contents

Preface

The impact of the West on the rest of the world is a recognized central theme of world history over the past two centuries. At present, when many historians are trying to avoid the ethnocentricity of their predecessors, that fact alone raises problems of interpretation. In the past, historians often concentrated on the history of their own society. Their central question was: How did we come to be as we are? The broader question of how the world around us came to be as it is pushed into the background. The more fundamental question of how human societies change through time was hardly approached.

Today, many historians in Western societies try not to overemphasize the activities of their own ancestors, but they are confronted by the fact that Western societies actually did play a central role in world history during recent centuries. The problem of European dominance is bound up with several interlocked problems in the interpretation of global history. One problem arises from the effort to identify an appropriate central narrative to follow the main line of human development on a global scale. Historians of the United States are used to tracing an account back from the present to the colonial period, and beyond that to Europe. Historians of Europe have arranged their narrative in the sequence of ancient to medieval to modern – and perhaps to postmodern. For the modern period, the building blocks of European history were often taken be national states, and one common theme was to trace the rise and fall of nations in a struggle for predominance within the European state system.

Already in the 1930s, Arnold Toynbee argued that the emphasis on the European nation-state was misplaced. The more useful unit of historical study was whole societies, such as those of the classical antiquity of the Mediterranean, the Western civilization of Europe and its offshoots overseas, or an East Asian society centered on China. Toynbee also gave special emphasis to those societies he considered to have reached the status of civilizations, as opposed to mere primitive societies. The rise and fall of these civilizations, and the relations between them, then provided the main line of development running through his ten-volume *Study of History.* More recently, Marshall Hodgson and William McNeill have been among the historians who have followed in this tradition of a civilization-based grand narrative.

Today, virtually all historians, whether or not they specialize in global history, agree that about the middle of the 1700s, if not sooner, the West became the dominant society in the world and ushered in a European age or an age of European empires. But the rise of the West did not merely introduce a new principal player in patterns of global interchange; it introduced a whole new era in world history. Empires had risen and fallen in the past, but no society had even approached the European degree of control over the whole world. By the end of the 1800s, Western powers had defeated virtually every other contestant on the field of battle, even the Chinese Empire, although they held back from formal annexation of China, and a scattering of other territories.

What was new about Western dominance was the fact that the age of European empires was also the dawn of a new era in world history. Specialists in world history now identify the industrial era as one of the three major periods in the longer run of human history, a tripartite division based not on the rise and fall of civilizations but on changing technology. The earliest of these periods, lasting up to about 10,000 years ago, was a preagricultural age. People lived by hunting and foraging, in groups that were necessarily small and scattered. Stone-age technology changed, but it changed comparatively slowly, presumably because the possibilities of intercommunication were small.

The development of agriculture introduced a new era. It was not simultaneous everywhere but spread outward from at least seven different and independent centers. With farming, population density increased, and with it the possibility of more intense intercommunication. Cities appeared in many different regions; writing was invented independently in places as distant from one another as Mesopotamia and Middle America. The new agricultural age was marked by arable farming, urbanization, literacy, and an increased pace of technological change, though the pace was still slow by recent standards. In all societies of this period, the vast majority of the population spent their lives producing food. Energy from fire was limited to heating and cooking; otherwise people and animals supplied what energy was available, with only a little help from wind and water power. Both birth rates and death rates were high; life expectancy at birth was forty years or less, even in the most successful societies.

Population grew slowly, and spurts of growth in some regions occasionally indicated a rising standard of living. But such spurts were most often cut short by natural disasters, disease, or human enemies. The fact that populations grew, however, implies a growing human ability to master the environment, even though economic growth per capita was comparatively rare and slow.

Then, in about the 1700s, the pace began to change again in some societies, introducing a transition from an agricultural to an industrial age. By the 1800s, contemporary observers began to talk about an industrial revolution, but the term is a misnomer. It was industrial in a narrow sense of dependency on steam power and factories, but rather in a broader increase in productivity per capita. For the first time in history, farmers and other food producers became a minority of the whole population – a minority capable of producing enough food for everybody else.

Nor was it revolutionary in the sense of rapid change followed by a return to stability. Technological change became more rapid than ever before, and the new pace continued through the past two centuries, with new sources of power, a broad victory over infectious disease, and new ways of mobilizing and transmitting knowledge. Life expectancy in the most advanced societies is now more than seventy years. The drop in death rates has been balanced by a decline in birth rates, so that the reproductive burden on women has been vastly reduced. This in turn brought revolutionary changes in relations between the sexes, as more women joined the nondomestic work force.

This sequence of a preagricultural, to an agricultural, to an industrial age was based on cumulative technical achievement, but it implies no general law of human progress. Humans have discovered more efficient ways of doing things, but there is no evidence that they are wiser than their ancestors in deciding what to do with their new abilities. After the bloodbath of European fighting in the First World War and the Second World War, the Holocaust, and the present threat to environmental resources, it is impossible to predict that humans will use their new technical prowess more wisely than they used their smaller powers in the past. In the past half-century, moreover, humans have achieved the technical ability to make the planet uninhabitable by their descendants.

These three stages in technology had a profound influence on the interaction of human cultures, including relations between the West and the rest of the world in recent centuries. In the preagricultural period, human cultures diverged. With little contact between sparse and scattered populations, opportunities to borrow ideas or techniques were rare. Most people had to make do with what they could discover for themselves. Languages diverged. Problems of adjusting to the natural environment had to be solved over and over again as humans left the African homeland. Even the agriculture that was to prepare the way for more rapid change was discovered several times in several places.

The more intense intercommunication that followed the agricultural revolution made it possible to learn what others had invented independently. Instead of diverging, human cultures began to converge, first in the regions of early agriculture, then bridging the gaps between them, and finally, only after several millennia, reaching the most isolated populations such as those of Australia and the Americas. The agricultural age did not arrive simultaneously everywhere, but when it did arrive, it created new patterns of culture change. Military innovations such as horse-drawn chariots, cavalry, and gunpowder spread to most of Afro-Eurasia. Religions that were to become the present-day world religions, such as Buddhism, Islam, and Christianity, spread broadly beyond their region of origin.

Outlines of cultures areas like those that Toynbee recognized emerged – an Islamic civilization growing outward from the Middle East, a broad south Asian culture based on India, and at least two in the Americas. During the past two millennia, the culture area we now call Western Civilization, or simply the West, emerged from a fusion of elements from the Roman Mediterranean and others from northern Europe.

The technological base of the industrial age first appeared full-blown in Europe, though it has derived in large part from innovations originating in other societies, of which the spinning wheel, the compass, the alphabet, and gunpowder are only the best known. It has since spread very broadly to the non-Western world, just as agriculture spread gradually to societies other than those that originated it. For a brief period of only about two centuries, however, the West was so much the industrial leader that the Western societies and industrializing societies were nearly coterminous. This temporary Western quasi-monopoly of the things that made the industrial age possible makes it difficult to achieve an even-handed perspective on the history of the world in this period.

It is easy to recognize the central theme as the globalization of human affairs under European leadership. Historians first began more than a century ago to deal with this theme in the context of European history, as the history of European imperialism. Other approaches to this grand narrative have centered on European economic achievement, on a capitalist world system centered in Europe, or simply on the process of globalization itself.

The essays that follow represent another approach to world history in a European age, centered on changing relations between the world and the West, this time through a series of cases studies rather than an overriding theory. This approach is based on the conviction that theory and broad generalizations often conceal so many exceptions that they are in danger of becoming only vague reflections of reality. Case studies, in turn, can only be a partial reflection of the broader processes of history, but they make it possible to stay closer to the empirical data on which all good history must be based. The whole truth is not available to historians in any case, and it is not possible to tell all possible partial truths at the same time. It may be that the sum of partial truths, arrived at by asking a variety of different questions about the past, may lead to a better understanding of how human societies change through time. Different questions also lead to different answers, and these essays represent an effort to ask a variety of different questions about relations between the world and the West in recent centuries. There is no recognized term for this attitude toward historical knowledge, but eclectic empiricism can serve as well as any other.

Historians must necessarily select from what is knowable about the past, and they have often concentrated on the doings of great men, top nations, or great civilizations, unconsciously setting aside the activities of women, the ordinary run of men, or societies whose achievements failed to attract Western admiration. Over the past half-century or so, many historians have shied away from the elitism of this approach. Looking at the relations between the world and the West through discrete case studies makes it possible to take some account of the affairs of the less successful and less powerful people and societies, whose role in history is often neglected.

Though it is important to deal with losers as well as winners, the rise of European power in the early industrial age is necessarily at center stage. The industrial revolution began in Europe, and the West was the first society to use the new technology to create an economic system capable of productivity per capita beyond the wildest dreams of the agricultural age – and to couple this new wealth with enormous advances in mass consumption.

These essays deal with the age of European empire and its background, concentrating on the period of the most overt empire building in the past two centuries. European industrial power was important, but it is not the principal concern of these essays. Nor is European imperialism, nor even the political and military responses of the non-Europeans the central concern, though they enter the picture. These essays focus on culture change, using the term in its broadest sense to represent a people's whole way of life. Culture is taken to include art and letters, religion, and values, but it also includes material techniques, kinship systems, agriculture, educational practices, and much more. Cultural history, however, is a rich and developing field of scholarship, but it is based in a different meaning of culture and it is not a concern in these essays.

The central theme is the recent appearance of a long-run aspect of world history. Just as human cultures diverged in the preagricultural period, they began converging with the beginning of agriculture, and continued converging on a vast scale in the industrial age. Human cultures are increasingly homogenized, for better or worse. Some of this process has taken place under the aegis of European empires, but not all. The pace of change was often as rapid outside the European sphere as within it, though often in direct response to the European threat, and it has continued and even accelerated after the liquidation of the European empires.

Some commentators have called this change a revolution of modernization, but modernization is dangerously ambiguous. It can mean change in any aspect of culture toward the model of the most successful societies at a particular time. *Modern* in this sense is obviously a changing concept. The effort to become more modern in the 1890s was different from a similar effort in the 1990s. The term can also take on overtones of Western ethnocentricity. In common Western usage, especially in the 1950s through the 1970s, modernization simply meant becoming more like the West. Social scientists at the time developed a body of modernization theory, largely concerned with how the rest of the world could catch up.

Much of modernization theory has gone out of fashion, and much of it can be set aside, but modernization is still a useful concept if the meaning of the term is strictly limited. It is used here to mean the aspiration to achieve, or the fact of achieving, some kind of society that is capable of the *kind* of high production and high consumption of goods per capita achieved by the most technologically advanced societies of the time. The definition is important because the term has been used so indiscriminately as to lose precision. It is also important to underline the possibility of being modern in this sense without simply imitating the Western way of life.

Modernization following this redefinition can involve borrowing from Western culture, just as the original achievement of Western modernization involved borrowing from others, but high economic productivity and high consumption can be achieved without becoming Western in other respects, or even capitalistic in a strict definition of that term. In this context, modernizing simply means trying to achieve the promise implicit in the technology of the industrial age.

The first three chapters deal with the technological sources of European power and with patterns of empire building around the world. The second part, also three chapters, deals with selected examples of culture change among non-Western people under European rule, with emphasis on the choices available and the choices taken by conquerors and conquered alike. The third part deals with culture change on non-Western initiative among people who felt the threat of Western power but were still free of Western rule. The final part deals with culture change in the important period of the European liquidation of overseas empires in the third quarter of the twentieth century.

Acknowledgements

I should like to thank, as always, the efficient staff of the express and interlibrary loan departments at the Eisenhower Memorial Library of the Johns Hopkins University. I am also especially grateful to friends and colleagues who have taken the trouble to read and criticize all or part of the manuscript at an earlier stage. They are Michael Adas, Anne Curtin, Charles Gilbert, Franklin Knight, and William Rowe. I alone am responsible, of course, for the occasions on which I have failed to take their good advice.

I should also acknowledge my indebtedness to Arnold J. Toynbee for the title *The World and the West,* which he used for his 1952 Reith Lectures, published by Oxford University Press in 1953.

Further Reading

Bentley, Jerry H., "Cross-Cultural Integration and Periodization in World History," *American Historical Review,* 101:749–70 (1996).

Curtin, Philip D. (ed.), *Imperialism* (New York: Walker & Company, 1971).

Gellner, Ernest, *Plough, Sword, and Book: The Structure of Human History* (Chicago: Chicago University Press, 1989).

Hodgson, Marshall G. S., *Rethinking World History: Essays on Europe, Islam, and World History* (New York: Cambridge University Press, 1993), edited by Edmund Burke III.

Jones, E. L., *Growth Recurring: Economic Change in World History* (New York: Oxford University Press, 1988).

McNeill, William, *The Rise of the West* (Chicago: The University of Chicago Press, 1963).

Smith, Bruce D., *The Emergence of Agriculture* (New York: Scientific American Library, 1994).

PART ONE

Conquest

The word *colonialism* is often a misnomer, used for any form of domination of one society over another. The original Greek meaning of a colony implied an outward migration from a mother city or metropolis to settle in a new place. True colonization in this original sense is represented today by examples such as the United States and Canada, where culture change took place but was mainly carried by a blanket immigration of Europeans who brought their culture with them. The Native Americans were pushed aside to become a small minority, sometimes culturally assimilated, sometimes not.

Another variety of so-called colonialism is demographically the reverse of true colonization. It is more accurately labeled territorial empire, where Europeans conquered a territory overseas but sent a negligible number of settlers beyond the administrative and military personnel required to control it. Examples of this type would be British rule in India and Nigeria.

A third, mixed case, midway between territorial empire and true colonization, also sometimes occurred. In these instances, European settlers were a substantial minority, living alongside other cultural communities of native inhabitants. The result is often called a plural society. A rough line between plural societies and true empires can be drawn when the settler community reaches more than about 5 percent of the total population. The important instances of plural societies in the past century or so are South Africa, Algeria, Israel, some Latin American countries, such as Peru or Guatemala, and many parts of the former Soviet Union.

The three chapters of Part I set the scene. The first deals with the emerging pattern of European dominance in the world. The second deals with roots of that dominance in European development and history. The third deals with the politics of European empire building overseas.

1

The Pattern of Empire

The conventional history of European empire building not only lumps dissimilar experiences under the rubric of colonialism, but it often, and too readily, accepts convenient fictions, concocted by long-dead publicists, historians, and government officials, in place of reality. Historians in recent decades have made great progress in correcting this European bias, but much remains to be done.

One tendency of past historiography, not yet altogether corrected, is the tendency to read backward from the clear pattern of European dominance in the recent past, assuming that it was the case in earlier periods as well. Territorial empire and large-scale true colonization have origins that can be traced to these earlier times, but they flourished only in the period since about 1800, or even later.

In earlier centuries, the most important modes of culture contact were commercial, mediated by trade diasporas or the settlement of merchants along a trade route to facilitate commerce. These commercial settlers came only in small numbers but were often extremely important in the process of culture change. They were, in a sense, professional cross-cultural brokers, facilitating trade between the home region and its commercial outposts. Examples can be found in the earliest urban societies of Mesopotamia and in the pre-Columbian Americas.

Many early trade diasporas were comparatively peaceful, living on sufferance with the permission, often the good will as well, of the rulers of the territory where they settled. Dating back to the medieval Mediterranean, European trade diasporas often took a more violent form, where Genoese and Venetian not only settled in alien trading

3

towns but seized the towns themselves and used them as bases for intercity competition in warfare as well as commerce. They rarely aspired to territorial control beyond those strong points, which is why militarized trade diasporas of this type are often called trading-post empires.

Between about 1425 and 1525, when the remnants of Magellan's fleet returned to Spain, European mariners revolutionized human ability to travel by sea and return. The achievement depended on a combination of improved vessels and navigational techniques with increased geographic knowledge, including the outlines of the world wind system. Before this time in world history, regular and routine navigation had been limited to coastal voyages and to some travel on inland seas such as the Mediterranean, though offshore voyages were common in the monsoon belt that stretched east and west from Indonesia to Africa and north through the South China Sea to Japan. After the 1520s, however, European mariners could sail to any coast in the world, though at considerable cost and danger at first.

This maritime revolution gave Europeans their first significant military advantage. They had, as yet, no technical advantage in the Mediterranean, where during the 1500s the Ottoman Turks were at least their equal. Overseas it was different. Maritime technology often made Europeans locally supreme in distant seas, where opposing ships mounting effective artillery were virtually unknown. Seapower also had the strategic advantage of mobility to concentrate the available force on a single objective.

It was the mobility of seapower that made it possible for Europeans to build trading-post empires at a time when they were still inferior militarily on land. In the early 1500s, when the Portuguese first began to send naval expeditions east of the Cape of Good Hope, they often chose as their bases islands such as Goa in western India, with secondary centers at Mozambique in East Africa, Melaka in Malaya, and Macau in south China. In the early 1600s, the Dutch established a similar network based on Batavia (now Jakarta) on Java, with connections westward to Ceylon and the east coast of India and north to an island in Nagasaki harbor in Japan. The English shortly entered the picture at Bombay, Madras, and Calcutta in India. France and other European maritime states followed with their own sets of competing trading posts. These trade enclaves were no threat to major Asian powers, but they were the entering wedge from which territorial empires were to spread in later centuries.

Overland trading-post empires soon began to appear as well. In the 1600s, French fur traders fanned out to the west of the lower St. Lawrence River valley by way of the Great Lakes. English fur traders reached south from Hudson Bay. Neither had any interest in controlling territory or ruling over the Native American populations; they only wanted a secure base for trade and protection from rival European traders. In Asia at the same period, fur traders from Muscovy were extending their trading-post empire eastward across Siberia to the Pacific. In time, these overland trading-post empires were to form the background for territorial empire and true colonization in both North America and Siberia.

Empire in the Americas

In the Americas, and in the Americas alone, European territorial empires date from the 1500s. Here, the European maritime advantage intersected with a particular American vulnerability. The ancestors of the American Indians had crossed the land bridge from Asia during the last Ice Age, up to about 10,000 years ago. Their passage occurred before the agricultural revolution, hence before the development of diseases like smallpox, which grew out of the interaction of humans and their domestic animals. Other serious diseases, such as falciparum malaria, evolved in tropical Africa only after agriculture had made dense human communities possible. Those postagricultural human pathogens came too late to be carried to the Americas by the original immigrants, and the Americas, in isolation, developed no diseases of equivalent seriousness. Meanwhile, the intensity of intercommunication across the Afro-Eurasian land mass made it possible for diseases originating at any point to spread much more widely. Elements of a common disease pool, though with local variations, existed over most of these continents.

Any disease environment tends to build up a pattern of countervailing immunities in the children who grow up there. Victims of most diseases, if they survive, emerge with a degree of protection against further attack. Measles and other so-called childhood diseases mainly affect the young because most people are infected in childhood and are relatively immune later in life. Some diseases are also benign in childhood but more serious for adults. Yellow fever, for example, is often so mild in children that it has no clinical symptoms, yet victims still acquire a lifelong immunity, whereas among adults, yellow fever is often fatal to more than half of its victims.

In the early 1500s, diseases from Afro-Eurasia were devastating for nonimmune American populations. Smallpox alone often swept away more than a quarter of the population, leaving the survivors incapable of an adequate military defense. As a result, major American empires such as those of the Aztecs and Incas were unable to withstand Spanish attack. The Portuguese also easily established bases here and there along the Brazilian coast. Even after the initial crisis, the disease impact lasted for decades as one unfamiliar disease followed another. Some of the new diseases, such as smallpox, were common to Africa and Europe alike, but the most commonly fatal of tropical diseases, yellow fever and falciparum malaria, were virtually unknown in Europe, though Europeans accidentally introduced them to the Americas through the slave trade. Amerindian populations declined steeply for about a century and a half after contact, before they stabilized and began slowly to grow again.

Patterns of disease are not, or course, a controlling variable to explain or predict what happens in history, but they can provide a first-level explanation of why a variety of patterns of cultural demography appeared in different places after Europeans mariners appeared. European maritime prowess allowed them to reach the Americas with an element of strategic surprise, before the Americans could reach Europe. Largely because of the disease catastrophe that followed, Europeans were able to establish their mastery over the shattered American societies. The first European territorial empires therefore appeared in the American tropics on the ruins of the Aztec and Inca empires in central Mexico and Peru, respectively.

Disease patterns were still more serious for the American tropical lowlands, where falciparum malaria and yellow fever from Africa joined smallpox and a range of childhood diseases from Europe. Native American communities in the Caribbean islands and the lowland coasts of tropical South America were virtually wiped out by the early 1600s. They made a genetic contribution to the Caribbean populations of the future, but most disappeared as a distinct cultural communities.

Only isolated communities in the Amazon basin have survived into the twentieth century.

In the new disease environment of the American lowlands, people from Europe also lacked protection from African tropical diseases, whereas those from tropical Africa carried childhood immunities to a wide range of Afro-Eurasian diseases as well. Their superior immune pattern made them best suited for the repopulation of the American tropics. Slaves could be bought on the West African coast, and the Atlantic slave trade began to supply them to the tropical Americas.

The resulting pattern is sometimes called the plantation complex. The Europeans used their seapower to establish political control, then used the same maritime skills to transport enslaved Africans as colonists to replace the dying Indians. In a more benign disease environment, they might well have brought European settlers to establish a true colony, but in the tropical lowlands they brought Africans instead. In the later 1700s, this pattern reached a kind of apogee in Jamaica and Hispaniola, but it also grew into a significant aspect of American development from the southern United States to south central Brazil.

Migration and Demographic Transitions

The mass emigration of Europeans is characteristic of the industrial age, beginning in the 1800s, although in any decade before the 1840s more Africans than Europeans crossed the Atlantic. Even though earlier European governments tended to think their best prospects overseas were trading-post empires, small true colonies were an occasional by-product. The Azores, in the mid-Atlantic at the same latitude as Portugal itself, were an uninhabited chain of islands discovered by chance. In the next century, after 1470, they were gradually settled by mainland Portuguese. By the mid-1500s they had become part of Portugal, producing the same wine, wheat, and cattle as peninsular Portugal. The Canaries and Madeira, closer to the African coast, went though phases of trading-post and plantation developments, but they too ultimately became true colonies of Spain or Portugal.

Brazil began as an adjunct to the Portuguese trading-post empire in the Indian Ocean. Ships bound for India had to pass close by. Though they did not often stop off, Brazil in unfriendly hands would have been a potential threat to the safe passage to India. When, by the 1540s, the French and some others became active as dye-wood traders on the Brazilian coast, the Portuguese crown decided to plant a colony there, mainly as the self-supporting nucleus for a garrison to protect a crucial strategic position.

The original expedition of 1549 shows the Portuguese intentions. It included 320 people in the pay of the crown, 400 convicts to supply labor, and about 300 assorted priests and free men as colonists and missionaries. Up to about 1570, European colonists were a majority, but, as the influx of African and Amerindian slaves shifted the balance, northeast Brazil became a plantation colony with European managers and an African and Amerindian working class. It was only in the 1800s that a significant amount of true colonization was again attempted, this time mainly in central and southern Brazil.

In the 1600s, the French and the Dutch pursued a similar strategy of commercial settlements. Some of their Caribbean posts followed the Brazilian precedent and in time became plantation colonies with a majority population from Africa, but others took another direction and became true colonies, more by population growth than by continuous immigration from Europe. The Dutch settlement at the Cape of Good Hope and the French settlement around the mouth of the Saint Lawrence can serve as examples. Both of these settlements were founded in the mid-1600s to protect commerce, but with enough European farmers to produce a local supply of food and to provide local manpower for defense.

New France along the Saint Lawrence was established to serve the fur trade, which required only a few thousand settlers, and that was all that France sent out. During the whole period from its foundation to the conquest by England in 1763, no more than 10,000 immigrants came from France, and some authorities think the number may have been closer to 4,000. Yet the net natural increase of less than 10,000 French settlers led, with only small later additions from Europe, to a French Canadian population of more than 5 million in North America today.

The purpose of the Dutch settlements at the Cape was similar – to serve as a way station for the Dutch East India Company's trade to Indonesia and India and to provide a garrison to protect the harbor at Table Bay. For several decades after its founding in 1652, Cape Town was a military post and little more. But then, in 1679, the Company decided to increase the number of settlers in order to make the post more nearly self-supporting. The settlers were not on the Company payroll, but they might be called out for militia duty. Meanwhile, they were encouraged to produce food for the garrison and for sale to passing ships. For a time, the Company subsidized the immigration of German, Dutch, and French Protestants. In all, it sent out some 1,630 people, but in 1707, it ended assisted immigration, and immigration died to a trickle. This European migration of two thousand or so before 1710 nevertheless grew by natural increase into a white Afrikaans-speaking South African population, which numbered about three and a half million by the early 1900s.

At the Cape of Good Hope, however, the result was not a true colony on the order of Quebec. The local Khoisan population survived and mixed with European settlers and with slaves from many shores of the Indian Ocean. The result is the present Cape Colored community, recently numbering more than three million people. The Cape Province thus became a plural society, but a plural society that absorbed many different cultures. Not only did the small nucleus of European settlers expand through population growth, but their culture became an important ingredient in the culture of the Cape Colored majority. The vast majority of Cape Colored people, for example, speak Afrikaans as their home language.

The European settlements at the Cape and in Quebec illustrate two important differences from other trading-post empires. In both, the settlers were not an all-male military force but included women. They soon developed a normal sex ratio, which led to a natural increase among the European community. European populations in the humid tropics rarely attained a net natural increase, even after many decades, partly for lack women and partly for lack of immunity to tropical disease. The disease environments of Canada and the Cape of Good Hope, however, were as favorable to European population growth as that of Europe itself, perhaps more so, and settler communities in North America and South Africa soon attained a higher rate of net natural increase than the European populations at home.

The demographic transitions in Spanish America were similar but more complex. By the 1570s, Mexico and Peru had overcome the anarchy of the conquest period to become the first territorial empires in the European world; yet two centuries later, they had become a complex network of plural societies, with little net demographic input from Europe. The Spanish empire in the Americas had begun, not on the initiative of the Spanish government but on that of the conquerors themselves, and they numbered in the low thousands. Their successors were few as well – soldiers, administrators, missionaries, and later on, mine and ranch managers. Spanish America, at any date in the 1500s, was a territorial empire controlled by a tiny European minority.

After that time, the flow of net Spanish immigration to the Americas is difficult to estimate. Some authorities give the figure of 150,000 legal emigrants crossing from Spain to the Americas over the whole period from 1509 to 1740. Others suggest a half million up to 1650 only. These estimates are uncertain because they seldom take account of a large but unspecified number of officials, merchants, and soldiers who returned to Spain after a tour of duty in the Americas. In addition, the migratory flow in the 1500s was largely male – less than 15 percent female before 1550, less than 35 percent female by the end of the century. This suggests that the second generation of Spanish-derived population would be *mestizos,* Spanish only on the father's side.

These patterns of disease, immigration, and reproduction formed the historical demography of Spanish America through the colonial period. No matter what the net migration from Europe, once the sex ratio of overseas Europeans reached parity among American-born Spaniards, the overseas European population rose by natural increase, just as it did at the Cape of Good Hope or in Quebec. So too did the mestizo populations. With time, the Native American decline slowed and stopped, and recovery began, but the timing was not uniform everywhere. Those Amerindian populations that first encountered the alien diseases had begun a strong recovery before the disease crisis reached more isolated regions.

The size of the pre-Columbian population of the Americas is a troubled problem for historians. Not only are census data unavailable, but some historians give high estimates to reflect the high value they place on Native American civilizations. Others derive their figures from archaeological and other samples, and the range of conclusions is very wide. High estimates of recent years are often ten times more than the low, and the greatest discrepancy is found in the early decades after the European arrival. After the establishment of Spanish colonial governments, the evidence is more secure. Central Mexico is a case in point. As of 1570, central Mexico had about 57,000 whites and mestizos and four million Indians. The foreign element was therefore less than about 1.5 percent of the total population, and the earlier disparity must have been much greater.

By 1700, 130 years later, there were only two million Indians (a 50 percent decrease) as against 400,000 whites and mestizos (a 700 percent increase). The foreign element at that time had risen to 18 percent of the total. Some of this increase certainly came from net immigration from Europe, but most of it was simply population growth. Local population dynamics rather than migration had changed this part of Spanish America from true empire to plural society, just as Quebec changed from trading post to true colony.

British North America passed through another kind of demographic transition during the 1600s and 1700s. The overseas-European population increased dramatically, as it did elsewhere outside tropical lowlands. The Indians that survived the disease crisis, however, were too few to form a working class, as they had in Spanish America. For the most part, the working class in the northern colonies was made up of indentured European servants and their descendants, a few African slaves, some convicts, and some free settlers.

The English, unlike the other colonial powers, sometimes founded true colonies in North America by intent. In the 1600s, it was a common opinion that England was overpopulated, and this opinion lay behind the colonization of Ireland as well. Some settlements were designed to reproduce the society of the mother country, but not all. New York was partly designed to anchor the fur trade through Albany to the west, just as Quebec was to anchor the fur trade of the Saint Lawrence. The South Carolina low country of the early 1700s was more a plantation colony on the West Indian model than it was a colony of settlement.

Nevertheless, more European migrants went to North America in the colonial period than to all other destinations, and their population growth after arrival was even more important. Recent guesses based on spotty immigration figures put the number of arrivals in the mainland British colonies at 360,000 to 720,000, depending on the mode of estimation. Whatever the actual number within that range, the rate of

11

population growth was so high that this small input produced an overseas European population of more than three million by 1790.

Even so, the volume of the European immigration was insignificant compared to the flow that would follow in the late 1800s. Imprecise estimates of all European movement overseas by 1790 indicate around a million and a half – far fewer than the total of around eight million Africans landed in the Americas before 1800, and insignificant compared to the European emigration overseas in an equivalent time period from 1800 to 1990, sometimes set at sixty million.

The Emergence of Territorial Empire

Territorial empire, like the massive European migrations overseas, belongs to the industrial age. Before about 1750, significant European control over territorial empires was still confined to the Americas, but even then the area governed was a shadow of what text-book maps show as Spanish and Portuguese America. The maps show European claims to sovereignty, whereas real government administration as of 1800 covered only the highlands from central Mexico to central Chile, most Caribbean islands, and much of coastal Brazil. Otherwise, the Europeans actually controlled only enclaves within territory they claimed but did not try to govern. Such enclaves to the north of central Mexico included scattered mining centers, trading towns such as Santa Fe, and bits of California surrounding mission stations. Elsewhere in North America, the pattern was similar. Real control extended over the coastal settlement areas from Quebec to Georgia, but beyond the Appalachians the dominant pattern was that of an overland trading-post empire. By 1800, not a quarter of the territory of the Americas was actually governed by Europeans.

North of the Black Sea and south of Muscovy, Europe had another frontier of expanding control to the east. At the beginning of the 1600s, this region had been mainly controlled by Tatar nomads left over from Mongol expansion of the 1200s and later, now contested by sedentary states on the borders – Muscovy to the north, Poland and Lithuania to the west, the Hapsburg domains to the southwest, and the Ottoman Empire to the south. The political and military contest between these sedentary states was more fluid than similar frontier struggles in western Europe. Ultimate political control of bureaucratic structures was less secure than in western Europe; populations were both sparser and more mobile. Over the period from 1600 to about 1800, however, the drift of power was away from the Tatars and Ottomans and in favor of the Russian Empire, and the military and political advance was accompanied by a massive settlement of what was to be Ukraine and southern Russia. It was the beginning of Russian colonization that would ultimately extend beyond the Urals as well.

Before 1800, however, the Russian presence in Siberia took the form of a trading-post empire that stretched eastward to Alaska. The bare beginning of true colonization centered in a narrow strip of land along the line of the later trans-Siberian railroad. In fact, the Russians had begun moving into that corridor a little before 1800, but the main Russian occupation came afterward, along with the Russian acquisition of territorial empire in the Caucasus and Central Asia. In this part of Eurasia, the pattern was that of incipient territorial empires in the south and overland trading-post empires in the north, with enclaves of true colonization scattered in both regions. The whole strategy of European expansion here was under the strong influence of older traditions of conflict between nomadic and sedentary peoples.

Along the southern and eastern coasts of Asia, the pattern of European empire was still that of the trading enclaves, though some territorial control was beginning here and there. In the Philippines, Spain had extended the patterns of control originating in Spanish America. Its bureaucratic administrative structure theoretically covered all the islands, but underneath, strong elements of control remained in local hands, Spanish and Filipino alike. The government in Manila did not even try to administer much, perhaps most, of the Philippine territory it claimed.

The most important European territorial empires in Asia were those ruled by the British and the Dutch East India Companies. They were chartered trading companies, originally intended to supervise trading-post empires. By 1800, the Dutch Company had considerable power over parts of the Indonesian archipelago, but it was mainly exercised for commercial advantage rather than tax revenue, much less day-to-day government administration. The Company's rule over territory, weak as it was, was confined to the western three-quarters of the island of Java. Otherwise it had genuine control over a number of trading-post towns and some islands of particular importance for the spice trade, like the Malukus.

In India as of 1800, the British East India Company was the dominant authority over the provinces of Bengal and Bihar, but the nature of that authority indicates the transitional stage between trading-post empire and real territorial control. Since the 1740s, European powers, especially Britain and France, had begun to be more than simple traders, even armed traders, and they transferred their European rivalry into Indian politics. The Mughal Empire, which had ruled north India through most of the 1500s and 1600s, was no longer a strong central authority except in name. Provincial rulers held the real power, though they might rule in the Mughal name. This fluid situation opened the possibility for the European companies to recruit Indian soldiers to oppose one another and to use their military power to participate actively in an Indian state system.

At first, the Europeans sought only to influence Indian rulers, but that influence gradually increased to the point that they were de facto rulers. In 1772, the British East India Company became, in theory, a corporate official of the Mughal empire for the provinces of Bengal and Bihar, in the hinterland of Calcutta. It assumed the post of revenue collector, or *diwan,* for those provinces but kept the revenue for itself instead of passing it on to the Mughal capital in Delhi. The actual tax collectors were Indian, as they had always been, but they now worked under supervision of British Company officials. Tax collection led the Company on to take over other administrative and judicial powers, at least over the top level of government. Still later, it began the indirect supervision of Indian "native states," which would agree to accept the authority of a British "resident," in effect a kind of ambassador whose advice the ruler was bound to accept in crucial matters.

Beginning with these convenient fictions, the authority of the British company increased until by 1805, it was the most powerful single territorial power in India. By the 1840s, the British East India Company was so powerful that its word could often be law even within most Indian states still not formally annexed to British India. Even so, the authority of the Company and of Crown officials above it was imbedded in a congeries of Mughal institutions, which were only gradually Westernized in the course of the 1800s.

The Changing Reality of Imperial Power

The powers of governments have varied over time, although the early industrial age made available a new technology of government, which, with local modification, has become worldwide. In the agricultural age government administration differed greatly from one culture to another. Feudal Europe was very different from Song China. Many historical atlases show a map of "Charlemagne's Empire," in a solid color and stretching over much of northwest Europe from a capital at Aachen. Charlemagne's overrule may have been recognized in some sense over this vast territory, but the levels of literacy and governmental efficiency in Europe at that time were so low that orders could not have been reliably transmitted everywhere, much less obeyed. It is doubtful whether a substantial minority of the population were conscious that they were part of an empire by any name.

Maps of later periods show such events as the transfer of Alsace and Lorraine from France to Germany in 1871. The meaning in that case was far more real. Taxes went to a new destination. Orders given were normally carried out; police and judicial authorities exercised control within a central framework of authority. Public education by that time was nearly universal, and changing the language of education from French to German meant something important, even though the people of Alsace continued to speak their own home language, which was neither. Hardly anyone, however ill-educated, could fail to be aware of the change. European governments in the early industrial age controlled a largely literate population through an increasingly efficient public administration, which controlled wide areas of public service. No preindustrial government had such extensive power to influence its subjects in so many aspects of their lives.

European empires overseas had increasing administrative power as well, but an enormous gap could sometimes exist between their claims to authority and the reality of power they were capable of exercising. The European use of grandiose titles to empire goes back at least to the early 1500s, when Manoel I of Portugal claimed the title "Lord of the Conquest, Navigation, and Commerce of Ethiopia, Arabia, Persia, and India." At the time, very few people in these territories had even heard of Portugal, but the claim is not as foolish as it sounds. In the European context of that time, it was merely the assertion of a

Portuguese monopoly over Asian trade, to the exclusion of other Europeans, and a warning that other Europeans who attempted to conquer Asian or African territory could count on Portuguese opposition.

At other times, Europeans underplayed rather than overplayed the reality of their power. In 1882, a British army occupied Egypt, but the European diplomatic setting of the time made it inconvenient for Britain either to annex Egypt or to withdraw. As a way out, the British Foreign Office established its control over major operations of the Egyptian government and ruled Egypt in fact for decades. British over-rule began in 1882, and a measure of control over Egyptian foreign policy lasted until 1952, but Egypt was a legal part of the British Empire only from 1914 to 1922. Everybody important knew what was going on, but it was a convenient fiction to call the British governor "consul general" rather than governor, and to rule the protectorate through the Foreign Office rather than the Colonial Office.

Openly disguised control of this kind was common in the age of empire. The map was dotted with *Schutzgebieten*, protectorates, overseas provinces, Socialist Soviet Republics, African Homelands, and other disguised forms of territorial empire. In most cases, the disguise was merely a legal fiction for the sake of public relations, not a serious effort to fool either the conquered people or the world at large.

The true degree of outside control, nevertheless, is sometimes hard to ascertain. It was theoretically possible a the height of European empire to set up a fully bureaucratic imperial administration, with the apparatus of the modern state at its command and with little or no participation on the part of the local population. But this kind of imperial government was rare outside of plural societies such as Algeria or South Africa, where a local population of overseas Europeans was available as administrators. Elsewhere, the vast majority of police, clerical workers, and low-level administrators were recruited locally. Sometimes high-level administrators were local as well, such as the rajas at the head of Native States in India.

The proportion of European administrators to population could vary greatly, but even in the most heavily administered colonies they were comparatively few. The Belgian Congo was tightly ruled, but it had only about one European administrator for 1,500 subjects. In other African territories, where the Europeans made a conscious decision to administer through existing authorities, the ratio might run as high as one to 50,000 or even more.

It was one question to decide how much authority to delegate to local subordinates, a second to decide how much authority to exercise at all. At one end of the spectrum, a European power might claim sovereignty over a territory in order to warn off European rivals but not attempt to rule over it. Actual influence might be limited to threats or an occasional punitive expedition. The Spanish and Portuguese claim to share sovereignty over the Americas in the colonial period was largely of this sort, and well into the twentieth century, Latin American republics left much of the Amazon basin and some of the Pacific coastal plain unadministered. Neither the Australians nor the Dutch attempted to administer all the interior of New Guinea until well after the Second World War. Unless the potential subjects had valuable resources such as minerals or oil, it was sometimes cheaper and easier to let them go their own way

Another possibility was to divide authority into a European sphere and a local sphere. Europeans often preferred to take over foreign affairs, the military, revenue collection, or posts and telegraphs, which seemed to affect their interests, leaving other matters to the local authorities, as the British did in Egypt. In other places, like parts of China in the late 1800s or the Persian Gulf sheikdoms in the early twentieth century, it is unclear whether Europeans were ruling at all or simply giving advice with a certain weight of power behind it.

A similar problem existed even with territories that were formally under European rule. Precolonial authorities could be left to rule their territory with the advice of European officials. Sometimes the advice was perfunctory, but at other times it was so detailed and precise that the advisers became the real rulers. The reality of imperial rule was therefore highly variable from time to time and place to place, even within a single colonial empire. Published maps colored appropriately to show French, British, or Portuguese territory merely showed claims to legal sovereignty, not the reality of power exercised on the ground.

Further Reading

Altman, Ida, and James Horn, *"To Make America": European Emigration in the Early Modern Period* (Berkeley: University of California Press, 1991).

Cavalli-Sforza, Luigi Luca, *History and the Geography of Human Genes* (Princeton: Princeton University Press, 1994).

Curtin, Philip D., *Cross-Cultural Trade in World History* (New York: Cambridge University Press, 1984).

Curtin, Philip D, *The Rise and Fall of the Plantation Complex* (New York: Cambridge University Press, 1990).

McNeill, William H., *Europe's Steppe Frontier 1500–1800* (Chicago: University of Chicago Press, 1964).

Menard, Russell R., "Migration, Ethnicity, and the Rise of an Atlantic Economy: The Re-Peopling of British America, 1600–1790," in Rudolph J. Vecoli and Suzanne M. Sinke, *A Century of European Migration,* 1830–1930 (Urbana: University of Illinois Press, 1991), pp. 58–77.

Moor, J. A. de, and H. L. Wesseling, *Imperialism and War: Essays on Colonial Wars in Asia and Africa* (Leiden: Brill, 1989).

Mörner, Magnus, *Adventurers and Proletarians: The Story of Migrants in Latin America* (Pittsburgh: Pittsburgh University Press, 1985).

2

Technology and Power

It would be hard to deny that imperial expansion in the past two centuries was in some way related to the beginning of the industrial age, with its enormous increases in per capita production and consumption, but historians of Europe disagree about what, precisely, that relationship may have been. Much of the discussion deals with aggregates of uncertain but familiar content, such as *industrial revolution, capitalism,* and *imperialism.*

Economic historians have not yet satisfactorily settled the problem of identifying the precise relationship between industrial technology and the Western form of economic organizations, broadly but loosely called capitalism. The term originated in the 1900s, but it has been extended, backward through time and forward to the present, to refer to a set of economic institutions that has changed so dramatically, even over the past two centuries, that it can hardly be considered a single entity. With one of these aggregates so imprecise a concept, it is is difficult to accept it as a prime mover, yet some authorities have suggested that capitalism caused both the industrial revolution and imperialism, and other relationships among these three aggregates have their advocates. Until the economic historians of Europe supply the rest of us with a sufficiently clear and plausible statement about the relations between capitalism and industrial technology, and with a convincing argument that either was the principal cause of imperialism, it is safer to proceed with a lower order of generalization.

Whatever the role of capitalism, most historians are convinced that Europe was the society that first produced the "industrial revolution."

Some authorities once thought that the achievement was essentially English and began in the late 1700s. More recently, historians have been exploring its origins elsewhere in Europe and further back in time, including technology borrowed from non-Western societies. Nor was the growth of productivity per capita unique to Europe. Song China and Tokugawa Japan, among other societies, moved toward sustained economic growth, without, however, crossing the line into a new industrial age in the way Europe did.

Historians have also dropped their early concentrations on a few spectacular inventions like machine textiles or steam power, followed by iron and steel. The technological revolution was much broader, and it was much earlier. In the era of the trading-post empires, the greatest source of nonhuman, nonanimal power was waterpower and sailing ships, and at sea, sail competed effectively with steam into the mid-1800s. The maritime age of sail not only witnessed enormous technical changes in sailing ships themselves, but in the whole technology of conducting trade at a distance, including mundane but important changes in banking and credit, insurance, or accounting. Economists sometimes refer to these as *transaction costs,* and their reduction over the centuries from the 1500s into the 1900s may have been an even greater contribution to economic growth than the improvement in sailing ships. By middle of the 1700s, a worldwide set of economic relationships had been worked out, in which gold and silver from the Americas paid for European imports from Asia, including the Indian textiles that were one of the chief commodities used on the African coast to purchase enslaved Africans.

Some non-European historians have sought to explain the industrial revolution itself by seeking its roots in such activities as the European trading-post empires and plantation societies of the preindustrial period. Early in the twentieth century, some historians in India emphasized the profits of the British East India Company and the European drain from the Indian-Ocean economy as the principal source capital of investment, making it possible for Britain to industrialize in the early 1800s. In the 1930s, Eric Williams, later prime minister of Trinidad, wrote a book called *Capitalism and Slavery,* which advanced a similar view, in this instance that the profits from the slave trade and the tropical American plantations supplied the "primitive investments" required for British industrialization.[1] The dawn of the industrial age is now recognized to be too complex to be explained in such a linear, monocausal fashion, but it is also widely recognized that the technology of long-distance economic organization and transportation, as they developed during the first centuries of European activity overseas, made a crucial contribution to the European organizing ability, including the ability to field the armies that would conquer and administer Europe's territorial empires.

Whatever the source, Europeans, from the later 1700s, began to produce a stream of goods per capita greater than produced by any previous society. With such resources, someone, or some few, had the power to decide how they should be used. Their use could take the form of new capital investment, including social investment in public goods like education and infrastructure, or they could be invested armies and navies to enhance the power of the state in its rivalry with other European states. They could be spent on social welfare for the disadvantaged members of society, or they could finance the conquest and government of other societies overseas. National advantage, individual wealth, and philanthropy were among the objectives advocated from time to time. Neither the new resources, however, nor the technology that created them, dictated the way they had to be used; the novelty of this all was the range of choice that had not existed in the preindustrial age.

Arms and the Military

The fact that Europeans had the power to conquer and dominate most of the world was a fundamental situation looming over all other relations between the West and the rest of the world. But the possession of power and the exercise of power could be different; the distinction between necessary causes and sufficient causes is useful in this regard. To have enough military power to dominate another society is necessary for its conquest, but the mere existence of that power is not a sufficient explanation of why that power should used in a particular way. European

---

[1] Eric Williams, *Capitalism and Slavery* (Chapel Hill: University of North Carolina Press, 1944).

technology, especially military technology, was nevertheless a necessary permissive fact in the background of world history in the imperial age.

Rivalries within Europe itself dictated that much of the first payoff of the industrial revolution would be spent on arms and armies. For that matter, the European ruling class of the preindustrial period was a military class. Churchmen and burghers shared power, but the share of the nobility was greatest. Whatever the sources of innovation in Europe, technology was not a strong point of the nobility, nor of the military classes as a whole. Their orientation and values emphasized bravery on the battlefield, not skill and inventiveness, not even creating new weapons. When artillery was first introduced, the guns were often served by low-status civilians. Into the 1800s, artillery was still a low-status branch of the service; cavalry had most prestige, in spite of the rise to top command of an occasional artilleryman like Napoleon.

Even in the 1800s, when the importance of industrial technology was fully recognized, the military classes in the principal Western powers still valued gentlemanly rather than professional qualities. One of the most important military reforms was to create a professionally trained officer corps. Prussia succeeded first in doing this, and the formation of the German Empire after the Prussian victory in the Franco-Prussian War was one result.

In spite of its disdain for technological tinkering, the European ruling class honored its military roots by spending an increasing proportion of the rising national income on the military, not principally for use overseas but for protection against European rivals. European armies increased from the tiny professional forces of the 1700s, through the *levée en masse* of the French Revolution to the formation of conscripted mass armies in the later 1800s, culminating in the mass slaughter of the war of 1914–18.

After the 1740s, major European wars were partly fought in places as distant from centers of power as Pondichery or Pittsburgh, but European statesmen thought first in terms of Europe and European rivalries. It time, however, these rivalries came to be transferred overseas; armed forces built mainly for use in Europe were used against European enemies on the fringes of empire and against non-Europeans as well.

On a world scale, the Europeans' first technological lead in warfare was at sea. They were the first to use seaborne artillery, with ships that were increasingly able to make long voyages in reasonable safety and with the knowledge of how to navigate over distant seas. During the two centuries and a half after Vasco da Gama appeared in Calicut on the first European voyage to India, Europeans were no more competent at land warfare than other leading societies of the Afro-Eurasian landmass. Yet Europeans retained their superiority at sea; no Asian society borrowed enough of that knowledge to establish a direct, Asian-controlled sea trade to Europe. A scattering of Asian merchants visited Europe, but, if they came by sea, they came on European ships.

Movement at sea was peculiarly hard to control with the maritime technology of the time. Almost any ship capable of sailing to the Americas, sub-Saharan Africa, or Asia could serve as a warship if necessary, and it had to be able to fight at times for its own protection. At certain periods, the terms of European peace treaties applied only to European waters, within declared "lines of amity." Into the early 1800s, commerce raiding in wartime was a private enterprise with government sanction, and out-and-out piracy persisted.

The advent of the industrial age ended that freedom on the high seas. Where once warships could belong to private firms, the new technology was so expensive that large warships could belong only to important governments. The turning point was a combination of steam power and armor, which also made warships too specialized for commercial use. The change began with river gunboats, steamers being especially effective in carrying artillery to the site of battle. The first armored steamers to be used in combat were built for the British East India Company, not for the technically conservative Royal Navy, and they were first used against China in the Opium War of the early 1840s. An iron-clad steamer called *Nemesis* showed its ability to silence the Chinese batteries along the Chinese rivers and was the technical star of that war of rivers. The line that begins with *Nemesis* leads down through the *Monitor* and *Merrimac* of the American Civil War and on to the *Dreadnought* and heavy battleships of the First World War.

European Land Power

European superiority in land warfare owed more at first to European organizational techniques than to the new weapons that would flow in time from European factories. Through the 1500s and 1600s, the weapons available to Europeans and non-Europeans were much the same, through the whole range of cavalry weapons, muskets, and artillery. Technical innovations were borrowed back and forth and used in different ways appropriate to the social and political structure of the state that used them.

European organizational ability came to the fore in two ways. One was the organization of weapons production; the other was the organization of the way weapons could be deployed in the field. The key early change was artillery. From the 1500s, light artillery suitable for field use rather than as siege guns was available, but only made of bronze and at great expense. Cast iron guns had to be much heavier for same muzzle size and velocity, hence less mobile. In the early 1700s, cheap iron field artillery made its appearance in European hands. Needless to say, all European-made guns did not remain in European hands. The initial superiority in weapons could be retained only if Europeans could continue to produce better and cheaper guns. In the 1700s, the European advantage was barely sustained. Again and again, European officers reported that the best of the Asian artillery was very good indeed, and they turned captured guns to their own use. In India, they often commented on the technical proficiency of the Indian gunsmiths, while complaining about the uneven quality of their product. The problem was not the techniques of production but the organization of quality control.

The other European organizational advantage, on the battlefield, went back to the 1500s and 1600s, with the rediscovery that infantry was more effective if it could be trained to maneuver and fight as a unit. This was a recurrent rediscovery in military history, but not because succeeding generations lost the knowledge of the tactical advantage of disciplined movement in battle. The key to success lay in the ability of a society to organize – to recruit, train, and maintain a professional army.

Like many military advantages, this ability was most effective when one side had it and the other did not, and the advantage of disciplined infantry was relatively independent of the weapons used. Nor was it open to the Europeans alone. In the early 1800s, a major military revolution took place in southern Africa, independent of the industrial changes in Europe. The Zulu and others among the Nguni people of present-day Kwazulu-Natal discovered the military advantage of a disciplined formation called *impi,* armed with short stabbing spears and shields, not unlike the Roman legions. The training was provided through the social and political innovation of using the existing age-grade system, by which males of a single age group went through instruction and initiation to adulthood together. The Zulu leadership reorganized this institution to form a permanent and trained army by recruiting all members of each age grade in turn and by keeping them in the army as long as it suited the ruler. This produced a force with a high esprit de corps and a high state of discipline.

By the 1820s, the Zulu and other Natalian kingdoms who adopted this system could easily defeat those who had not. The result was to favor the use of the impi against those who had not yet adopted it. Aggressive impi-using armies spread outward onto the high veld, northward into Swaziland, Mozambique, into central Tanzania, and northwest into the upper Zambezi valley in western Zambia. After a few decades, the military migrations settled down, and ultimately they were overtaken by other empire builders who came with the new firearms from Europe.

Elsewhere in the world in the mid-1700s, the success of the new tactics from Europe spread in a similar pattern against opponents who had not yet mastered the organizational skills to answer in kind. This was first apparent in India, where the British and French East India Companies trained Indian troops to fight in the European manner. They added another European innovation, maneuverable light field artillery, which horses could draw rapidly into action. A good gun crew could serve such an artillery piece so as to maintain a rate of fire faster than that of musketeers of the time. Supporting infantry was now equipped with flintlock muskets, which first came into use in the 1690s, and with bayonets enabling them to replace the pikemen who had formerly made up most infantry units.

It was this combination of tactics and training that the European companies took to India, beginning in the 1740s. In that decade, the French Company began to strengthen its role in the politics of southern India by recruiting armies of Indians, trained in the European manner of the time by noncommissioned officers from Europe. The original effort was not designed to conquer India nor to create a territorial empire, but merely to strengthen the French political position in the Indian state system. The ultimate enemy was the British

Company, which responded by creating a similar army of sepoys. The rivalries in Europe thus gave the European Companies a military advantage over the less organized Indian forces, which fought in the old way. That advantage was the basis of the British Company's first territorial empire. By 1782, the Company in Bengal had a standing army of more than 110,00 men, 90 percent Indian. More significantly, the major cost of that army was paid for out of revenues drawn from Bengal itself. The conquest of India began, in short, with the aid of European tactics and organization, not principally with the new weapons that were to come with the industrial era, and it was largely paid for by Indian taxpayers.

Indian armies were, of course, capable of imitating the European style of tactics and training, as the experience of the British East India Company in confronting successive Indian states was to demonstrate. Before the tactical revolution, European and Indian armies of the same size were roughly equal in battle. Then, in the battle of Plassey in 1757, the Company, with a European-style army of only three thousand men, defeated a Mughal army of fifty thousand cavalry. While that particular victory was partly accidental, the Company advantage was temporary. In the series of Mysore wars in south India between 1767 and the 1790s, the forces needed for victory gradually increased. Whereas the British Company won the first of these wars easily with armies that were outnumbered by 7:1, in the final war the numbers were nearly equal because of larger contingents of French and French-trained troops fighting for Mysore. A similar sequence of declining advantage occurred in the three Marattha wars between the 1770s and the early 1800s. There, the British Company began outnumbered by 12 to 1 and ended the last war with a close-called victory over a stronger set of opponents, again stiffened by French training and advisors.

In the early 1800s, the rise of the Sikh state in the Punjab showed what military modernization could accomplish. The opportunity on the Indian side occurred about 1805, when the Sikh religious community, neither Hindu nor Muslim, began to consolidate its political power over Punjab. The initial leader and military commander until his death in 1839 was Ranjit Singh, who began to build a disciplined army following European principles of organization. He also built political unity by using the Sikh community to provide a kind of cohesion that would attract a following of Hindus and Muslims alike, and he recruited European military officers. He mainly fought to unify Punjab rather than trying to conquer abroad, but his movement had elements in common with secondary empires elsewhere.

At Ranjit's death, the Punjab army was probably the most powerful in India, but the Sikh state began to lose its organizational unity. In the two wars against the British Company, in 1845–6 and 1848–9, in retrospect and from a strictly military point of view the victory could have gone either way, and there were political mistakes on both sides. The British Company won, however, and the victory cleared the way for the Company to annex Punjab and emerge for the first time as the paramount power in India. This victory, like the foundation of the Company's territorial empire in India, owed more to its organizational success in marshaling Indian resources than it did to the technological superiority of its weapons. The superiority of European weapons was to come later in the century.

The Rise and Fall of a Weapons Gap

About the middle of the 1800s, a weapons gap between European and non-European armies began to appear, and this advantage gave the Europeans the military lead that lasted through the age of imperialism that began in the 1870s. Though artillery improved through the course of the century, the revolutionary change in colonial warfare was in infantry weapons. Into the 1850s and later, the standard weapon for most European armies was the flintlock muzzle-loader with a smooth bore, first introduced during the 1690s. A soldier rammed powder and ball down the barrel and fired with flint and steel through a touchhole. These guns were so much more reliable than previous firearms that they allowed infantrymen to substitute the bayonet for the variety of pikes, lances, and swords they had previously carried. Though a good infantryman could load and fire a musket only about once a minute, disciplined infantrymen firing by ranks could maintain a steady fire. Musketeers became the dominant foot soldiers of European battle-fields.

After more than a century and a half of dominance, flintlock muskets were displaced in the 1860s by major improvements in accuracy and rate of fire. The improved accuracy came from rifling the interior barrels with spiraled grooves, causing the projectile to emerge spinning. The principle had been known for many decades, and rifles were sometimes used for military purpose in the late 1700s. Though the earliest rifles were accurate to at least four times the range of a smooth-bore musket, the projectile could not simply be rammed down the muzzle, so that the loading time could be three to five minutes. After decades of experimentation, the solution was to use a bullet that would expand slightly as it was fired, so as to catch the grooves of the rifling.

The firing speed improved with the development of a bolt-action breech mechanism. The bullet and powder could then be introduced as a single cartridge and fired when the bolt struck a percussion cap in the base on the cartridge. By the 1860s, the breech-loading rifles could be fired six times a minute, with accuracy at a range eight times that of a smooth-bore musket. Breech-loading rifles were used in the later years of the American Civil War, and their effectiveness had a spectacular demonstration in Europe with the Prussian victory over Austria-Hungary in 1866.

Even greater speed of fire was possible if the cartridges could be fed into the barrel automatically. Americans began working on such guns even before the end of the Civil War. During the 1880s, European armies replaced single-shoot breech-loading rifles with magazine rifles. In the same decade, the first effective machine guns were brought into use, with an even greater speed of fire, and nitrocellulose (smokeless powder) replaced the old gunpowder with an explosive that was much more reliable and less visible.

The British domination of India was virtually complete before these new weapons were available, but they were to be crucial in the very rapid European conquest of Africa and Southeast Asia. The difference is most apparent in West Africa, where for decades the European had been selling trade guns similar to the model of the 1690s flintlock. Because of this near equality in weapons, combined with the high mortality rates for Europeans in the West African disease environment, European had made no significant attempts to build territorial empires before the 1870s. They made occasional military interventions, like the British march on Kumasi in Asante in the first two months of 1874, but the British force withdrew and the Asante returned to control of their own affairs. The British did, however, somewhat perversely annex the territory of the African states that had been their allies against Asante, founding in the process the first British colony in tropical Africa that extended beyond trading-post dimensions.

The French in the Western Sudan first showed what the combination of European tactics and weapons could do against enemies still armed with flintlocks. The tiny force available to the French on the lower Senegal in the 1880s consisted mainly of locally recruited Africans fighting under French officers, backed by small numbers of French marine infantry and artillery. The French strategy was to organize annual dry-season campaigns lasting less than six months, beginning with a force of less than a thousand men and rising to less than two thousand at later stages in the early 1890s. Armed with magazine rifles and light artillery, with machine guns added toward the end, this force conquered for France an area several times the size of France itself, with a population of 10 to 15 million people, even though they were sometimes outnumbered by as much as 50 to 1.

The French navy, whose operation this was, began with the strategy of a trading-post empire composed of fortified posts along the Senegal to the head of navigation and supplied by steamers on the river. They then sent strong but lightly armed columns into the interior each year, establishing a line of higher posts, each fortified and defended by small garrisons after their main army withdrew at the beginning of the rainy season. A railway line followed the line of posts until it reached the Niger at Bamako, and French steam gunboats were operating on the Niger even before the railroad had reached it. The strategy was important. A force of this size could neither occupy nor rule over all the territory that ultimately fell to France. Any threat to the French presence could be met by a sharp military lesson; otherwise, the African authorities who accepted "French protection" were allowed to go on ruling their territories with only minimal interference.

The French navy was always heavily involved in colonial affairs, and all this was done on the initiative of the French naval officers, with little direction from Paris – sometimes without permission. The cost to the French treasury was insignificant, and while the losses from disease were heavy, the troops at risk were mainly African, and the apparent gain in territory was immense. The military prowess of traveling columns laid down a claim to rule; making the claim a reality could be postponed for a decade or more. It was only in the 1890s and later that the French government took the new colonies away from naval and marine officers and established a civil administration that actually began to rule, though French West Africa remained one of the most lightly administered territories in Africa.

With variations, this kind of advance went on all over tropical Africa in the 1880s and 1890s, based militarily on light artillery, magazine rifles, and machine guns against people who had no such weapons. The British conquered northern Nigeria with a force of much the same magnitude as the French force in the Western Sudan, and against similar odds. In Central Africa, King Leopold of Belgium established his control, as a private citizen with a private army, over what became the Belgian Congo. By end of the 1890s, the conquest of Africa was nearly completed, with only a few remnants left; but the weapons gap was already closing, just as the gap in organizational efficiency had begun to close in India by the time of the Anglo-Sikh War of 1848.

Even before the 1880s, some African authorities had recognized the importance of the new weapons: If they could secure a supply, they would have the same advantage as the Europeans. Here and there, in places widely scattered through Africa, African rulers began to extend their territory in much the same way as the French marine officers in the Western Sudan or Leopold in the Congo. Historians of Africa often call this secondary empire building, because the territorial expansion was built on the military hardware of industrial Europe. Egypt had begun building a secondary empire in the Nilotic Sudan as early as the 1820s, based on European-style military organization and tactics.

In the 1890s, three African kingdoms had rearmed themselves so successfully that they had at least an outside chance of standing off a European army. Madagascar had begun this course as early at the 1850s. One Ethiopian emperor tried in the 1860s and failed, but he was then succeeded by Menelik, who, in the 1880s and early 1890s, increased the size of the Ethiopian Empire several times over. In the late 1880s, the Dahomean kingdom in West Africa began systematically raiding its neighbors for slaves, sold to Europeans as "contract laborers" in return for modern weapons.

Only the Ethiopian Empire survived the age of imperialism in Africa. Menelik acquired enough rifles and modern artillery to inflict a decisive defeat on an invading Italian army at Adwa in 1896, and the demonstration victory was enough, until Mussolini's invasion of the 1930s, to discourage other European threats. Dahomey, on the other hand, was unable to train its army to use the new weapons effectively and went down to defeat by France in 1892. While the Malagasy kingdom organized a modern-looking army with European technical assistance, it collapsed in 1895 in the face of a French invasion, though more from internal dissension than from military defeat.

The extravagant European weapons gap began to narrow about 1900, though few people realized it at the time. Europe had by now become accustomed to winning overseas, even when outnumbered. Menelik's victory at Adwa appeared to be a fluke. The European press misunderstood the military lesson of the Anglo-Boer War, though it is clear enough in retrospect. The Boer republics discovered that they held the largest gold deposits discovered so far. They began to use some of the gold revenue to buy modern weapons in order to stand off pressure from British mining interests. When the crisis came in 1899, the British expected a quick victory, but in the war, which lasted until 1902, Britain sent a force of nearly a half million against a Boer force of 60 to 65 thousand. The military lesson that emerged later in the twentieth century was that an offensive war against people with equal arms requires at least equal numbers, but to defeat guerrillas armed with modern weapons requires a force that outnumbers the guerrillas many times over.

These new realities were not readily apparent the time. During the 1890s, the Dutch learned about the effectiveness of guerrilla war in operations against the Aceh on Sumatra. In the Spanish-American War, the Americans easily defeated the Spanish forces in the Philippines, but to defeat the "Philippine Insurrection" of 1900–01, the United States required a force that outnumbered the insurgent by two to one.

The new disparity continued in the remaining colonial wars of the interwar period. The French and Spanish force needed to conquer the Rif Mountains, a mere corner of Morocco, was more than 500,000 men – far more than was necessary for France to subdue all its sub-Saharan territories taken together. The Italian Ethiopian campaign of the 1930s required a half million Italian troops, whereas the force under Italian command at the battle of Adwa in 1896 was barely 15,000. On that occasion, the Italians fought outnumbered by about seven to one, but they might nevertheless have won under more able leadership. By the interwar period, the end of the weapons gap was obvious. By then, machine guns were generally available, and a machine gun was a superb defensive weapon.

After the Second World War, the price of an antiguerrilla campaign had became extremely expensive. By then, even when the colonial powers did not face a direct military threat, the price of holding colonial territory was known, and it had became part of the bargaining equation. In the early 1950s, the Dutch gave up Indonesia rather than pursue their reconquest at the price that was then required. The French gave up Indo-China and Algeria for similar reasons, and the United States retreated from Vietnam, although the United States was the foremost military power in the world. By the mid to late 1960s, most optimistic military estimates held that guerrilla tactics like those of the Vietnamese would require a modern army to outnumber the enemy by five or six to one.

Administrative Technology

Behind the weapons and behind the industrial system that produced them was a body of organizational technology. Europe's ability to organize lay behind the efficient production of goods, including weapons, and the efficiency of armies in the field. Both were closely related to the means of government administration. It is sometimes forgotten that efficient bureaucratic infrastructure is relatively recent in the history of the world. It is easy to assume at first glance that the Carolingian Empire and the German Empire of 1871 were close enough to the same thing to deserve the same name. Even in the late preindustrial period in European history, governments had difficulty reaching down from the centers of decision making to the actual individuals they wished to control or to tax. In the 1700s and earlier, governments in Europe worked with something remarkably close to the system of indirect rule that they later used in their overseas empires. They had too few paid, appointed, removable officials to carry out their orders directly, though they did have members of the feudal class, landowners, men who could be designated as justices of the peace as they were in England, and in return for favor from the central government, these people could be allowed to carry a great deal of the burden of day-to-day administration.

European society of the preindustrial period was also highly corporative. People were considered as members of groups that were in fact informal corporations with differing privileges and disabilities. Some such groups were legal corporations as well including guilds, universities, towns, or the church. The bureaucratic servants of a monarch had little choice but to rule through such groups or through local magnates, landowners, or informal corporations. They had to locate and depend on people who already had local influence. The government could afford to offend some powerful citizens, but not many at the same time, much less all of them at once. Once chosen, such local instruments of royal power were hard to remove, even when they were inefficient or when they actively sabotaged the intentions of higher authority. In short, bureaucrats in Europe had some of the same troubles as the rulers of colonial empires, seeking to rule through "natural leaders" under several varieties of indirect rule.

As industrial society became more complex, governments needed to establish sanitary facilities, inspect factories, control child labor, police the growing cities, plan railways, control currency and banking, and tax in new and complicated ways. Once applied to European conditions, similar techniques could used overseas. Their very existence made overseas empire appear more valuable. Imperial control was of little use to the colonial powers unless they could run the conquered territories cheaply and effectively in ways that suited their interests. Once Europeans had a corps of removable personnel, with typewriters, mimeograph machines, and all the rest, they could sometimes manipulate subject societies in intricate ways, although often without understanding the long-run consequences of all that they were doing, as we shall see in later chapters.

In some ways the manipulation was straightforward. The overseas subjects paid for their own defense, and they often paid most of the cost of imperial expansion. By the late 1800s, the vast majority of the troops serving in the French, British, German, and Netherlands armies overseas were non-European, and the cost of maintaining those armies fell to the local budget. The Indian Army, including the troops of British origin, was paid for by the Indian taxpayers, and these costs were a large part of the Indian budget. The Netherlands Indies also had a military organization separate from the Netherlands Army and paid for mainly by local taxpayers. In about 1900, that army consisted of about 30 percent Dutch recruits, 20 percent other Europeans (mainly German), a smattering of Africans, and 50 percent East Indians. Military expenditures between 1871 and 1914 accounted for about 35 percent of the Netherlands Indies budget.

Some have said that Europeans forced the overseas subjects to pay for their own subjugation, and to some extent that is true. On the other hand, defense is a normal cost of life for any society. The role of the military in non-Western societies, precolonial and postcolonial, is ambiguous enough to leave unanswered the question of whether ordinary citizens got their money's worth. Whatever the overall balance sheet of empire, however, the imperial powers at the height of empire exercised military power overseas at bargain rates for the taxpayers at home.

The administrative structure on which that power was built was sometimes fragile. After independence, the colonial states created by the Western powers sometimes lost the power to govern, as they have done for long or short periods during recent decades in places as diverse as Cambodia, Somalia, Rwanda, Zaire, and Liberia. Techniques of public administration remain largely unstudied on a comparative basis from a world-historical perspective, within the European empires and outside them, though several later chapters will deal with non-European efforts to strengthen their own government administration to counter the threat of Europe.

Medical Technology

The developing body of medical knowledge was another powerful influence on the course of European empires overseas, though its actual implementation sometime lagged behind scientific understanding in Europe. Even before the discovery of the germ theory of disease or the mosquito vector for malaria and yellow fever, European military medicine made great strides in protecting European soldiers in the overseas world. These soldiers had grown up with immunities appropriate to the European disease environment. In a new disease environment overseas, especially in the tropical world, their deaths rates on garrison duty increased to become many times those of soldiers who served at home. Yet, between the 1840s and the 1860s, purely empirical advances, especially in preventive medicine, made a striking difference in the death rates of men in barracks in the tropical world (Figure 2.1). Annual death rates from disease dropped 50 to 70 percent from a combination of quinine, new drugs for treating dysentery, and greater care to provide clean water and better ventilation.

Some authorities have taken these improvements as evidence that Europeans had solved the problem of keeping their soldiers alive in the tropics. Tropical medicine seemed to be another technical source of European power. In the 1800s, however, the improved disease mortality of European troops in the tropics occurred mainly in barracks. On campaign, death rates remained high, even aside from enemy action, even though some unusual campaigns showed signs of victory over tropical disease. In 1874, British military authorities made much of the medical record of their two-month march from Cape Coast to Kumasi and back with a loss of life from disease of only 17 per thousand among the European troops involved. In fact, that campaign was an anomalous fluke; no other tropical campaign before the end of the century equaled its health record, though that campaign did raise some false expectations.

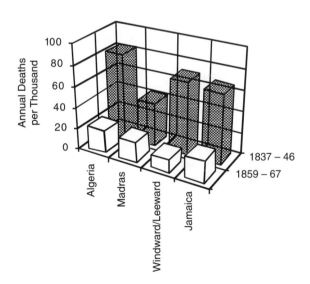

1. Disease mortality of European troops serving overseas – change between the 1840s and the 1860s.

Death rates from disease in barracks continued to improve, because medical officers on duty there were relatively free to do what they thought best. On campaign, they were subordinate to the line officers whose first concern was to win in the field. Available knowledge of preventive medicine was often not put into practice. Throughout the tropical world, preventive medicine on campaign was mainly ineffective until after the turn of the century, when the European conquests were virtually finished.

Military Power and Phases of Empire

In summary, the phases of European political and military activity overseas correspond to broad changes in European technology that accompanied the rise of industrialism. The earliest period, up to about 1750, was marked by rough technical parity between the West and the most advanced regions of Afro-Eurasia. Asian powers were militarily superior on land, European at sea. The special epidemiology of the Americas set those continents aside as one place European could create territorial empires with relative ease.

In the late 1700s and early 1800s, the Europeans began to gain a military edge in some parts of Asia – India, for example – but it was not yet based on industrial prowess; it was based, rather, on organizational skills, apparent in the tactical lessons European instructors gave to their Indian troops. Even before the marked weapons gap of the later 1800s, Britain had established its rule over a majority of the people of South Asia.

The period of approximately 1870 to 1900 was the central period of European military superiority based on the new weapons. These were the decades of the European conquest of the humid tropics, when Europeans partitioned sub-Saharan Africa, seized the remains of monsoon Asia, established genuine control over previously unadministered parts of the Amazon basin, and laid claim to the remaining islands of the Pacific.

After 1900, the weapons gap was no longer so great, but little remained still to conquer. There was some mopping-up in North Africa and the Middle East. Other conquests were begun and left unfinished. Russia and Britain both established a degree of competitive informal control over Persia and Afghanistan, but they stopped short of formal annexation. International rivalries also slowed or prevented the partition of Siam and China. The European powers divided China into spheres of influence, but the Europeans were preoccupied by the rivalries leading up to the First World War. Beginning in the 1930s, Japan was the industrial power that finally *did* attempt to conquer China, but that effort ended with the Japanese defeat in Second World War. By the 1940s, empire building had diminished benefits and rising costs. The reversal of the weapons gap was one of these costs, but it was only one problem among several in the international setting of the early cold war.

It would be a mistake to overemphasize a permissive factor such as the expectation of a cheap victory, though it was clearly important in some African conquests, like those of France in the Western Sudan and Britain in northern Nigeria. At times, Europeans, like others, went to war in circumstances where a predicted cheap victory was not forthcoming, or remained at war after the cost of victory was beyond any rational calculation. The sacrifices of the European powers in the First World War are a case in point, but it is evident throughout human history that rationality has not played a major role in the decision to wage war.

Further Reading

Cipolla, Carlo M., *Guns and Sails in the Early Phase of European Expansion, 1400–1700* (London: Collins, 1965).

Curtin, Philip D., *Death by Migration: Europe's Encounter with the Tropical World in the Nineteenth Century* (New York: Cambridge University Press, 1989).

Curtin, Philip D., *Disease and Empire: The Health of European Troops in the Conquest of Africa* (New York: Cambridge University Press, 1998)

O'Brien, Patrick Karl, "Intercontinental Trade and the Development of the Third World since the Industrial Revolution," *Journal of World History,* 8:75–133 (1997).

Parker, Geoffrey (ed.), *The Cambridge Illustrated History of Warfare: The Triumph of the West* (Cambridge, U.K: Cambridge University Press, 1995)

3

The Politics of Imperialism

Historical discussions about the causes of imperialism during the past century have often centered on the materialist interpretations called Marxist, though that interpretation probably owes more to J. A. Hobson than to Karl Marx. Hobson's most important book, *Imperialism: a Study,* appeared in 1902 and was strongly influenced by the recent events of the Anglo-Boer War in South Africa. Hobson's central point was that the capitalist and industrial economy of Europe produced more funds for investment than the European economy could absorb, and that these surplus funds therefore tended to be diverted overseas in search of higher profits or higher interest rates in a less competitive market. European governments, anxious to protect funds their nationals invested overseas, were hence lured into the expansion of their overseas empires.

This theoretical discussion of the material roots of imperialism and the variants that have ensued over the course of the past century is akin to other debates about the relations between capitalism, industrialism, and imperialism, and it is a proper concern for historians of Europe. For these essays, however, it is more useful to be content with a more practical level, to be concerned with the actual policies various European governments said they were following at various times and the processes of decision making that lay behind them.

Intent and Fact

We can assume at the outset that material interests were present at any and all levels where people have made decisions. We can also assume that political decisions had to be made in a world where industrialization (whether capitalist or not) was remaking power relationships, whether or not all actors were well informed about these changes. It is an ancient quip that Great Britain acquired its Indian empire "in a fit of absence of mind." The statement applied to the early 1800s, and the reality behind it was that no British Government made a clear statement about its intention to allow – or to forbid – the East India Company to create the territorial empire it was actually in the process of setting up. The conquest of India by a private concern, though chartered by the Crown, made it a shade less than official policy, though in the end consecutive Governments accepted the result.

In the official policy of central governments in Europe, viewed broadly, absence of mind toward empire-building was more common than not. Though it is difficult to separate declared intentions from undeclared and covert aims, periods of overt empire-building were comparatively short for most of the European powers. The declared German drive for a "place in the sun" lasted less than a quarter-century, from about 1884 to 1907 or 1908. Dutch official policy was anti-expansionist through the first half of the 1800s. The turn toward overt expansionism can be dated from the beginning of the wars for the conquest of Aceh in northern Sumatra in 1873 and ran on into the first decade of the 1900s, a period of about three decades, and it was confined to Southeast Asia. Portugal was expansionist only from 1883 onward into the first decade of the 1900s.

The British absence of mind is the classic case. In spite of acquiring the largest overseas empire of all, official policy was consistently non-expansionist after Waterloo. In the peace of 1815, Britain returned some captured overseas territories to Holland and France without serious qualms. Overtly expressed expansionism only returned with the Salisbury ministries between 1886 and 1902. Even within that period, Gladstone was in power with an officially anti-imperialist ministry from 1892 to 1894. This adds up to only fourteen years of more or less open empire building.

The pattern is clear: most European powers were self-consciously and avowedly out for conquest only during a relatively short period from about 1870 to 1910, and with a much heavier concentration of interest during the two decades of the 1880s and 1890s. This relatively brief period of overt European intent is, of course, the defining characteristic of the age of imperialism. It was, however, far form being the only period of Western empire building.

France was an exception to the common pattern, in timing if not in outcome, and the difference arose more out of international rivalries in Europe than events overseas. Following the French loss to the Allies in the Napoleonic Wars, French policy overseas went through an expansionist spurt, in an apparent attempt to compensate for losses in Europe. France was then briefly active in Guiana, Senegal, and Madagascar, but the objective was still that of the plantation complex or else trading-post empire, not territorial empire like of the British East India Company. Then, from the early 1820s to the early 1850s, France was as much a declared nonimperialist as any other power, though in fact it was creating a territorial empire in Algeria to match the British activity in India.

When Napoleon III came to power in 1851, French policy changed again. The government tried to capitalize on past Napoleonic glory with adventures in Mexico and elsewhere, but that phase ended in 1871, after defeat in the Franco-Prussian War. From the 1870s to the First World War, French policy passed through a period of comparatively rapid alternation. At least two ministries fell because they tried to organize forward moves in the face of anti-imperialist sentiment. Yet France in this period built the second largest of the European empires overseas.

Swings of opinion in the Chamber of Deputies reflected changing perceptions of France's place in Europe. The French loss of imperial wars and overseas territory, as happened in 1763 and 1815, brought, for one segment of French opinion, a desire to compensate by conquering still more territories overseas. Another segment called for France to rebuild French military power in Europe in order to reestablish its proper position of leadership there. Between 1871 and 1914, both of these sentiments were strong. Both sides agreed on the importance of restoring national prestige; they differed only on the means of going about it. A parallel circumstance occurred in 1962, when Charles De Gaulle gave up the fight to retain Algeria in favor of policies designed to reestablish the rightful place of France within Europe.

Overt empire building outside of western Europe was a more significant exception to the European pattern. Japan was clearly out of phase, partly because of its later acquisition of industrial technology –

more still because of its different political and cultural orientation. Japan attacked Taiwan and Korea in the 1870s, but the overt expansionism only began with the Sino-Japanese war over Korea in 1894. Japan's rule over Taiwan began in 1898, and its control over that island lasted as long as European rule lasted in most of tropical Africa. The Japanese empire on the Asian mainland dated only from the victory over Russia and the occupation of Korea in 1905. After that, while imperialist sentiment declined in western Europe, Japanese expansionism, however subdued in the 1910s and 1920s, flourished until the end of the Pacific War in 1945.

The United States and Russia

The United States and Russia are often absent from lists of Western empire builders of the 1800s. The United States was not territorially European. Though Russia was geographically European, its earlier history and orientation often departed from the general pattern, and its empire building was overland, not overseas. Both Russian and North American expansionism was almost continuous from the 1600s onward, first taking the form of overland trading-post empires based on the fur trade, then moving gradually into a pattern that began as territorial empire but often turned into a plural society, as settlers streamed in from the Slavic parts of the Russian empire to the west.

In neither case was desire for territorial empire the main intent, though both Russia and the United States participated along with the others – Russia extensively in the Caucasus, Central Asia, and Korea, and the United States equally dramatically in the 1840s by annexing most of northwestern Mexico and moving overseas in the 1890s by seizing the Philippines and Puerto Rico.

In the American case, expansion followed a legal fiction of acquiring territory already claimed by other Europeans, often territory the other had only incompletely under its administration. The Louisiana Territory was so far unknown to France that the United States had to send Lewis and Clark to discover what it had purchased. The actual conquest from the Native Americans followed later and was comparatively easy against sparse populations, even then undergoing the first attacks of exotic disease of the kind experienced by populations of central Mexico centuries earlier. Nor was most of the territory acquired from the Republic of Mexico in 1848 actually administered by Mexico, any more than all of Alaska was actually governed by Russia. These were simply transactions in claims, with only part of the territory under actual control of the seller. Some currents of opinion in the United States favored territorial acquisition of densely populated regions in Latin America and elsewhere, but in general, the Americans preferred land to the west that appeared open for settlement. The idea of "manifest destiny" was to expand true colonization on the model of the Atlantic seaboard, not to create a territorial empire on the model of India. The annexation of Hawaii, Puerto Rico, and the Philippines was an anomaly justified to the public mainly on strategic grounds.

Russian expansion was even more strategically oriented. From the core of Muscovy, the most direct route to the sea was northward to the Arctic Ocean. Russia therefore had a long-term strategic objective of gaining control of year-round warm-water ports. Beginning in the 1600s, Peter the Great had led the drive for ice-free ports – St. Petersburg to begin with. Later, similar efforts led south to the Black Sea and the search for an opening into the Mediterranean. Others led to the Persian Gulf by way of Iran and to the Pacific along the route of the trans-Siberian railroad. In one sense, Russia expanded continuously as a matter of avowed national policy, but seldom for the sake of ruling alien territory.

In general, then, European empire building was rarely an overt and declared policy at the centers of power in Europe, except for a very limited period centered in the 1880s and 1890s. A great deal of territorial expansion took place, not as a matter of central intent but guided by forces on the periphery. The absence of mind was in the imperial center, and that was not where the action was.

The Political Environment on the Periphery

Theorists who deal in world-systems analysis use the terms *center* and *periphery* with special meanings. The terms are used here in a non-technical sense, simply to locate a decision-making individual or group both geographically and within the political structure of a European empire. Long before the 1800s, European bureaucrats had developed the notion that orders should come down from the center of government, often in the king's name, to a hierarchy of subordinate officials, who passed them on down the line. In Europe, the people at the top of this hierarchy tended to be at the court or in the capital city, whereas subordinates were most often located elsewhere, at provincial capitals or in principal towns.

The spatial aspect of this hierarchy was not so important in Europe itself as it was to become when similar institutions were used to govern subjects thousands of miles away. Before the era of underwater telegraph cables, the distances involved meant that communication necessarily took weeks or months. Orders went from the colonial ministry or equivalent body to governors-general, to subordinate governors, and finally to military commanders and other subordinates at the point of contact or friction with non-Western neighbors or opponents.

Decision making thus was decentralized, with important consequences. People at different levels of the hierarchy, in different places, had different sources of information and different assessments of the political or military situation. As always, the man-on-the spot had a vastly different assessment from those at other levels of command or with different perspectives.

Each official with the power to make decisions had a particular circle of vision determined by his location and the information available to him, in addition to whatever other predispositions he may have had. Individual acts of imperial advance often depended on the interaction of a set of individual decisions, each reached within the context of a particular circle of vision.

The Anglo-Burma War of 1852

This proposition can be illustrated by examples of imperial advance. One classic example is the British acquisition of a large part of southern Burma after the Second Burma War of 1852, which became classic partly because it was publicized at the time in an important pamphlet, "How Wars are Got Up in India," by Richard Cobden, a leader of the free-trade movement.[1]

---

[1] Cobden, "How Wars are Got Up in India," in *The Politial Writing of Richard Coben,* 2 vols. (London: T. Fisher Unwin, 1903), 1:399–458 (First published 1853).

The relevant decision makers in this case were the British Government, acting through its control of the East India Company, the Governor-General of India, Lord Dalhousie, based in Calcutta, and the British men-on-the-spot in the delta of the Irrawaddy River in southern Burma. An earlier treaty had provided for a British resident in Rangoon and a Burmese ambassador in Calcutta, but that diplomatic representation was not yet in place.

In 1851, the Burmese authorities in on the lower Irrawaddy arrested two British sea captains on trumped-up charges. In the immediate situation, this was a case of cross-cultural misunderstanding. It had been the occasional practice in this part of Asia to bring serious charges against foreign merchants, then to let them go in return for a substantial fine. In this case, the demand amounted to less than £ 1,000 sterling, but as with waves spreading out from a stone dropping in water, its repercussions spread until they intersected with several different circles of vision.

The sea captains were angry to be treated in ways that were illegal in their own society, and so they appealed to authorities in Calcutta. The second circle of vision was that of Dalhousie and the government of India. The British position in India and in Asia generally depended on the power of the Indian Army and the Royal Navy, but the use of that power was constrained by financial considerations; wars, even punitive expeditions against weak rivals, were expensive, and so was the seizure and administration of still more Indian territory. Seen from Calcutta, the ideal strategy was to take advantage of Britain's known military power without actually using it. The very threat of force could be cheaper and sometimes just as effective as the use of force itself. Financial constraints were still more important when seen from the circle of vision of the imperial government in London.

Dalhousie in Calcutta, meanwhile, was engaged, like other viceroys before and since, in trying to increase the sphere of British influence among the "native states." In his time, the government of India put forward the Principle of Paramountcy, a little like the Monroe Doctrine in American policy toward Latin America, in that it was simply a diplomatic statement by a strong power that others would do well to heed. According to this doctrine, British power was so overwhelming on the subcontinent that Britain had the right – indeed the obligation – to intervene in the affairs of any Indian state that did not maintain adequate standards of government administration. Furthermore, the British Raj was to be the sole authority deciding what those standards should be.

A doctrine of that sort is hard to maintain. It required a delicate balance between the willingness to use punitive force if required and the knowledge on the part of potential opponents that force would indeed be used in certain circumstances known to all parties. In the language of the time, it was often spoken of as "white man's prestige," but behind it was the power and prestige of the Indian Army.

From Calcutta's perspective, therefore, the extortion of a few hundred pounds from a few British merchants was not what counted; what counted was the opportunity to underline the strength of British authority in the region. Dalhousie therefore sent a small naval expedition to the lower Irrawaddy with a demand for reparations, set at a higher figure that the probable losses of the merchants, with punitive intent as a lesson to others who might offend against British subjects.

The Burmese circle of vision then entered the picture. The Burmese court in Ava saw the danger of the British threat and withdrew the offending governor of Pegu on the lower river. The new governor, however, had arrived with military reinforcements, and he overestimated his own strength. He refused even to discuss the British demands.

The British naval commander, a man named Lambert, then entered the picture. He could have referred the matter to Calcutta, but he was hot-tempered and fell into the trap of cultural arrogance and racism of his time and class. He saw himself personally insulted by a petty Asian official and contrary to his official orders, proceeded to blockade Rangoon. He silenced a shore battery with his shipboard guns and began to take reprisals against Burmese shipping. The Burmese authorities still refused to give in, and Lambert only had three ships under his command. The situation on the Irrawaddy was then a stalemate.

Back in Calcutta, Dalhousie had a choice between forgetting the whole matter, or doing what the strong often do in such circumstances, escalating the scale of force applied. He ordered a full-scale invasion of coastal Burma, still pressing for a settlement of the original claims, but Burmese court politics intervened, and the British were still unable to get a settlement. In the end, Dalhousie simply declared the annexation of the part of the lower Irrawaddy that the British forces had seized in spite of the fact that the seizure was contrary to orders from London and called the war finished. The British Empire ended with a slice of Burmese territory that no one on the British side intended to acquire when the affair began.

In London, the situation was understood quite differently. Naval officers and governors-general were supposed to obey orders. The Government censured Lambert and brought Dalhousie under severe criticism for having got Britain into a useless and expensive war that ended by gaining territory it did not want. London nevertheless found it physically and diplomatically difficult to reverse what its agents had done. It became a classic instance of acquiring empire in a fit of absence of mind.

Leaving aside the Burmese perception of these misunderstandings – and wars for empire always had at least two sides, in spite of the common European-centered way they were often reported – the war and the annexations came about because of differences of opinion based on three circles of vision. Lambert's view was common enough for those with many guns at their disposal who think they have been insulted. Dalhousie escalated the controversy because of his concern for British prestige in India. The home Government was concerned by the expense of an unnecessary war that brought one more piece of unwanted territory overseas but was unable to prevail against a fait accompli.

Britain in Malaya

The territorial expansion of British holdings on the Malay peninsula is another and somewhat different example of unintended empire building. The British interest here in the early 1800s had been strictly a trading-post operation, even though its territorial empire had been growing simultaneously in India. Britain had, in fact, occupied the Dutch holdings in Southeast Asia during the Napoleonic Wars but returned them to the Netherlands at the peace of 1815. During the wars, Stamford Raffles had founded Singapore to further British trade in the region. With the coming of peace, Britain kept Singapore, along with the trading cities Melaka and Penang on the straits of Melaka. In the 1850s, these posts, collectively called the Straits Settlements, were detached from the government of India and put under the British Colonial Office.

The rest of the Malay peninsula consisted of a series of small states, each centered on a port at a river mouth and each attempting to dominate the trade of the sparsely populated hinterland, but with ineffective control over that interior. At mid-century, the settled British policy was not to encroach on the authority of the Malay sultanates. The governors of the Straits Settlements judged them to be well enough organized to preserve the peace and protect European commerce. Singapore's interest was limited to the defense of the Malay rulers from the potential expansion of Siam to the north or of the Dutch from their settlements on Sumatra across the straits to the west.

The sultanates, however, were weak in two respects, and this weakness became more obvious as the mid-century approached. They were not capable of controlling piracy by some of their subjects and neighbors. They were also ineffective in controlling the spread of tin mining along the western part of the peninsula, and tin mines attracted tens of thousands of Chinese miners, mostly young men without women who were a disruptive element in Malay society. The British were against piracy, but their economic interests were only indirectly involved in tin mining. Raffles had opened Singapore as a free port, which attracted immigrants from all over Southeast Asia, including southern China. The Chinese immigrants were so numerous that they soon far outnumbered the native inhabitants, as well as the small number of British attached to merchant houses in Singapore and other towns of the Straits Settlements.

Tin mining increased markedly from about 1848, first in Perak and then in the sultanates of Selangor and Negri Sembilan. Most of the tin mines belonged to Chinese capitalists, many of whom were British subjects resident in Melaka and Singapore, and most of the tin was exported to Europe, especially to Britain. The Malay sultans had only rudimentary administrative systems, which were unable to control the miners and keep the peace, and what order was kept was that maintained by Chinese "secret societies." Yet the sultans welcomed the mines for the wealth they could provide. Through the 1850s and 1860s, the sultans found these problems increasingly difficult, and the commercial and mining interests in the Straits Settlements found disorder increasingly bad for business. At that point, they turned to the colonial government for help.

Several different circles of vision were involved. The sultans found their position more and more untenable; they valued the economic return from mining, but the mines and miners were slipping out of their control. The mining and commercial interests in Singapore, from still another point of view, feared for their investment and wanted better preservation of law and order. London had still a third perspective; no British economic interests were directly involved as long as tin was available. London's position was to preserve the status quo and avoid the expense of forceful activity or increased territorial responsibilities in Southeast Asia.

A kind of crisis emerged in the early 1870s. The Singapore government asked London for permission to intervene, and London refused. Finally, in 1874, London conceded that it might be permissible for the governor of the Straits Settlements to send an official to reside at certain courts in the Malay States, if this were done at the expense of the Straits Settlements, not of the British taxpayers. London had in mind a kind of diplomatic agency. The governor, Sir Andrew Clark, however, interpreted the permission in his own way. After a minor military intervention, he persuaded the sultan of Perak to sign an agreement that not only welcomed a British resident at his court but also provided that the resident's "...advice must be asked and acted upon on all questions other than those touching Malay Religion and Custom." London's orders had been followed; no annexation took place, but the Perak agreement was only the first of series of similar agreements with other sultanates. Within a few decades, they constituted the foundation of what became the British Malay States and ultimately the present Malaysia. As in Burma some twenty years earlier, the London government was backed into an acquisition it had initially forbidden, on the initiative of its man-on-the-spot, largely responding the local problems and local interests.

Man-on-the-Spotism

In the Anglo-Burma War of 1852 and the British encroachment in Malaya later in the century, the impetus for empire building came from the periphery, not the imperial center. A similar tendency could be traced in patterns of French expansion into West Africa or Dutch expansion in Southeast Asia. It was, indeed, so common a tendency that the phenomenon has been identified as "man-on-the-spotism."

Some of its sources are clear enough. Peripheral policy-makers interpreted their task as one of maximizing the power and advantage of themselves and their fellow countrymen within that narrow local range. If, for example, a particular project would cost more than the local budget would bear, it was always possible to ask the center for more money, justifying the request as furthering the common good. It was also possible to make commitments that the center would be forced to honor in the longer run, even though it would have refused if permission had been asked for in advance.

Policy makers at the center, on the other hand, were closer to the taxpayers' representatives and others concerned about a wider range of costs and responsibilities. From the central point of view, it was necessary to balance the demands from different parts of the world and from various agencies within the central government. French cabinets after the 1870s had to balance the claims of revenge against Germany against those of expansion in Africa, Indochina, or elsewhere. They also had to balance the demands of the Ministry of the Navy, which controlled most overseas colonies, against those of the War Ministry, with its principal responsibility in Europe and North Africa, to say nothing of the broader international concerns of the Ministry of Foreign Affairs. British imperial affairs were divided and balanced in much the same way between the Colonial Office, which ruled over most colonies, the India Office, which ruled India, and the Foreign Office, which was in charge of Egypt, the Anglo-Egyptian Sudan, and a few other territories. These multiple balancing acts increased the central tendency to say "no," or at least to set limits on requests that came to it from the periphery.

Men-on-the-spot were also those most likely to encounter cross-cultural confrontation. Whether they were merchants, missionaries, or administrators, they had to deal with people, within the imperial frontiers or beyond, who were culturally different from themselves, with different values and different ways of conducting business. Dealing with those beyond the frontiers was more difficult because it required compromise with the "barbarians" at every turn. If, on the other hand, the outsiders were within the empire and a colonial government could make the rules, compromise might still be necessary, but the dominant political authorities would at least be those that shared one's own culture and values.

In the 1800s, men-on-the-spot had two additional incentives to expand. The weapons gap based on industrialization lowered the price tag of any use of force against non-Europeans. Men-on-the-spot were therefore in a position to relieve their cross-cultural frustrations more cheaply than ever before. In addition, that same industrialization in Europe tended to bring about new economic and social dislocations overseas. The preindustrial resources of public administration were often inadequate. Europeans had newly developed reasons to think they could handle the problems.

Malay tin mining is only one instance of a worldwide process. European industrial demand for goods from overseas encouraged non-Europeans to meet the demand, and that very process brought about disruptive changes, which, as in this instance, were bad for trade and damaging to a cheap source of tin. In other instances as well, it appeared to Europeans that more efficient government was required than the "natives" could furnish, and they saw no prospect for improvement except in European hands. Europeans in general were influenced by the new pride in the new organizational power of European governments, and this pride was itself a major source of the cultural chauvinism and racism that was so marked in European thought in the late 1800s. On the periphery, the frustrations of trying to deal with people with a different way of life were more severe, and consciousness of the organizational and industrial power of Europe gave men-on-the spot a heightened sense of the value of empire, combined with the promise of victory at a decreasing price.

At the same time, and especially in the middle decades of the century, European governments distrusted intervention, even at bargain basement prices. This was the era of the *imperialism of free trade,* when European commerce was expanding to new markets throughout the world. It seemed to many observers that, by any rational calculation, the best policy was to buy from the cheapest source and to sell at the highest possible price wherever a well-run state could keep the peace and see to it that contracts would be honored – at most only a degree of "informal empire" was required.[2]

These considerations, however, cannot be taken to explain European imperialism in the era of overt empire building in the 1880s and 1890s, but they can be used to illustrate some of the stresses and strains that lay behind imperial decision making even in that period.

Further Reading

Curtin, Philip D., "Location in History: Argentina and South Africa in the Nineteenth Century" *The Journal of World History*, 10:41–92 (1999).

Marshall, P. J. (ed.), *Cambridge Illustrated History of the British Empire* (Cambridge: Cambridge University Press, 1996).

Mommsen, Wolfgang J. and Jurgen Osterhammel (eds.), *Imperialism and After: Continuities and Discontinuities* (Boston: Allen and Unwin, 1986).

Steinberg, David Joel (ed.), *In Search of Southeast Asia: A Modern History*, rev. ed. (Honolulu: University of Hawaii Press, 1987).

---

[2] The classic treatment is by John Gallagher and Ronald Robinson, "The Imperialism of Free Trade," *Economic History Review*, 6(2nd ser): 1–15 (1953).

PART TWO

Culture Change and Imperial Rule

Historians once characterized the development of European empires with a process model based on one-word names for a series of stages: voyage, factory, fort, empire. Two additional stages, decolonization and modernization, would have to be added to take account of the past half-century. The reality behind these one-word descriptions began with the European ability to sail anywhere in the world, to establish a place for their factors to trade, to fortify these shore establishment, and finally to see them turn into territorial empires. When the stage of empire was reached, the model became more complex. The overseas territory included a government administration with Europeans on top. Many local people had to be drawn into government administration. Some local social groups became richer and more powerful, whereas others became poorer and weaker.

Among the leading social groups demanding further change was an élite class conscious of Western material achievements. Its members became the modernizers who wanted some aspect of the material promise demonstrated in the industrializing world – for themselves, for their country, or both. Many came to want the high per capita incomes they saw in the West. They sought a variety of different means to that end – capitalist or socialist of various kinds. The promised goals could be very different, though they almost always included due respect for aspects of the local culture, which they rarely wanted to discard altogether. The European presence often included missionaries trying to convert people to a Western religion, and the

Europeans brought some degree of Western education and economic change through the impact of a world economy.

Then came decolonization, a process common to virtually all of the former colonial world. It was most often led by the modernizing élite, which became frustrated with the colonial situation and began to organize political action on the Western model. To do so, they had to draw in the less Westernized elements of society – to find a mass base for protest. The colonial rulers then had to make a choice. They could try to make their exit gracefully and relatively peacefully, as the British did from India, or they could try to continue in power by force. Whenever the colonial power fought, either it lost or, if it won militarily, international and domestic pressure at home forced it to withdraw, as the Dutch did from Indonesia and the French did from Algeria.

The final one-word stage is modernization. The goal is almost universal in the world today, where virtually everyone wants to enjoy the high productivity and high per capita consumption that the most advanced countries began to achieve almost two centuries ago.

This six-stage process model is, however, incomplete. It leaves out the non-Western countries that were never fully conquered and ruled by Europeans, such as Japan and in varying degrees, China, Thailand, Afghanistan, and Iran. It also leaves out Taiwan and Korea, where the colonial master was Japanese, not European. Those who escaped European domination required enough military modernization to make the prospect of conquest expensive for any aggressor, and that military modernization also had a price. The modernizing leadership usually had to push aside the former rulers. That in itself was a revolutionary change, forcing the modernizing élite to act much like the modernizing nationalists in the former colonies. These never colonized countries thus entered the process model, but only at the final stage of postcolonial modernization.

The three chapters that follow deal with culture change at the stage of empire. The purpose here is to use individual examples to illustrate some of the variety of circumstances in which non-Western people reacted to the policies colonial governments sought to impose. Chapter 4 deals with the special case of plural societies, where the colonial overrule was accompanied by a substantial minority of settlers from Europe. Chapter 5 deals with examples of culture change in parts of the Americas, where relatively dense Amerindian populations sought to resist change or to accommodate their way of life to that of the dominant segment of Mexican society. Chapter 6 deals with comparative cases of change resulting from imperial policies regarding administration and land tenure in some of the territorial empires of southern Asia.

4

Culture Change in Plural Societies: South Africa and Central Asia

The process model of voyage, fort, empire takes little or no account of plural societies that also sprang up in the gap between territorial empire on the one hand and true colonization on the other. The earliest to be formed were in Indo-America, the countries along the backbone of the Americas from Mexico south to Bolivia, Paraguay, and parts of Argentina and Chile. The cultural mixture there is highly diverse: in some countries separate Indian communities live in relative isolation; in others, such as Mexico, Indian and Spanish cultures have integrated over the centuries, so that the majority culture is more Mexican than either.

Another set of American plural societies emerged from the plantation complex in the Caribbean and eastern South America. People from Africa were present almost everywhere, and their cultures blended to create a new, Creole culture. After the end of the African slave trade, massive immigration of indentured laborers from India created in some places a separate East Indian cultural community. The European community was often very small, but it was a majority in some islands such as Cuba and Puerto Rico.

A similar group of plural societies exists in Southeast Asia, where cultural pluralism resulted from migration within the tropical world, not from a significant community of European settlers. The largest immigrant group was Chinese, whose arrival, especially in the 1800s, made them the majority ethnic community in Singapore and a large minority in Malaysia, Thailand, and Indonesia. Indian immigrants at this same period became an important cultural community in Singapore, lower Burma, and Malaysia.

Several kinds of cultural pluralism existed in the Soviet Union at the time of its break-up. Some ethnic sentiments reflected differing nationality feelings among people whose culture was a subdivision of the general European culture. The separation of the Baltic republics, Moldava, Ukraine, and Belorus was like the division into nation-states elsewhere in Europe. It belongs to the sphere of European history, not that of European empires.

To the south and east, beyond the Slavic lands, a variety of non-Western people had fallen under the control of the Russian empire. Many reproduced the cultural demography of territorial empire, but others received so many Slavic settlers that they belong to the category of plural societies. These non-Western Soviet territories fall into three groups. The first lies along the southern frontier of the Russian advance toward the Caucasus between the Black Sea and the Aral Sea. This region includes the former Soviet republics of Georgia, Armenia, and Azerbaijan.

A second group is located in Central Asia, east of the Aral Sea and west of China. Russia conquered these territories mainly between 1860 and 1890, with a timing similar to that of the age of imperialism elsewhere. This region became the most important group of plural societies in the Soviet Union, and, after its break-up, emerged as the five independent republics of Turkmenistan, Uzbekistan, Tadzhikistan, Kirghizia, and Kazakhstan.

A third group consists of a number of non-Slavic regions, recognized as autonomous republics within the Russian Soviet Federated Socialist Republic, which have continued as such in the present Russian republic. They are twenty-one in number, relatively diverse, small, and scattered, and they include Chechnya, which has tried to claim independence from the Russian republic. In the early 1990s, ethnic Russians made up more than 80 percent of the population of the Russian republic as a whole, but they were often a minority within the autonomous republics, as they were in Chechnya. Other autonomous republics were highly varied and they were located in European Russia as well as Siberia. A group of six along the Volga River had been within the Russian sphere for centuries, but ethnic Russians were a minority in four of these six.

South Africa: the Formation of a Plural Society

The plural societies in Africa were found in the far north and far south, where European immigration created substantial European cultural communities in Algeria and again in South Africa and Zimbabwe. The mass withdrawal of the French settlers from Algeria after 1962 greatly reduced the size of the French community there, leaving the only important plural societies on that continent in the far south.

It used to be common to divide the world into hemispheres, as though there were only two, one centered on the Americas and the other including most of Afro-Eurasia. There are, of course, an infinite number of possible hemispheres, depending on the point in space from which you look at the globe. Southern Africa is isolated at the southern end of a long extension of the Afro-Eurasian landmass. If you turn a globe to place South Africa at the center of your field of vision, you will see a hemisphere that is mostly water. South Africa is literally at one of the ends of the earth.

By the 1600s, when the Europeans first established themselves on the coast, South Africa was broadly divided linguistically between the Khoisan-speaking people of the southwest and the Bantu speakers of the southeast, whose language and culture could be traced to tropical Africa. The Bantu speakers mainly practiced agriculture with an important element of stock raising, and they were distinct from Khoisan people who spoke the click languages. The Khoisan were divided between the San, who were hunters and foragers, and the Khoikhoi, who were mainly pastoral nomads. The cultural differences reflected the basic three ecologies of mixed farming, stock farming, and hunting, but centuries of interaction around the fringes of all three groups had produced a great deal of intermarriage and cultural mixture. The ethnic divisions recognized today within these the basic groups are recent, going back no more than a few centuries.

In the mid-1600s, Europeans began to arrive in the Western Cape Province of South Africa, and two Afrikaans-speaking communities developed, one mainly of European descent and the other, the Cape Colored people, a racial and cultural mixture of the local Khoisan people with immigrants from Europe, East Africa, and several different parts of Asia. In the 1800s and after, two other groups of immigrants began to arrive, the English-speaking Europeans and the Bantu-speaking Africans mainly from the Eastern Cape Province.

In the other provinces of South Africa, other population movements created a variety of other patterns where different cultural communities lived side by side. The Europeans, both Afrikaans- and English-speaking, settled in pockets throughout the country. The English went first to the Eastern Cape, then to Natal, and later to the cities where economic development was concentrated. Nor were all the immigrants who joined English-speaking South Africa from Britain. Many came from continental Europe, but once in South Africa they integrated linguistically and culturally with the English speakers who were already there rather than with the Afrikaners.

White Afrikaans speakers also moved from their original home at the Cape. In the 1840s and 1850s, the migration called the Great Trek brought them onto the high veld, where they set up the new republics of the Orange Free State and Transvaal and established their economic and political dominance over the African majority. A final major immigrant group was Indian, introduced mainly in the second half of the 1800s to the Indian Ocean coast of Natal as indentured workers in the sugarcane fields. By the 1990s, their descendants has grown into a community of just under a million people, almost 3 percent of the population.

As a result of these different migrations, various immigrant communities were diversely scattered in pockets through out the countryside and in the urban centers. The African populations also tended to be ethnically concentrated. As the Europeans moved in, they seized the best land, though Africans continued to provide most of the farm labor, and Europeans settled in the urban centers of mining and industry. Early in the twentieth century, the South African government marked out certain regions as reserves for exclusive possession of the Africans, who were not permitted to own land elsewhere. In time, the reserves were recognized as ethnic homelands, each for a particular linguistic group – Zulu, Xhosa, Tswana, and so on. Most of the land was reserved for whites, but whites still needed African labor, so that the majority of the inhabitants of "white" South Africa were in fact Africans.

Creating a Plural Society in Central Asia

Central Asia, far from being at an end of the earth, is at the heart of its greatest landmass, historically a crossroads of interchange between India, China, Europe, and the Middle East. If you turn a globe to center on central Asia, on a point such as the city of Samarkand, the hemisphere you will see is the most land-filled of all the possible hemispheres. Until the past millennium, migrants mainly moved overland, not by sea, and a great many of them moved through central Asia. The result is a range of central Asian populations that are more diverse and culturally mixed even that those of South Africa.

As in South Africa, the most stable division over time was that between nomads and sedentary farmers. The nomads lived mainly in the arid regions to the north and west, while sedentary farmers lived in the mountains to the east and south or along the rivers flowing toward the Aral Sea. The terrain offered few ecological choices; the more arid plains were suited only for pastoral nomadism. When nomads conquered the river valleys, as they did from time to time, they had little alternative but to adopt the technology and some of the culture of their sedentary neighbors.

Central Asian people cannot be divided culturally or historically into the five Soviet Republics now recognized as independent states, any more than the South Africans were culturally divided between the "tribes" recognized by the apartheid government of South Africa. In physical appearance, central Asians tended to be a mixture of Mongoloid types more prevalent in the east and north and a Caucasoid or Iranian physical type prevalent in the south and west, though linguistic divisions do not always follow physical appearance. Central Asian languages are divided between the Mongolian, the Turkic, and the Iranian language families, again with a rough tendency for Iranian languages to predominate southwest toward the border with Iran, the others to the north and east. No region spoke a single language before the Russian conquest or after, and the Soviet period simply added a variable Slavic element to regions that were already culturally mixed.

As early as the 1600s, European settlers had been infiltrating into Asia east of the Urals and north of Kazakhstan, but migration to central Asia proper came mainly after the 1850s. As in South Africa, suc-

cessive stages of settlement took different forms with different consequences. The first wave came in the last four decades or so before the
First World War, when Russian and Ukrainian peasants moved into
what became northern Kazakhstan, where plow agriculture was possible. As early as 1911, fully 40 percent of the population of that region
was Slavic. In 1989, Russians were 41 percent of the Kazakhstan population, and Ukrainians were another 6 percent. The Kazakhs themselves were down to 38 percent in the country that bore their name
(Table 4.1).

The proportion of settlers in the total Kazakh population, however,
was less stable than the comparison between 1911 and 1989 suggests.
The Stalinist years were a period of great disruption and high mortality. Between 1926 and 1939, in the period of enforced collectivization,
the Kazakh population apparently dropped by one million people, per-

Table 1 Ethnic Balances in Soviet Central Asia and Successor States

SSR	Population (millions)	Ethnic Groups	Percent Russians in 1991
Turkmenistan	3.5	Turkmenians 68%	
		Russians 13%	9%
		Uzbeks 9%	
Uzbekistan	19.6	Uzbeks 69%	
		Russians 11%	9%
		Tatars 4%	
		Kazakhs 4%	
		Tadzhiks 4%	
Tadzhikistan	5	Tadzhiks 59%	
		Uzbeks 23%	
		Russians 10%	7%
Kirghizia	4.2	Kirghizians 48%	
		Russians 28%	21%
		Uzbeks 12%	
Kazakhstan	16.5	Kazakhs 38%	
		Russians 41%	37%
		Ukrainians 6%	

Source: 1989 USSR Yearbook; 1991 data, Goskomstat.

haps a quarter of its total. Some people died after they lost their cattle. Others simply fled; nomads are mobile, and those seeking to escape forcible settlement could cross into Xinjiang in western China, which was culturally similar and from where they were in a position to return when the situation in Kazakhstan improved. Meanwhile, Russian and Ukrainian farmers continued to move in.

Other Russian and Ukrainian migrations further south into the oasis country along the Syr Darya and Amu Darya rivers were a different process with different timing. Some Slavs came before the First World War as administrators, soldiers, technicians, and commercial people, but the Russian population of what was to be Soviet Central Asia was only 6 percent in 1911, and that was concentrated in the north in a belt between Lake Balkash and the Chinese border, leaving the south as territorial empire. For that matter, the two khanates of Bukhara and Khiva were still only indirectly under the czar at that time.

The heavy population movement of Russians and other Europeans into the southern central Asian republics came mainly after the Second World War. At the end of the Soviet period, the Russian population in the three southernmost provinces was about 12 percent of the total, or about the same proportion as that of the French in Algeria at the end of French rule. Most were not workers or peasants like the settlers in Kazakhstan, but relatively well-educated, well-paid technicians and bureaucrats.

Comparative Demography: South Africa and Central Asia

In spite of the enormous internal variety in the cultural demography of South Africa and Central Asia, the distinctive social patterns of the two territories were remarkably similar. In 1988, the population of Soviet Central Asia was 49 million, or when 25 percent were Europeans. In 1987, the total population of South Africa was 35 million, of whom 14 percent were considered to be white. For some purposes in South Africa, the more significant proportion is that of all people of Western culture, both white and colored, which in 1987 would have been about 23 percent of the whole.

In recent decades, differential population growth rates for Europeans and non-Europeans were similar in Central Asia and South Africa; non-Europeans increased faster than Europeans. Because both had long been a part of a larger Afro-Eurasian disease environment, the entry of European colonists did not provoke a die-off of the indigenous peoples like that in the Americas. Two distinct demographic phases nevertheless occurred in both Central Asia and South Africa. Up to about 1950, the settler populations grew both in numbers and in proportion to the whole population. This result came partly from immigration, partly because the settler community had better diet and medical attention. In Central Asia in the Stalinist period, the non-Slavic peoples suffered more than the Slavs in the struggles over collectivization. As a result, the European population in all of Central Asia rose from 6 percent of the total in 1911 to 30 percent of the total in 1959.

Sometime after 1950, however, the growth rate of the Slavic population slowed, and the more recent demographic phase set in. For a time, continuing immigration offset the declining natural growth, and brought the European population to a peak of about 33 percent in about 1970, after which it declined to about 25 percent in 1989. The population growth rate for the Russian Republic was 6.8 per thousand, while the growth rates in the five central Asian republics varied from 18.1 per thousand in Kazakhstan up to 35.2 per thousand in Tadzhikistan. The result is the highly diverse pattern of plural society illustrated in Table 4-1. In 1989, the dominant local ethnic group, which was the one that gave its name to each republic, was a majority in each republic except Kazakhstan, but it was nowhere more than 70 percent of the total. The Russian minority was at least 10 percent everywhere and was the second largest ethnic group everywhere except in Tadzhikistan.

These swings in the settler proportion were similar in South Africa, as Table 4.2 indicates. In 1870, the whites had been 17 percent of the total, and the whites and colored together had been 27 percent. By 1987, increasing African population meant that the whites alone had fallen to 14 percent of the total and the whites and colored together to 23 percent.

In South Africa and Central Asia alike, settlers were distributed unevenly. Some regions, such as northern Kazakhstan or the Western Cape Province, approached the conditions of a true settlement colony. In the native reserves that were renamed homelands in South Africa, the European population was often less than 1 percent of the total, as it was in the rural parts of southern Central Asia.

Table 2 South African Population by Race*		
Category	Number	Percent
African	25,981,635	74.5
White	4,911,000	14.1
Colored	3,069,000	8.8
Indian	913,000	2.6
Total	34,874,635	100

* Estimate as of June 1987.
Source: Legum Colin, African Comtemporary Record, 1987–8.

Education and Culture Change

In Central Asia and South Africa, culture change took place at a different pace in different ways. It was most rapid among both Asians and Africans who moved to urban areas in search of work. Cross-cultural contact was most intense in these regions of rapid economic development, but cross-cultural friction was also most intense there. As everywhere else in the world in the twentieth century, feelings of ethnic identity were called up most vividly in communities with marked ethnic difference. The European rulers of Central Asia and South Africa were conscious of the problems of ethnic conflicts. South African governments tended to identify the problem as one of race. Soviets saw a "nationalities problem." In other respects, the two governments viewed ethnic conflict in ways that were sometimes closely parallel and sometimes very different.

Education and religious policy were two areas of government decision making that most obviously involved culture change. After the Russian Revolution, every Soviet citizen was theoretically equal to every other, and the Soviet intention was to form all to a common standard managed by the Communist Party. This effort involved such institutions as the Young Pioneers, similar to west European Boy Scouts; the management of all media of communication, from the press to literature and the arts; the formative experience of universal military service for men; informal pressures in the workplace; and, of course, the formal educational system at all levels. The superiority of Russian over other Soviet cultures was more often taken for granted than consciously embedded in policy.

In the 1800s, in Western Europe and pre-Revolutionary Russia alike, theory about appropriate education for the empire overseas had emphasized the value of spreading civilization to the "natives," but the task was often left to the private effort of missionary societies. It was a logical choice at a period when public education in Europe itself was only gradually being introduced; mass public education was expensive, given the other demands on the colonial budgets. Few indeed considered the possibility that metropolitan taxpayers might pay for colonial education; the idea of spreading civilization was more often a justification for empire than a serious policy. If the intention to spread European culture were serious, the place to begin was free and compulsory elementary education, followed by a reasonable degree of open entry into secondary schools and university for bright children. In fact, none of the major territorial empires proposed any such thing, even as a distant goal. The only Western empire to move in this direction was the United States in Hawaii and Puerto Rico, with a more modest effort in the Philippines.

South Africa is an example of this broader pattern of neglect. In the 1800s, the governments provided little public education for children of any race. Until the 1950s, the only education available to Africans came from the Christian missions, and it was neither compulsory nor free, since the missions often charged school fees. It was only then that the government took up public education for Africans under the Bantu Education Acts, but only with the intention of providing Africans with an inferior education, slightly better for Colored and Asians.

The distinction made theoretical sense; Africans were barred from most skilled or professional positions in any case. It would have been counterproductive to educate them for positions reserved for others. Toward the late 1960s, however, the policy began to change as the apartheid government discovered that an industrializing country needed a better educated work force, but drastic differences in quality of education remained. In 1963, the government spent twelve times as much per capita for education of whites as it did for Africans. In 1988, it still spent five times as much. The difference shows up in the 1984 literacy rates: 93 percent for whites, 71 percent for Asian, 62 percent for Colored, and only 32 percent for Africans.

At that same time, the Central Asian literacy rate was nearly that of white South Africans. The Soviet Union introduced public education in Central Asia earlier and on a larger scale than most other imperial powers, though educational opportunity remained less than was available in the Russian Republic or western Europe. In 1930, the Soviet Union nevertheless set a goal of free and compulsory primary education for Central Asia, though schooling was only compulsory for four years, and implementation took time. By the 1940s, however, about 90 percent of children of school age were in school. Opportunities to move up the educational ladder were also more open than in most tropical African colonies or South Africa.

Religion

Religion is another key area where the Soviet and South African governments had different goals. Christianity was a proselytizing religion in prerevolutionary Russia, in western Europe, and in settler South Africa. Orthodox Christians, however, made very little use of the opportunity to convert the people of Central Asia, and Christian missionaries often found it difficult to convert Muslims in any part of the world.

Christian missionaries made a far more serious effort in South Africa, and they were better received, in spite of the fact that many Africans came to resent the racial exclusiveness of the missionary churches and that some aspects of Christianity fitted badly with older African social and religious traditions. As a result, many African Christians joined separatist African churches rather than the official mission churches run by the whites, but South Africa is nevertheless one of the high points of Christian success in Africa. An African aphorism runs to the effect, that "In the beginning we had the land, and you had the Bible. Now you have the land and we have the Bible." But even that was not quite accurate. The Europeans in South Africa at the end of apartheid had more than 80 percent of the land, but about half of the African population was officially classified as "heathen."

In comparison, Russian Christians before the revolution were far less successful, and the Soviets tended to discourage religion of all kinds, but they were no more successful in suppressing Islam than the Christian missions had been. Some educated Central Asians, like some Russians of similar background, moved over to a vaguely secular disbelief, but Islam held most of its followers in the oases. In Kazakhstan, Islam even made some gains among people who had previously been pagan.

Economic Development

Economic growth was an area where Central Asian and South African government intentions and achievements were more nearly parallel. Both the Soviet Union and the South African government favored high productivity, though they differed as to how the product was to be distributed. In theory, the Soviet state wanted to use the material increase for state purposes, which would include high rates of mass consumption only in the long run. The South African state policy tolerated and sometimes encouraged a racial division of income, which would give most to whites, less to Indians, still less to Colored, and least of all to Africans.

The means chosen to reach these goals were different in the two cases. The Soviet system in Central Asia, as elsewhere in the Soviet Union, was basically a directed economy. The South African system was capitalist, but with considerable government intervention to implement the social goals of apartheid, and it included some government ownership of economic enterprises, especially heavy industry.

Both the South African and Central Asian economies were moderately successful over the decades, less so than the most developed countries but far more so than the least developed. For about a quarter of a century after the Second World War, Soviet Central Asia led all of the Muslim world in economic growth, and South Africa led all of Africa. In about 1960, per capita incomes in Central Asia and South Africa were nearly the same. They would have been five or six times greater than incomes in poorer countries such as India or Pakistan, but only about one-fifth or one-sixth of the per capita incomes in rich countries like Canada or the United States.

Then came the oil shocks, the foundation of the Organization of Petroleum Exporting Countries (OPEC), enormous gains for the Persian Gulf states, and the rise of the new industrial economies on the Pacific rim. The South African economy continued to grow more successfully than the economy of most of Africa in the 1970s and 1980s, but it slipped behind the industrial growth of Taiwan or South Korea. Central Asia slipped behind even more, beset by the economic problems of the Soviet Union as a whole.

The distribution of income within the Soviet Union was nevertheless more equitable than it was within South Africa. Money wages in Central Asia were the same for Asians and Europeans. Estimates in about 1970 indicate a living standard about 20 to 25 percent less than that of the Russian Republic, simply because more people in Central Asia held low-paying jobs. In South Africa, on the other hand, skilled or high-paying jobs were reserved for whites by law. This policy began to be modified somewhat beginning in the late 1970s, as Africans were allowed to belong to trade unions and an effort to equalize wages began. In spite of some progress, the total picture by 1987 was still abysmal. The average black income per person was not even one tenth of the average white income. Thus, while South Africa was the most developed country in sub-Saharan Africa, the incomes of ordinary Africans were not always higher than those in the more fortunate parts of tropical Africa.

Nationalism

Nationalism, in the sense of opposition to European rule, has been endemic in the colonial world from the late 1800s. Nationalism, in the other sense of loyalty to people with shared language and customs, can be expected to thrive where different cultures are present in the same society. Plural societies such as South Africa and Central Asia were prone to nationalism in both senses, and the rulers of both were sensitive to their dangers.

Before the 1980s, it was a common opinion that the Soviet Union had succeeded in assimilating the ethnic majorities of Central Asia, where as white South Africa had failed. South Africa was the pariah state in world opinion, ultimately subject to sanctions for its attempt as a minority government to impose racial dominance. The Soviet Union was sometimes applauded as a place where the conquered people were welcomed into the fold of common citizenship – like Hawaii, the French West Indies, and other assimilated bits of former colonial empires. The judgment of South Africa remains, but that on the Soviet Union has been reconsidered recently in the light of ethnic violence in its former republics from Georgia and Azerbaijan into Central Asia, to say nothing of the problem of Chechnya in Russia itself.

South African and Soviet Policies on nationalities had certain points in common, and each was conscious of what the other was doing or not doing. The Soviets, however, tended to see their nationalities problem in their own political and cultural setting. In the early years after the revolution, they perceived the threat of an Islamic revival beyond Soviet borders, which could turn into anticolonial nationalism and a demand for independence. To counter the universal claim of Islam, the Soviets tried to encourage the claims of linguistic nationalism as a form of divide and rule. In 1924, they subdivided the old Turkestan into the five units that make up present-day Central Asia. Each became a separate Socialist Soviet Republic, with areas of autonomy from the central authorities. Each was expected to encourage local culture, hence to emphasize its differences from the others, and to minimize the fact that the community of Islam gave them all a common religion. The overt autonomy was deceptive, since each of the five governments was actually controlled by the Soviet Communist Party, a unitary party dominated by Russians. The policy may have reduced anti-Soviet feelings, but local resentment remained, especially during the Stalinist period from the mid-1930s to the mid-1940s. During the Second World War, many Soviet soldiers from Central Asia deserted to the Germans.

After the Second World War, returning economic prosperity made it possible for the Soviet government to reduce its insistence on separate nationalities. It tended, instead, to emphasize common Soviet citizenship, while at the same time allowing local political leaders to play larger roles in each of the republics, a source of trouble for the future because local control made possible an increase in political corruption. When the Soviet reform movement of the 1980s attacked government corruption, present in Central Asia as elsewhere in the Soviet Union, the policy was sometimes viewed as a Russian attempt to suppress local leadership, and economic hard times also raised ethnic tensions within the republics. In either case, a common response was to revive the ethnic sentiments that had lain dormant. The problem was not solved, merely put off, by the break-up of the Soviet Union. The tensions of a plural society were still present in different ways in each of the independent republics.

For South Africa, the apparent success of the Soviet nationalities policy was so striking in the 1950s that the National Party took over the Soviet idea and decided to set up its series of *homelands,* informally called Bantustans, even imitating the Soviet terminology. The intent was similar to that of the Soviets – to divert people from potential solidarity as Africans and to emphasize their potential loyalty to smaller ethnic units such as Xhosa, Zulu, or Tswana, thus leaving the white minority still a minority but the largest of several minorities, with a continued ability to divide and rule. The apartheid government furthered this policy by setting up separate universities for some of the major ethnic groups – one near Cape Town for the Colored, one for the Indians in Durban, and others for African subdivisions. It also encouraged home-language education in primary schools, though that policy met so much opposition that it had to be dropped.

Ultimately the homelands policy aimed at a grant of formal independence to each of the Bantustans in turn. Thus, the Africans assigned to that homeland would lose their South African citizenship, however small the rights they might enjoy under it. As of 1987, 20 million Africans were counted as living in South Africa, with 5.8 million counted in the homelands, but international opinion regarded homelands independence as a fraud, and no other country gave them diplomatic recognition.

After 1990, the leadership of the ruling National Party abandoned the homelands as it abandoned apartheid in general. After its election victory of the 1994, the African National Congress (ANC) reincorporated the former homelands into the republic. The homelands African leadership was thoroughly discredited and generally seen as corrupt, like the Communist party leadership in Central Asia. The new constitution of 1996 divided the country into nine provinces in place of the earlier four, though South Africa remains a unitary state, not a federation like Canada or Australia.

In South Africa the policy of divide and rule failed, just as it partly succeeded in Central Asia with the emergence of five new independent states after the break-up of the Soviet Union. Most Africans continued to claim political rights in South Africa as a whole, rather than settling for lesser privileges in a restricted area. The relaxation of apartheid allowed the ANC to emerge as the dominant African voice, and the ANC has consistently held out the goal of a democratic South Africa with equal rights for all. It was opposed by the Panafricanist Congress, which for a time demanded full political rights for Africans only. It was also opposed by the Zulu Inkatha movement under Chief Mangosuthu Buthelezi, which was the only significant political voice appealing to the divisive ethnic nationalities like those of Central Asia. It is too early for confident prediction, but, at the end of the 1990s, it looked as though ethnic nationalism had triumphed in Central Asia, whereas it failed in South Africa in face of a continued majority faith in a greater nonracial South African nationality.

Plural societies were a significant by-product of the age of Western empire building, and the formal end to European colonial power has not diminished the problems of ethnic conflict that they brought about. The recent histories of South Africa and Central Asia are evidence enough. On the other hand, ethnic conflict is a worldwide problem of the recent past and an easily predictable problem stretching into the future. The age of European empires was an important contributing factor, but it was not alone. The commencement of the industrial age with its globalization of human activity has to be counted as an overriding influence on an enormous variety of culture change and culture conflict. People have had to make individual decisions about their response, and their decisions have been various, as we will see in the next chapter from the example of Mexico.

Further Reading

Bacon, Elizabeth E., *Central Asians Under Russian Rule: A Study of Culture Change* (Ithaca, NY: Cornell University Press, 1965).

Curtin, Philip D. (ed.), *Imperialism* (New York: Walker & Company, 1971)

Thompson, Leonard, *History of South Africa,* 2nd ed. (New Haven: Yale University Press, 1995).

5

Culture Change in Mexico

One residual error of the once-popular hemispherization of the world is the view that the history of the Americas in general is much like the history of the United States and different from that of other continents. In fact, Canada and the United States have more in common historically with Australia and New Zealand than they do with most of the tropical Americas. The plantation complex that flourished on the tropical east coast of both continents had intimate connections with Africa as well as with Europe. The plural societies of Indo-America had something in common with other plural societies, such as those of central Asia or Africa – more, in fact, than they had in common with the settler societies of North America or with the plantation societies of the Caribbean.

The European conquest of Mexico and Peru began in the 1520s, whereas the European conquest of North Africa and of Bantu-speaking South Africa began only in the 1830s. The Russian conquest of Central Asia began even later, in the 1860s. Amerindian and European cultures were therefore in contact within the Spanish empire for about three centuries before the European cultural penetration of Africa and central Asia had seriously begun.

All cultures change over time, but one simplistic idea about change in Amerindian cultures is that they gradually accepted cultural elements from their European neighbors in a process often called acculturation. They sometimes did that, but Euro-American cultures were simultaneously borrowing Indian patterns, and both were also constantly changing for internal reasons. In some places, central Mexico for example, the result over more than four centuries was the creation of a dominant cultural pattern that was neither Indian nor European, but Mexican. It is sometimes called *mestizo* or mixed, but the same term is used for people of mixed race, usually Spanish and Amerindian. The races did, indeed, mix, but the significant aspect was the creation of a new cultural blend of Spanish and Indian. The term *ladino* in Spanish has other meanings, but it can be used here for the Indian-Spanish cultural blend that became Mexican.

Like the term *modern,* ladino means different things at different times and places. Ladino culture was not a simple continuation of the initial melding that began in central Mexico in the 1530s, nor was the form of Ladino culture unchanging. The early Ladino culture, like other cultures, continued to change, and it changed alongside the Spanish version of European culture and a variety of Indian cultures, which were also changing. This process, which has been carefully studied in recent years, was most rapid in central Mexico and continued over a long time, but it is not the concern of this essay.[1]

This chapter will deal instead with some of the smaller and less central Indian populations that managed to retain evolving versions of their earlier culture into the 1800s, in some respects down to the present. Two have attracted special attention because of their long-term struggle to preserve what they most valued in their older way life. Both were far from the Valley of Mexico, the true center of the power and influence of New Spain. One is the Maya on the Yucatan peninsula. Another, and the much smaller society, is that the Yaqui in Sonora, originally inhabiting a single valley where the Yaqui River flows west from the Sierra Madre into the Gulf of California.

The Encounter with Spain

The encounter with Spain took place in stages that were similar through most of what became Spanish America. The initial conquest of the core regions occupied roughly the decades from the 1520s to the 1570s. After that, a more stable period followed, often simply called the colonial period in Spanish-American history. The end of

---

[1] See especially James Lockhart, *The Nahuas after the Conquest: A Social and Cultural History of the Indians of Central Mexico, Sixteenth through the Eighteenth Centuries* (Stanford: Stanford University Press, 1992).

Spanish rule in the early 1800s, however, was only one of a series of changes that affected Indian-Spanish relations about that time, beginning in the 1760s with the "Bourbon reforms," so called after the new Spanish dynasty. These reforms centered on an administrative rearrangement of Spain's empire, including increased freedom of intercolonial commerce for Spanish subjects.

For Indians under Spanish rule, these reforms are often associated with the so-called second conquest, where, after a period of benign neglect, the Spanish sought to establish firmer control over the Indian communities, and the Republic of Mexico continued with similar policies after the break with Spain. In one sense, the second conquest, in its various forms throughout Latin America, was a regional equivalent of the more aggressive European annexations in Asia and Africa. The ultimate driving force in either case was the beginning of the industrial era.

The impact of these two conquests of indigenous America, however, were very different for different regions, even within what became Mexico. The first conquest was most intense for central Mexico. The Spanish destroyed the Aztec capital of Tenochtitlán and built Mexico City on its the location, which continued as the most important urban center in the Americas. For central Mexico, the first conquest was the most physically shattering; the impact of the alien diseases was most intense there, and the cultural influence of the Spanish missionaries was most concentrated.

The acceptance of Christianity in central Mexico is sometimes regarded as one of the most successful Christian missionary efforts anywhere in the world, but as elsewhere with the spread of the world religions, formal acceptance could be superficial. So many aspects of the old religion entered Mexican Catholicism at this time that it was possible for many to become Christian without breaking all of the core matrix beliefs that belonged to the Indian way of life. The great epidemics so overshadowed religious change that it is impossible to say what course it would have taken without them. With the population decline, however, many aspects of the central Mexican cultures withered and died, although others continued as major contributions to a mixed culture that was to be Mexican.

A Spanish cultural community came into existence in Mexico between the middle 1500s and the middle 1700s. Its first members were soldiers and administrators, later joined by miners, ranchers, commercial people, and some manufacturers. But comparatively few Spaniards came to Mexico as permanent residents, and many fewer women than men. Race mixture was the result, and mestizos retained some of their mothers' culture. Some hispanicized Indians also moved into the Western cultural sector and made their own contribution. By the late 1700s, this Spanish culture of most people born in New Spain had already become distinctly Ladino.

By that time, two distinct kinds of cultural matrix had come into existence. One was Ladino, Spanish-speaking but with many features borrowed from the Indians. On the other hand, there were a variety of different mixtures in which the Indian tradition was still dominant. By the eve of the second conquest, neither cultural type was changing as rapidly as it had done during the first century after the Spanish arrival. It was almost as though the Indians had borrowed what they wanted, and the Europeans had done the same. The second conquest of the 1800s was to change that.

The First Maya Encounter with the Spanish

Both the Maya and the Yaqui met the Spanish challenge in its early centuries in ways that were atypical of the experience of most other communities that now make up the Mexican republic. For the Maya, the European challenge came at a special time in their own history. When the Spanish arrived, the Aztec domination of central Mexico and the Inca empire in the Andes were close to the peak of their power over their respective regions. The Maya of the mid-1500s, on the other hand, were close to a nadir of their political, material, artistic, and intellectual achievement.

The Maya people, in any case, had never been united in a single empire. They inhabited and still inhabit three different regions with different regional histories. Two of these are in the Yucatan peninsula, commonly identified as the northern and southern lowlands. The northern lowlands are a flat, limestone plain, with the lightest rainfall in the northwest corner of the peninsula, where the natural vegetation is a low forest. Rainfall becomes heavier toward the south and east, making a transition toward the rain forest that dominates the southern lowlands, now divided politically between Belize, the Mexican state of

Chiapas, and lowland northern Guatemala. The final Maya region is the highlands, which rise above the Pacific coast of Mexico and extend to the east and north through highland Guatemala into Honduras.

The classic florescence of the Maya civilization occurred in the southern lowlands, an unusual feature because most early urban societies have developed in settings other than dense tropical forest, most often in river valleys like those of the Nile or the Indus. The Maya, however, created one of the most outstanding urban and literate societies of the Americas. Many elements of this complex society were present near the beginning of our era, leading to the Classic period of monumental building about 300–800 C.E., with the late classic florescence in the southern lowlands in the last centuries before 800 marking the pinnacle of Maya achievement in many spheres.

Then, between 750 and 850 C.E., Maya society in the southern lowlands passed through a crisis of probable material and environmental origin. Monumental building in most cities of that region stopped, and population declined drastically to stabilize at a new, lower level. The rich architectural record continued for a time in the northern lowlands, where cities such as Chichén Itzá flourished till about 1000 C.E., but Maya civilization was already five centuries past its peak of achievement. The Maya, after the postclassic collapse, nevertheless preserved some of the social institutions that had made possible their earlier achievement, among them a cohesion of the farming communities and a sharply graded class structure, where the population as a whole recognized and acquiesced in the leadership of an élite.

The Spanish first appeared on the coast of Yucatan in 1517, but they soon passed by to concentrate their effort in central Mexico, although the Maya suffered the imported diseases, beginning with the first smallpox epidemic in 1519. The Spanish effort to conquer Yucatan began in 1527, and the first phase ended in 1547 with the suppression of a Maya "revolt." Even after that, Spanish control was only partial, since they were forced to rule through Maya intermediaries, and some substantial Maya states existed completely outside the Spanish sphere of influence until the 1690s. Even later, the Spanish (and the Mexicans after independence) lacked secure administrative control over the whole of Maya territory until well into the twentieth century.

The elaborate priesthood and state structures of the Classic period had already been partly lost before the Spanish arrived, and the Maya were able to adjust to the Spanish imposition of power without drastic change in their culture. Individual communities could graft Christianity onto the roots of their own religion without fundamental changes in their former beliefs. Some Spanish priests and administrators came to live among them, along with a few Spanish-speaking representatives of Ladino New Spain, but the Ladino culture was confined to the towns, and its representatives were a small minority.

The First Yaqui Encounter with the Spanish

During the early centuries of Spanish presence, northern Mexico had an altogether different experience from that of central Mexico, or from the first two and a half centuries of contact with the Europeans in Yucatan. By the 1700s, central Mexico, with its relatively dense population, was beginning to recover from the disease die-off of earlier centuries. Ladino culture tended to dominate in the cities, in certain haciendas, ranches, and mining areas, interspersed among other populations that were still mainly Indian. In the Ladino regions, the population was mainly Christian, though with lingering pre-Christian beliefs. It was Spanish-speaking, though often bilingual in Spanish and at least one Indian language. The densely populated outlying regions of the south, such as the isthmus of Tehuantepec and the Pacific coast, were more like Yucatan. Most people were at least nominal Christians, but more than half knew only Indian languages, as compared to an estimated 20 percent Indian monolingualism in central Mexico.

In the north, the arid and semiarid country was again different. It was separated from central Mexico by an irregular line, sometimes called the Chichimec frontier. The name Chichimec came from the Aztecs, who used it for all people they considered to be the wild barbarians of the north. The frontier line approximates the division between the sedentary and urbanized farmers of the south and the nomadic peoples of the north, and it can be traced from east to west about 150 miles north of Mexico City.

It is nevertheless possible to distinguish the various northern cultures according to basic ecology and community size. Some were hunting and gathering peoples, but they were few in number and lived mainly in the far northwest in California. Others were seminomadic and practiced some agriculture, as did the Navaho and Apache. Still others were agricultural people with fixed villages. Among these, the Pueblo of present-day New Mexico could be considered urbanized. Still others, with smaller though permanent villages, would include the Pima and Tarahumara of the Chihuahua mountains and the peoples of the coastal valleys in Sonora including the Yaqui and Mayo.

The original Spanish conquest of Mexico was confined to the south of the Chichimec frontier, and it was limited even there. North of the frontier, occasional Spanish exploring expeditions marched through the country, and Spain used those occasional entries to claim the territory as against other Europeans, but the Spanish did not even set up an indirect administration as they did in Yucatan. Instead, they created a series of enclaves of Spanish control and activity, which served as centers for the spread of the Ladino culture from the cities of central Mexico.

The main value of the Mexican north was its mineral wealth, though the local Indians rarely exploited the gold, silver, and copper of this region, as they did in central Mexico. The Spanish introduced mining, managed by Ladinos who recruited local workers when they could or imported labor from the more densely populated central Mexico when they had to. The mining centers were not self-sufficient in food, and they soon attracted satellite centers of Spanish agricultural activity in the form of ranches and haciendas, based on the crops, sheep, and cattle introduced from Europe. Up to the late 1700s, however, neither the mines nor the haciendas were centers of Spanish rule. They were Spanish enclaves in territory that was culturally and political Indian, reproducing the pattern of the trading-post empires that the Europeans spread around the shores of the Afro-Eurasian landmass or overland across Siberia or the northern American forests in pursuit of furs.

It was through missionary activity that the Yaqui first encountered the Spanish, and missions were a third kind of Spanish enclave in the Indian north. In Sonora and the northwest, missions were assigned to the Jesuit order. Before 1617, when the first Jesuits arrived, the Yaqui were about 30,000 people settled on the valley bottom in an area about 60 miles long and 15 miles wide. At about 30 people per square mile, this was the densest population in the region that became northwest Mexico.

Coastal Sonora was much too dry for rainfall agriculture, but greater rainfall in the higher elevations of the interior fed streams such as the

Yaqui and Mayo Rivers, which watered the coastal valleys. The long and dense settlement in these valleys gave a sense of identity to the Cáhita-speaking peoples who lived there. In spite of their small numbers, the Yaqui may have made up about a quarter of the population of the region that became the state of Sonora. Some Yaqui lived by fishing along the desert coast or by hunting and gathering in the mountains, but the core population in the valley was settled in hamlets with an average size of only about 400 people. Each hamlet was politically independent for most purposes, but the people of the valley had a sense of identity as Yaqui and a sense of difference from such neighbors as the Mayo in the next valley, even though their language and culture were similar. The people of the Yaqui valley could unite from time to time in impermanent alliances for common action, such as warfare.

Spanish expeditions had passed north up the Sonora coast before 1617, with no permanent result, but the Jesuit arrival was different. They established settlements beyond the Spanish frontier in order to convert Indians, who were for the most part nomadic, and to encourage the converts to settle around the missions, creating a series of Indian villages or towns under missionary control, as they did elsewhere in Brazil and Paraguay.

In northwest Mexico, they moved beyond the range of secular Spanish authority and without military support. In effect, they were the government of New Spain within their settlements. Their declared long-run intention was to turn over political control of their charges to the ordinary Spanish government and their spiritual care to the secular clergy. In fact, they rarely did so, and the missions became a new and different political and cultural enclave in the north.

We only know about the Jesuit missions from the Jesuit records, and the Yaqui understanding of these events would inevitably be different. By the Jesuits' own account, and with the concurrence of later Yaqui memory, a handful of Jesuit priests entered the Yaqui valley and reorganized Yaqui society over a period of hardly more than a decade. They persuaded the people to move from their small hamlets to eight Spanish-style towns centered on eight churches. The Jesuit fathers appointed elders and other subordinate governors to rule over the towns on the fathers' authority. This was the first united government the Yaqui people had ever had.

The Jesuits also introduced new agricultural methods, cattle, plows, new crops, and a new system of land tenure, dividing the land into plots, which family members could work during three days of each week, and communal fields, on which all able-bodied males were obliged to work a further three days each week. The Jesuits kept the output of the communal fields as a reserve, partly for insurance against bad times, partly to aid the Jesuit Order in extending its activity even further to the northwest, ultimately to California. Under this regime, the Yaqui passed through the demographic crisis of their encounter with Old World diseases. The period of Jesuit rule was not all sweetness and light, but by the late 1700s, the old ways the Yaqui remembered and sought to preserve were the mixture of Christian and indigenous culture that had grown up under Jesuit rule. The later Yaqui traced their identity to the formative period of Jesuit rule and the original eight mission pueblos.

The apparent peace and acquiescence ended in 1740, when the Yaqui rose against the Jesuits in a widespread Indian revolt that extended north into what was to become Arizona. Even then, the rebels demanded the reform of Jesuit government, not its abolition. The revolt was suppressed, but reforms that followed gave the Yaqui more say in their own affairs. By the 1760s, however, the Jesuit Order as a whole came into conflict with the Bourbon dynasty throughout the Spanish empire. When the order was expelled from Spanish America in 1767, the political structure of the eight pueblos continued, now under Yaqui control.

The Yaqui held onto their land, and they managed to avoid paying the usual tribute. Their bargaining position was strengthened because, by supplying labor to the northwestern mines, they were able to make themselves indispensable to the advancing Mexican economy. As nominal Christians, they were strengthened in their effort to withstand much of the pressure on the cultural norms they had created for themselves in the previous century. The Indian community thus earned relative peace by making itself indispensable to important people in the provincial government.

A similar tacit compromise had helped to preserve the integrity of Maya culture through most of the 1700s, but under very different political forms. In Yucatan, the Spanish had been content to rule through the Maya upper class, which continued to control the land

and most community affairs. In the Yaqui valley, the Jesuits had created a more nearly classless society with themselves in charge at first. After they left, the Yaqui leadership was more democratically chosen, and it was Indian, not Spanish, but up to the eve of the second conquest the political and cultural order that the Jesuits and the Yaqui had created together had a remarkable stability and a potential to withstand new pressures from the Ladino world when they came.

The Second Conquest of Mexico

The second conquest began before the wars of independence of the 1810s and continued in the background of the North American invasions of the 1840s, the French intervention of the 1860s, the reform movement under Benito Juárez, and the dictatorship of Porfirio Díaz from the late 1870s to 1910. Some aspects of this second conquest were Mexico-wide; others were limited to a single region or locality. Military aspects, in particular, often involved only particular peoples, for example the Yaqui or the Maya, or even smaller segments of these cultural communities, especially of the Maya, a large group who lived scattered in several jurisdictions. Even in the Maya segment that fell to Mexico, separate revolts, called *caste wars,* occurred separately in scattered Maya regions of Yucatan and Chiapas.

Many central political and military events of Mexican history during the 1800s did not involve the Indians directly. They centered on the national politics of the emergent Mexican Republic, played out through a kaleidoscopic sequence of pronouncements that rarely meant precisely what they said and announced plans that rarely materialized. The pronouncements and plans, however, represented a struggle between three blocs of political interest within Ladino Mexico. One bloc was broadly conservative, made up of the upper clergy, the landed classes, and the wealthy in general, plus what followers they could attract from other classes. A second was broadly liberal, in a sense common in the 1800s, including a belief in private enterprise, coupled with strong suspicion that the corporate interests surviving from the colonial period were unfavorable to Mexico's proper goal of catching up with industrializing Europe and North America. The vast body of unassimilated Indian communities, perhaps a third of the Mexican population as of about 1850, might have figured as a third bloc, but they were disunited and mainly served as cannon fodder for the liberal and conservative blocs.

At the all-Mexico level, the most serious damage to the Indian communities came from a curious interaction of the liberals and the conservatives between the 1850s and 1910. In 1854, after four decades of fighting among rival military leaders and the lost war with the United States, liberal forces led by Benito Juárez were able to overthrow a military dictator and begin working toward a new constitutional order that would make a reality of the liberal program. The movement was known as the Reform, and its program was generally democratic and modernizing, in the sense that it sought to make Mexico the kind of society the reformers admired elsewhere in the Western world. They favored education, free thought in religion, free private enterprise, and political liberty for the hispanicized middle class.

The liberal bloc saw their program impeded on two fronts. One was the special corporate privileges still held by the church and the army, which gave them inordinate power within the Mexican state. The second was the ignorance and cultural conservatism of the Indians. Some liberals held that the Indians were racially inferior and talked of the desirability of encouraging immigration from Europe, but this was a minor strain. Benito Juárez was himself of largely Indian descent, though he was a typical middle-class Mexican lawyer with liberal ideas who had never been a member of an Indian community. In its main lines, the liberal program was not anti-Indian, only opposed to the surviving Indian cultures. It called for public education, though it supplied little, and it set out to break the solidarity of the Indian communities. The liberals identified communal land holding as a special bar to agricultural improvement. They believed that by individualizing land holding, they could turn the Indians into self-reliant peasants who would compete against one another in the market.

The liberal program hardly had a chance. From 1857 to 1860, Juárez won a three-year war against the conservative opposition, and then from 1862 to 1865, he spent another three years fighting the French intervention in favor of a puppet emperor, Maximiliano, originally of Austria. Maximiliano was barely overthrown and peace restored when Juárez himself died in 1872, and the liberals were once more replaced by a military dictator, Porfirio Díaz, who ruled from 1876 to 1910.

Díaz had been a liberal, and his regime continued at least one part of the Liberal program, setting out to abolish communal Indian land holdings. As of 1810, about 5,000 Indian towns held communal lands. These were mostly in central Mexico, mostly on relatively good land, and they made up about 6 percent of the total area of the republic. By 1910, when Díaz had completed his land reorganization, the Indian communal holdings had been reduced by 60 percent, and the Indians had lost most of their best land and virtually all that lay in the core area of central Mexico. The original liberal program intended to make the Indians into peasant farmers, but most of the land they lost was transferred to large haciendas. The former communal owners became landless laborers, and most became debt peons rather than free workers, slipping into a form of forced labor close to slavery. As a force for culture change, this undoubtedly accelerated the process of hispanization that had already begun; it drew many Indians from their previous communities and inserted them in the lowest ranks of Ladino Mexican society, though it was not the kind of modernization Juárez and his followers had hoped for.

The Second Conquest of the Maya

For the Maya, some aspects of the second conquest began as early as the 1770s, when the financial reform of the Spanish empire reached into Yucatan. Indian communities there had been left alone under their own aristocracy with a measure of financial independence, which now came under attack. Their cash holdings were transferred to the colonial treasury, where they were, perhaps, more safely overseen. In any event, this put a stop to alleged corruption within the community, but it opened the possibility of transferring funds from community treasuries to the central government. In much the same way, the church began to take control of funds that had been kept by lay confraternities in the Maya community for the cult of saints. Church authorities now began to use them for more general religious purposes with Ladino overtones. By the 1790s, administrative reforms had cut deeply into the freedom of the Maya aristocracy to run their own affairs under Spanish overrule.

More serious still, beginning in the 1770s, Ladinos began to take over the land and assume control of agricultural production. The population density in Yucatan had not been great, and the early Spanish agricultural enterprises had been mainly extensive ranching. Although the Maya population was by now increasing again after the disease crisis of earlier centuries, Maya communities began to lose their land through a variety of expropriations, and the Ladino hacienda sector grew by leaps and bounds. By the 1790s, the Ladino landowners began to shift from maize and beef to cotton, sugar and henequen, largely for export. By the time of independence, the hacienda sector may have become the most important part of the Yucatecan economy. It was certainly the most important sector for Yucatan's relations with the outside world.

At that time, people who were culturally Ladino had become nearly a quarter of the Yucatecan population – imprecise estimates indicate a population of about 300,000 at first contact with the Spanish, dropping to perhaps 150,000 by 1700, rising to perhaps 360,000 by 1800, and to 580,000 by 1845, with progressive Ladinization increasing after independence. Some of the trend toward hispanization was the product of immigration from central Mexico, but most of it had local roots. The key process was the break in the solidarity of Maya communities. Up to this time, social order had been maintained by continued prestige and authority of the nobility, who controlled the land and important ritual functions and preserved the core meaning of Maya religion, in spite of the Christianity that had been grafted onto it.

When the Maya communities lost their land, individuals were forced to seek work on the Spanish-controlled haciendas, and most soon fell into debt peonage equivalent to slavery, since the debts of the father could be passed on to the children. The corporate identity of the Maya community was replaced by the hacienda communities of the sugar and henequen plantations, linked by a common obligation of service to the *patrón*. For most Maya hacienda workers, this transfer was the beginning of the loss of Mayan identity. It began with the subordination of the Maya elite, the suppression of community religious rites, the linguistic replacement of Maya by Spanish, and the progressive infiltration of the market economy. All this was not immediate in the first generation, but, over the decades the shift of community membership from the Maya to the Ladino world was cumulative. When the caste wars broke out in the 1840s and 1850s, the hacienda Indians took almost no part in the defense of other Maya communities or of Maya culture.

This growing Ladino Yucatan was firmly centered in the towns, especially in Mérida in the northwest, served by its subordinate port of Sisal. A second tier of towns included the fortified port of Campeche at the southeast corner of the peninsula and Valladolid, the chief center for the frontier district of Ladino expansion to the east and southeast. Finally, at a lower level of population and importance, was the town of Bacalar, a port link to the Caribbean just north of British Honduras. But most of the eastern and southern forest region was not administered by the Mexican authorities. Yucatan in the early 1800s still had an imprecise frontier line between the Ladino world controlled from the cities and the lightly administered or unadministered regions that were still fundamentally Maya.

The Caste War and Chan Santa Cruz

The major political and military event of Maya resistance was the Indian rebellion known as the Caste War, actually the most prominent of several caste wars. The name came from the Spanish word *castas* referring to those who were not recognized as truly Spanish, including mestizos, mulattos, Africans, Indians, and combinations of these groups The great Maya Caste War broke out in 1847 as a by-product of fighting already in progress between Ladino factions in the aftermath of the North American invasion of 1845. At its height, in mid-1848, the Indians had captured virtually the whole of Yucatan beyond the principal cities, but their forces then fell apart as individuals felt the need to plant corn for the new season. By 1855, the Ladino counterattack succeeded almost everywhere except in the eastern forest area that was to become the territory of Quintana Roo.

During the early years of the Caste War, a new form of Maya political organization appeared at a place called Chan Santa Cruz (later Felipe Carillo Puerto), in the eastern forest area about twenty-five miles inland from the Caribbean coast. The new state centered on a holy cave and a *cenote* or pool at the bottom of a deep vertical chasm, a formation common in the limestone of Yucatan. The new political leadership began using the ritual symbol of a speaking cross which gave instructions through an interpreter. In time, the new state developed a political structure centered on the cross. The chief official was the "patron of the cross," who combined the authority of a Catholic bishop with that of a Maya priest, just as the cross was simultaneously a Christian symbol and a Maya symbol based on the Maya belief in the importance of the four cardinal directions. Other officials included the interpreter of the cross and the secretary of the cross, and, lower down, military officials whose titles of rank corresponded to those of the Mexican army. In time, the military stepped into the place formerly occupied by the village leadership. In effect, the new state remained Maya, but it borrowed from its Ladino opponents some aspects of their religion and other aspects of their military organization.

Chan Santa Cruz was by no means impregnable. It was captured several times during the Caste War, but most often, the garrison simply disappeared into the forest, to reappear when the Mexican army withdrew. After the end of the Caste War in 1855, forces of Chan Santa Cruz continued their raids against the Ladino-held areas, capturing slaves just as the Ladinos captured Maya slaves for sale to the Cuban sugar plantations. Mexican raiders sometimes entered Maya territory, sustaining heavy losses, but in the 1880s and 1890s the situation began to stabilize. Chan Santa Cruz remained the strongest independent Maya force, but two or three other independent Maya polities maintained diplomatic relations, sometimes military conflict as well, with Chan Santa Cruz, with the British in Belize, and with the government of Yucatan. Periods of formal peace and de facto truce were common. The background problem for all the independent Maya was that theirs was the poorest part of the peninsula and could not sustain a large population, perhaps no more than 10,000 by the 1890s.

The Mexican government under Porfirio Díaz decided to end Maya independence once and for all, as part of his similar policy against Indian hold-outs elsewhere in the republic. In 1899, the Republic of Mexico mounted a major expedition against Chan Santa Cruz, supported by repeating rifles, machine guns, and artillery, while building a road into Maya territory from the west and a light railroad inland from the Caribbean coast. The Mexican government this time not only conquered but occupied Chan Santa Cruz; it organized the conquered region as Quintana Roo, not as a separate state or annexed to the state of Yucatan, but as a non-self-governing territory under federal control.

By 1902, the second conquest appeared to be over as far as Yucatan was concerned.

Chan Santa Cruz remained under Mexican control until 1912, when the violence of the great Mexican Revolution reached Yucatan and forced the Mexican troops again to withdraw. This time, the Maya of Quintana Roo did not reoccupy their former capital but continued to live their own lives under a very weak Mexican administration. It is possible that effective Maya political independence in some parts of that region lasted into the 1960s, but more generally in the twentieth century the Maya of Yucatan entered into patterns of culture change that are worldwide as well as Mexican. The Maya language is still widely spoken, and elements of the ancient Maya religion are still vital in Yucatan and the broader Maya culture area. Overt rebellion by other Maya against the Mexican government occurred as late as the 1990s further west in the state of Chiapas. As to Yucatan, however, the impact of the European and North American tourist invasion in recent decades may have brought about more fundamental changes in Maya life than occurred in any equivalent period in earlier centuries.

Yaqui Resistance

The Ladino advance and Yaqui resistance in Sonora had a timing similar to that of the Maya stand in Yucatan. The wars of Mexican independence from Spain brought on a series of regional battles between Ladinos, Indians, and mixed forces that included both. A major Yaqui revolt from 1816 to 1833 was a part of that general turmoil, led by a Yaqui who took the *nom de guerre,* of Benders. Its declared object was to set up an Indian state that would be the legitimate successor to the Aztec state of three hundred years earlier, and it attracted the support from Mayo and other Indians of the region.

The Mexican government crushed that insurgency, but the Yaqui were able to reemerge whenever the Mexican state was weak, as it was following the liberal-conservative civil wars of the mid-century. For the decade 1875–85, a new Yaqui leader, Cajeme, managed to create a virtually independent republic in the Yaqui valley. When Porfirio Díaz emerged as centralizing dictator, Mexican troops again reoccupied the valley, and Ladino hacendados took title to the valley land.

Yaqui resistance was then reduced to guerrilla warfare from the nearby mountains, but the resistance was sustained through the 1890s over an area that stretched from the northern fringe of the valley almost to the Arizona border. The Díaz government occupied the valley itself and began to seize Yaquis suspected of supporting the guerrillas and deporting them to distant parts of the republic. Many were sent as virtual slaves to work on the hemp plantations of Yucatan, just as many Maya prisoners had been deported as slaves to the Cuban plantations.

By the time of Díaz's fall in 1910, the defeat of the Yaqui in Sonora, like that of the Maya in Quintana Roo, looked final. Both had sustained their culture and identity by changing with the times, adopting something of the Ladino way of life, particularly in the field of political organization, as did the eight pueblos of the Yaqui or Chan Santa Cruz in Yucatan. Both adopted Ladino weapons and the knowledge of how to fight with them. After 1910 however, the fate of the Indian heritage in Mexico was caught up in Mexican revolution.

Indian Mexico and the Revolution

It is sometimes difficult for historians to say when great political revolutions began and ended. The Mexican revolution began with the fall of Díaz in 1910, but it was slow to establish a new direction for the republic. Its most stable achievements came no sooner than the presidency of Lázaro Cárdenas from 1934 to 1940. By that time, the principal spokesmen for the revolution had placed the Indian heritage firmly in the center of the fabric of Mexican nationalism. The Spanish heritage was respected as well, but, as symbols of national pride, Cuauhtemoc and Moctezuma had won out over Cortés. A considerable *indianista* literature dates from those first three decades of the revolution, venerating the Indian tradition in literature and the arts. The Cárdenas government made political concessions at times; in 1937, it granted the Yaqui an autonomous zone in their valley, consisting of about half the territory they claimed as their own, and allowed them to reconstitute the eight pueblos.

But respect for the Indian past did not include the goal of returning to it. The revolution also stood for mass education as an essential step toward catching up with the most developed nations, including mass education in Spanish. Over the decade of the 1930s, the percentage of

89

the Mexican population that knew any Indian language dropped. The percentage that knew only an Indian language dropped still more. Even so, literacy in Spanish was a little short of 50 percent by 1940, and, if the curve of hispanization for that crucial revolutionary decade were projected into the future, not all Mexicans would know Spanish until after the year 2000.

The geographical incidence of language change is also significant. Most came in the fringe areas, where resistance to Mexican rule had been most pronounced during the 1800s. The loss of Indian-language speakers was greatest in the coastal regions, in the north, and in Yucatan. It was minimal in the old core area where Ladinos had been dominant longest. In fact, the absolute number of speakers of the four largest core-area languages – Nahuatl, Mixtec, Zapotec, and Otomi – actually increased during the 1930s through population growth. The only major language that declined in absolute numbers was Yucatecan Maya.

This suggests that cultural pluralism was weakening in Mexico with increasing industrialization, urbanization, and internal migration. It is fair to say that the Indian and European cultures in Mexico are now so far integrated that at least three-quarters of the people are neither culturally Indian nor culturally European, but simply Mexican. On the other hand, the Mexican way of life, in common with others throughout the world, has been meeting the influence of global homogenization. This includes not merely the influence of worldwide television or that of the flood of tourists to the Mexican coasts, but perhaps more important still, the enormous two-way traffic of migration between Mexico and the United States.

In comparison with plural societies in South Africa and Central Asia, the European element in the Mexican gene pool is sometimes evaluated at about 10 to 20 percent of the total, the rest being Indian and some African. This would indicate a physical movement of Europeans into Mexico on an order of magnitude similar to that of Europeans into South Africa or Central Asia. Compared with those areas, however, European migrants were fewer in number, but they arrived much earlier and their high natural increase balanced a natural decrease among the Native Americans.

This difference in demography and timing largely accounts for the more integrated culture of Mexico, compared with either South Africa or Central Asia. Yet local factors were also in play; large regional differences exist within Mexico. Spanish immigrants came to Peru or Guatemala in similar numbers and with similar timing, yet Mexico as a whole is now more culturally integrated than either. The cultural heritage of the Mexican revolution is certainly part of the explanation, but a fuller explanation will have to wait for the comparative study of other cases equivalent to the Yaqui and Maya elsewhere in Latin America.

Further Reading

Clendinnen, Inga, *Ambivalent Conquests: Maya and Spaniard in Yucatán, 1517–1570* (New York: Cambridge University Press, 1987).

Farriss, Nancy H., *Maya Society under Colonial Rule: The Collective Enterprise of Survival* (Princeton: Princeton University Press, 1984).

Hu-DeHart, Evelyn, *Missionaries, Miners and Indians: Spanish Contact with the Yaqui Nation of Northwestern New Spain, 1533–1820* (Tucson: University of Arizona Press, 1981).

—, *Yaqui Resistance and Survival: The Struggle for Land and Autonomy, 1821–1910* (Madison: University of Wisconsin Press, 1984).

Reed, Nelson, *The Caste War of Yucatan* (Stanford: Stanford University Press, 1964).

Restall, Matthew, *The Maya World: Yucatec Culture and Society, 1550–1850* (Stanford: Stanford University Press, 1997).

Spicer, Edward H., *The Yaquis: A Cultural History* (Tucson: University of Arizona Press, 1980).

6

Administrative Choices and Their Consequences: Examples from Bengal, Central Asia, Java, and Malaya

Government administration has been a long-standing concern with those who have managed European empires overseas, as it was for those trying to govern Europe itself in the industrial age. It was one thing to decide what policies to follow, and a quite another to see that they were carried out on the ground. This involved the same sort of management techniques that were so important to the rise of the West in many different fields. Political and diplomatic history attract more attention that administrative history; they have the excitement of a game with winners and losers and clever moves by the players. Administrative history, on the other hand, is concerned with the way political decisions are carried out, which is often more important that the decisions themselves. The efficiency of government depends on the machinery for transmitting whatever orders come from the ruling group down through lower ranks of society until the lower orders are finally forced to do something or to refrain from doing something.

It is increasingly clear that government administration is properly a part of the technology of management, and the rise of administrative competence in Europe itself was long and gradual. In the Middle Ages, many of the powers associated with maintaining peace and order and directing the course of society were in the private hands of feudal lords. The pages of Western Civilization textbooks describe a succession of government authorities who sought, among other things, to create a centrally controlled and effective bureaucracy. The "new monarchs" of the 1400s and 1500s were followed by the "absolute monarchs" of the 1600s and the "enlightened despots" of the 1700s.

Toward the end of the 1700s and into the 1800s, the growth of administrative technology paralleled the growth of industrial technology, just when it was most sorely needed by a complex and rapidly changing society. To a degree, the new level of productivity owed at least as much to organizational as to mechanical tools. The new legal uniformity of the Code Napoléon, along with equivalent adjustments in English common and statute law, came just when the economy needed to respond to new conditions. Governments' concern with regulation of the new factories increased just when the early industrial age was creating new social problems that demanded government action. Much of that action was weak and tardy, but this systematic increase in the powers of government continued throughout Europe in the 1800s and through the 1900s.

We have here a significant covariance: industrial technology improved and government administrative technology improved simultaneously. For the moment, it is not our concern which one caused the other. It is noteworthy that similar changes were taking place as they became necessary for the governance of the European sphere overseas. Up to the middle 1700s, European companies east of the Cape of Good Hope had confined themselves to running trading-post empires or militarized trade diasporas. They rarely sought either to seize territory or to send out settlers to occupy it on the model of North America – and never to conquer and rule over indigenous populations on the model of Mexico or Peru.

On the fringes of the Indian Ocean in the second half of the 1700s, however, they *did* begin to acquire territory and to govern Asian populations. With that, they ran into the same administrative problems that had plagued European monarchs at home and had thwarted Spain in its effort to govern the Americas.

Initially, the European monarchs and their bureaucratic advisors tried to solve the problems overseas in much the same way as they did in Europe. At home, they sought the support of local notables, towns, the church, or important corporations such as guilds, and, in return for their support, recognized the power of these authorities to dominate other and lesser members of society. Overseas, they conquered by military force, but they ruled by recognizing the authority of local rulers or other notables who could be persuaded to cooperate.

The pattern emerged at the very beginning of European empire-building in the early 1500s, when the Spanish were first trying to govern the Caribbean islands. There they found a class of local notables through whom they could rule, called *caciques* in Arawak. As they advanced to the mainland of Mexico and South America, they carried the precedent with them, along with the Arawak term. In the longer run, the Arawak are gone, but their word *cacique* is still found in the Philippines, half way around the world and five centuries later, as a term for the local ruling class which, over the centuries, managed to build on Spanish recognition of their ancestors' power. Their local political power, land ownership, and wealth made it possible for them, as a class, to maintain their position though centuries of Spanish, a half-century of American, and a half-century of independent Philippine government.

During the 1800s, however, administrative history in Europe took a different turn from administrative theory and practice in most European empires overseas. In Europe, a major concern was to sweep away the remains of noble or corporate privilege. In extreme cases in the twentieth century, they were so successful that the term *totalitarian* could be used of governments that sought total control over society.

The Europeans, however, never had enough of their own personnel overseas to establish a fully European administration. Even in southern Africa, sufficient Europeans were present to govern the settler society but not enough to govern the Africans as well, and as a result, it was necessary to add local administrative help. Sometimes, in Africa and elsewhere, the colonial powers did this by recruiting local individuals directly into the colonial service. Governor Félix Éboué of the French Congo is an example of an African official whose loyalty to the Free French was to be important during the Second World War.

Theorists of empire in Europe made a virtue of necessity. Dutch commentators on Dutch rule in Java praised the wisdom of ruling through the "natural rulers," or at least those whom the ordinary peasants were accustomed to obey. Java already had class of quasi-hereditary administrators called the *priyayi*. These Dutch theorists argued that the priyayi were natural chiefs, *volkshoofden,* whose inherited prestige made a useful front for Dutch rule in what has been called political theater – indeed, the natural chiefs were sometimes called puppets. These European theorists sometimes called this combined rule by the Dutch and the natural rulers a benign system of dualism. The Dutch intended, of course, to remain in charge but removed themselves as much as possible from actual contact with the populace.

In India, the British East India Company had been intermeshed with Indian governments since the mid-1700s, leading gradually to a formal division between British India and the Native States, which the British ruled only indirectly. Toward the end of the 1800s, many British theorists believed that Indirect Rule, with initial capitals, was the proper goal for African administration, which should rule only "through the chiefs." A group of similar theorists in France promoted policies of *association* with the local élite in each colony, in preference to the total *assimilation* of the local society and culture to French norms. Lord Lugard in Britain and Robert Delavignette in France, both of whom governed in African colonies in the early twentieth century, were among the prominent spokesmen for these policies.

The advocates of dualism, association, and Indirect Rule were all deeply influenced by European racist views that were prevalent at the time. They argued, in effect, that because of deep-seated racial and cultural differences, what was good government in Europe was not necessarily good government for European empires overseas. The "natives" were so different that it was better to let them govern themselves "in their own way," even if the African way did not correspond to the forms of local government Europeans thought most suitable for their own society.

The fundamental decisions, however, were most often made in the early decades of European control, and theorizing often followed the fact. In the first instances, the Europeans took over a society with an established government, inevitably linked to the whole structure of that society. Government, in short, was an integral part of local culture. Europeans, being unable to create a government de novo, had of necessity to adopt some part of the existing government apparatus, modified to suit their interests and biases. Their choice of some local people rather than others to carry out their orders inevitably changed local government, sometimes even more than the orders themselves.

The precolonial government usually represented some kind legitimacy based on a balance of power within society. Any ruler, however despotic, had to respect what the most powerful in the rest of society would accept. With a colonial regime inserted at the top of the pyramid, the local rulers at the next level had, overtly at least, to obey the Europeans, but they no longer had to be quite so careful to mollify their subordinates. European rule could thus circumscribe their power from above, while increasing their authority over those below. The result could be a thorough remaking of local societies as some groups moved into positions of real power while others dropped out, sometimes permanently, from the charmed circle.

Historical Examples

These general considerations can be illustrated by historical examples from the experience of diverse societies in South and Southeast Asia. The colonial power's initial choice of intermediaries often had unforeseen consequences, which lasted through the colonial and into the postcolonial period.

Bengal Land Tenure

The British rearrangement of Bengal land tenure is a classic case. In 1772, the British East India Company assumed the role of *diwan* of Bengal under the overrule of the Mughal Empire, an anomalous situation, since the Company was, in theory, a trading company. It became, still in theory and in its corporate capacity, an official in the Mughal government, but it also was able to use that theoretically subordinate role to make the Company the dominant authority, replacing the Mughal government as the ruler of Bengal.

The East Indian Company, however, had no means of knowing what went on all over Bengal, much less exercising real control, even control as light as George III's government exercised in Great Britain, and the Company had no intention of ruling in detail. It was still a commercial firm with political and military functions on the side. Its reason for stepping forth as diwan of Bengal was to secure a share of the land revenue that had previously been passed on to Delhi. The Mughal Empire, like most Indian empires before it, has been called a landlord state whose main source of revenue was land revenue, paid by all those who worked the land, in theory to the emperor. In theory also, the land belonged to the emperor in something like the Western sense of ownership, not merely in the Western sense of sovereign political control.

In general, land revenue was partly paid directly to the imperial court, but another part was allocated to certain imperial officials, who were assigned the revenue of certain lands in place of salary. These were *jagir* lands, and the holders of jagir lands did not collect the revenue themselves. Instead, they had long ago assigned the actual revenue collection to a subordinate class known as the *zamindari,* hereditary revenue collectors whose ancestors had done much the same thing even before the Mughal Empire had been founded in the 1500s.

The land revenue was considerable, a third to a half of the whole harvest, and the zamindari were allowed to keep about 10 percent in return for their services as collectors and also for preserving law and order and supplying troops in time of war. The size of the primary zamindari holding could vary considerably. It might be so small that the zamindar himself worked the land with the aid of a few hired workers, or it might be several villages. In either case, the zamindar's rights to the land were heritable and alienable; they could be sold on the market.

Furthermore, some rights were held in a series of stages, so that the revenues might pass from a primary to a secondary and even to a third-level zamindar, each of whom was supposed to help preserve law and order and to give military aid in emergencies. In return, each was allowed to keep something like 2 to 10 percent of the revenue that passed through his hands. Below the zamindari of all levels were the peasants who actually worked the land, and they usually held their land in heritable leases, so that they too had permanent rights to a particular piece of land.

What this system amounted to, for all its complexity, was an agrarian economy where the land theoretically belonged to the state, but where in fact many different individuals and families had certain defined rights to particular pieces of land. None of these rights amounted to ownership in the Western sense. None of the payments was clearly either a tax or a rent in the Western sense. Nor was the value of these rights tied to the scarcity value of the land itself; since population densities were low in the 1700s, claims to land meant very little without people to work it.

When the East India Company took over Bengal, it sought a way to make revenue collection as efficient as possible without arousing strong resistance. While the company might have gone through hired officials directly to the peasants who worked the land, as it did later on in other parts of India, company officials were impressed by what they saw as the social benefits of the English system of land tenure. Under that system, much of the land in England was owned by large landowners, often members of the nobility. Agricultural production was actually managed by farmers, who paid rent but were men of substance who hired farm laborers to do most of the actual work. The English landowners were simply gentry who collected their rents, though they were tacitly expected to fill such useful public offices as justice of the peace or member of Parliament and to supply their sons as officers in the army and navy. These posts carried some salary, but the salary was far lower than the cost of maintaining a gentleman in one of these positions.

In Bengal, with the English system as a model, the Company's officials sought to place the zamindari in a position modeled on that of the idealized English landlord. The Company recognized them as the owners of the land, responsible for paying the land revenue. It also decided in 1793 to set the revenue at a fixed sum of money for each piece of land, which would not change over time. This arrangement came to be known in Indian history as the Permanent Settlement of Bengal.

The general result of this settlement was to vest the various rights over the land in a single group, which was identified as landlords. These were the primary zamindari who made the first collection from the peasants. Both the upper-level zamindari and the peasants at the bottom lost their customary rights. The settlement brought about important shifts in the income of various past claimants, which also changed with the passage of time.

In the first instance, everybody with a claim to the land or its products lost out to the primary zamindari. Within a few decades, inflation reduced the real value of revenue, and the British Raj itself lost out relative to its earlier position. As population grew, land became more valuable, and those who held zamindari rights grew wealthy from windfall profits, but the actual social change was more complex. In many parts of Bengal, the original zamindari were unable to hold onto their positions because the original payments they owed the Company had been set at too high a level. They were therefore forced to sell to others, often to men of wealth from Calcutta and other urban centers who were willing to invest in future land values. The new owners neither resided near the land nor had personal ties to the peasants who worked it, so that the official social goal of approximating the English landlord class, became increasingly distant.

Functionally, the position of the zamindari also changed as their previous administrative and military obligations were shifted to other branches of the new bureaucracy. Instead of being a part of local government at the lowest level, they became simply rent collectors – in fact, land owners who paid part of their income to the government.

While the long-term history of the Bengali zamindari as a class could be traced through the later economic and social history of Bengal and Bangladesh, the point for the moment is that any new revenue policy would have brought about some redistribution of income and social position. The Company officials in Bengal sought one outcome, but another actually occurred, and the Permanent Settlement of Bengal became a classic instance of the unintended changes that came about when the rulers of European empires intervened in local systems of land tenure.

Russia in Central Asia

Before the 1860s, Russian advance into non-Slavic territory of central Asia had only reached the fringes of the important sedentary societies along the irrigated valleys of the Syr Darya and Amu Darya Rivers flowing to the Aral Sea, where the main political units were the khanates of Kokand, Khiva, and Bukhara. Between the 1860s and the 1890s, the Russian military advance was rapid and complete. The Russians annexed Kokand directly, along with parts of the other two khanates, but they left the bulk of Khiva and Bukhara with less actual Russian direction than was generally the case with the Native States in India.

From the 1860s onward, the Russians had very nearly the same land tenure options in the annexed territories as the British had in Bengal. As in Mughal India – as, indeed, in Muslim law generally – all land was in theory the property of the ruler, but actual control of the land in central Asian sedentary areas was in the hands of the local aristocracy and some Muslim charitable foundations. The Russians might have followed the British lead in Bengal and treated the land holders as land

BELMONT UNIVERSITY LIBRARY

owners, but they wanted to maximize government revenue, and they were suspicious of the local aristocracy. They therefore declared that the title to all land still belonged to the state, but actual possession was assigned to others who actually worked it. The only local authorities they retained were the village officials who controlled irrigation water, who were judged to be independent of the old aristocracy.

This move was not only revolutionary for central Asia; it was far more generous to the local peasants than the treatment of the Russian serfs at their emancipation earlier in the 1860s. The motive, however, was not to create a free peasantry as a desirable social goal but to collect greater land revenue. The Russians assumed that by removing intermediate claimants to the land and using the services of hired and removable tax collectors, they could wring more out of the peasants.

This Russian land settlement of 1868, like any other that could have been chosen, had social consequences. The most significant was the impoverishment of the local aristocrats, who gradually lost their importance in local society. By the time of the First World War and the Russian Revolution, they were largely gone from the annexed territories, though their power and influence continued in the two quasi-independent khanates.

With the coming of the Revolution, the only sources of local leadership were at the village level or among the Muslim religious educated élite. The wartime disorders might well have provoked some central Asians to try for independence from Russia – or from the Soviet Union after 1917 – but no such thing happened. In 1916, there were widespread central Asian protests over labor conscription, but no significant independence movement emerged either then or immediately after the revolution. The strongest resistance to the new Soviet regime came from Khiva and Bukhara, led in large measure by the local aristocrats whom the previous Russian regime had allowed to remain in power as indirect rulers.

By the late 1920s, the Soviet Union felt strong enough to try its own measures to remold the structure of central Asian society. In the irrigated lands of Turkestan, the Soviets took over all of the former state lands that Russia had distributed to the peasants a half-century earlier and converted them into large collective farms, usually under Russian Soviet management. Russification of the administration was now possible because the number of Russian settlers had created an incipient plural society, with enough Slavic outsiders to staff grassroots management. In the background was the fact that cotton was so important to the Soviet state that it was willing to invest the resources needed to collectivize it.

Even so, the Soviets also found it necessary to employ local administrators, partly for political reasons, but their attempt to "nativize" the administration also had social consequences. The Soviets might have tried to work through those who had been local leaders in the past, but the aristocracy was gone, and Soviet officials, now distrustful of the peasants, sought instead to employ people who met Russian educational standards. In doing so, they created a new elite, which, though trained in the Soviet system, was not in the long run more loyal to the Soviet Union than it was to the local Socialist Soviet Republic, which became independent at the collapse of the Soviet Union.

Java

The Dutch regime on Java presents an example of a different kind of administrative choice. At the Dutch arrival early in the 1600s, most of Java was ruled by a bureaucratic empire, the empire of Mataram. The island was densely populated, and villagers produced paddy rice as the basic food crop. At the top of the bureaucratic pyramid was the imperial court, which maintained relatively inefficient control over the *bupati,* or provincial heads. The bupati were not so much royal appointees as important men in the region, whose authority the court officially recognized, and the court usually passed the office on to their heirs.

The bupati ruled through a subordinate élite class called *priyayi,* separated from the ordinary peasants by a deep gulf of culture and tradition. The classical Javanese culture, with its shadow plays, music, and religious writings, was essentially a priyayi culture and distinct from the cultural life of the peasants.

The Dutch traders who arrived in the 1600s had no intention of taking over Mataram, even if they had the power to do so, but they needed a local base and they seized the port city of Jakarta, which they renamed Batavia. The Dutch East India Company, called the VOC from its Dutch initials, was established as a commercial firm, though it was also authorized to make war as necessary to further commerce. It used Batavia as a base for trade and for negotiations with the other powers of the region through commercial pressure, warfare, and diplomacy.

The VOC thus entered into the maze of politics at the court of Mataram, seeking always to gain commercial advantage and the security of its base. It relied mainly on diplomacy, but it occasionally played one ruler against another with military intervention. As a result of diverse pressures, the VOC gradually acquired territory from Mataram, mainly at first in the vicinity of Jakarta. The VOC was in business to trade, with such monopoly advantages as a moderate use of force would bring; it had little interest in actually governing. Unlike the situation with the English Company in India, land revenue was not a serious concern, though it was to become important after the Netherlands Indies government took over from the VOC in the 1800s.

The VOC left its Javanese territory under the control of the same class of bupati who had previously served Mataram. At times, it simply recognized the same individual official in the same post with the title of *regenten* (Dutch for rulers). The literature on Javanese history in English usually calls them regents, though the English term usually has a somewhat different meaning. In any event, the system of ruling through regents continued as Dutch territorial control increased and that of the Mataram court declined, until the Dutch came to control the whole island.

The actual powers of the regents changed over time. Through the 1700s, they were probably stronger than their predecessors had been under Mataram. They had a fairly free hand in their own territory; the Dutch had few concerns beyond their commercial advantage. The VOC provided the regents with a strong master, whose support freed them somewhat from the danger of overthrow from below. In return, the Company made the regents responsible for seeing that the peasants cultivated and delivered certain products for the European market.

In 1800, however, the VOC failed financially, the Dutch government took over its territory, and the new rulers began to reverse the former tendency to let the regents rule in their own way. The British occupation from 1811 to 1816 continued the tighter central control and introduced a new emphasis on land revenue, following the Indian example. Land also began to be assigned to European planters for direct exploitation, which itself required more supervision.

When the Dutch returned after the Napoleonic Wars, they assigned a Dutch resident to the court of each regent, with authority to overrule any of the regent's decisions, and they imposed a detailed set of administrative orders, using the regents to enforce whatever economic policy was in effect at the time, whether it was collecting land rents for the central government, demanding certain crops for delivery as tribute, or supervising encroachment of Dutch-owned plantations at the expense of the traditional village agriculture. These new aims and methods suggest that the Dutch were moving in the direction of a European-style bureaucratic administration, but that movement was cut off by other developments.

The Java War of 1825–30 began as revolt against the government of the Netherlands Indies under the charismatic leadership of Prince Dipanagara. His movement had millennarian and Islamic elements, which brought the Prince a broad following among the rural population. The Dutch won the war with the support of most of the regents, but the victory was expensive. The lesson they drew from the experience was that support from the regents was essential to the stability of their regime – they were, after all, the natural leaders the Javanese people were accustomed to obey. This lesson confirmed the value of dualism in colonial government and helped to ensure the position of the regents as rulers of Java – and of their subordinates drawn from the priyayi – until the Japanese occupation of 1942.

Change did, of course, take place, but Javanese did most of the grassroots governing. In 1865 the Dutch ruled a Javanese population of about 12 million with only 175 Dutch civil servants, governing through 69 regents with authority over some 400 priyayi district heads, who in turn tried to keep order among the thousands of village heads. By the twentieth century, colonial government had become still more complex, though in 1930, there were still only 75 regents for all of Java.

The Dutch were ambivalent about colonial administration. They were impatient with the traditional outlook of the regents, yet through the first half of the twentieth century, they counted on them as important allies. They sensed that the serious danger to their regime came from two sources: at the village level it came through the religious claims of the Muslim leaders, and at a political level it came from the Western-educated urban nationalists with their demands for independence. While the Dutch government supported the regents, it also worked where possible with the lower priyayi who had learned Dutch and had a Dutch-style education.

The regents valued their Dutch support partly because they themselves were unpopular with the religious and the nationalist wings of the opposition. Their offices remained largely hereditary, in practice though not in law. In 1930, about two-thirds of the 75 regents were the sons or near relatives of regents from some part of Java. Finally, during the turmoil of the Japanese occupation and the war for independence that followed, the office of regent disappeared, but many of the traditions of the priyayi as a larger class passed over into the vastly expanded civil service of independent Indonesia. After the mid-1960s, the new military governors of Indonesia came to occupy something of the position of the Dutch central government in Batavia, and the descendants of the priyayi contributed heavily to the membership in the new bureaucracy that had taken over the role of the priyayi through whom the Dutch and the regents ruled.

Malaya

The Malay peninsula is similar to Java linguistically and culturally, and it also passed through a period of dual control divided between the Malay sultans on the one hand and British officials on the other, but the nature of the encounter and its long-run outcome were altogether different. To begin with, the British interest in Southeast Asia in the 1800s was more strictly commercial. The British territorial empire was in India, and Britain had been happy enough to return Java to the Netherlands after the Napoleonic Wars. It retained a few small ports on the Straits of Melaka and founded a new port city at Singapore to guarantee the passage through the straits and the diffusion of their trade in the neighborhood.

On the Malay peninsula, the only political entity approaching the power of Mataram or even Yogyakarta was Siam, whose authority stretched south into what is now northern Malaysia. Between the Siamese sphere and the British Straits Settlements were a series of small river-mouth states, each of which sought, with little success, to dominate the trade of its hinterland. Hardly any of the sultans of these states approached the power exercised by middle-level bupati serving Mataram or by regents serving the Dutch at that same period. The Malay peninsula was, in any case, far more sparsely populated than Java. We have already seen in Chapter 3 the crisis of disorder that led to the British protectorates over the Malay States. The Pangkor Engagement, and other agreements modeled on it, superficially resembled the relations between the Netherlands Indies and the regents on Java. Unlike the arrangement with the *residenten* on Java, however, the Malay agreements provided that each sultan must ask the advice of his resident and act on it "on all questions other than those touching Malay Religion and Custom." In the next decades, similar agreements with other sultans laid the foundations of the Federated Malay States and ultimately a wider entity called British Malaya – still later the present independent country of Malaysia.

The crucial question was how much and what kind of advice the new residents would give. The British empire had practiced a variety of forms of indirect rule, but in this case the Malay sultans lacked the administrative machinery to deal with their most pressing problems, Chinese immigration and economic growth based on tin and plantations. The residents' solution was to create a new, Westernized government administration, theoretically under the sultans but in fact under their own control.

The residents swept away the Malay forms of government and brought in British officials and British legal forms. Where they needed subordinate local officials, they recruited them from among Western-educated local people. Whereas the Dutch on Java had kept Javanese law for all cases where Dutch individuals were not involved, the British in the Malay States introduced the Indian Penal Code, which was basically Western. For civil cases, they introduced a new legal system based on British civil law. The sultans became a series of constitutional monarchs, with the trappings of power but little real authority outside cultural and religious life. The British needed the sultans as a representatives, and the Sultans needed a Westernized administration.

The Dutch had been moving in a similar direction before the Java War, but, after the 1830s, their search for security led them to rely on the regents exercising real power in traditional ways. The Malay residents' solution of turning to more Western forms of administration was acceptable to Singapore and the sultans alike, and London knew little about the actual policies until they were an accomplished fact. At the same time, the Malay residents were not ordinary members of the Straits Settlements government. They therefore had something of a free hand; Singapore was not deeply concerned about what the residents did in the Malay States, as long as it was not a major item in their own budget. Through actions initiated by the residents, the powers of the sultanates increased enormously while those of the sultans declined, but what the sultans lost in power, they gained in increasing wealth, status, and prestige. As the protectorate over the individual Malay states became more fictional, the ceremonial position of the sultans became more secure.

One result of this process was that the Malay sultans became a powerless, yet integrated set of figureheads, who were no threat to the nationalist leadership at the time of independence in 1957. The whole group of sultans was kept on as a kind of corporate constitutional monarchy, and they periodically elect one of their number to serve as head of state of Malaysia for a five-year term. In the longer run, the sultans of Malaysia formed one of the very few non-Western monarchies to pass through a European protectorate and emerge into independence without being overthrown by their own people.

Discussion

Of these two pairs of examples, the first two, Bengal and central Asia, are examples of land tenure changes that moved in opposite directions. The zamindari of Bengal were chosen from among several groups with a claim to the land and elevated to land ownership. But relatively few individual zamindars passed their privileges on to their descendants. New men were bought in, and the old sold out.

In central Asia, on the other hand, the equivalents to the zamindari were deprived of their titles, and something close to land ownership passed to the peasants, but they too lost out in the 1930s to collectivization. Real control passed to modernizing, Soviet-trained technicians and bureaucrats.

A somewhat ironic point is that Europeans seeking to maximize land revenue had other social and political goals as well. The pursuit of these social goals moved them to change traditional systems of land tenure. The result was a fundamental change in Bengali society, and not at all the consequences they intended.

The second pair of cases has to do with administrative and political modernization rather than land tenure, but the gap between intentions and outcomes was much the same, for Europeans and non-Europeans alike. The regents, in serving the Dutch, transformed themselves over a century or more into a class of officials more secure in their power than their predecessors, the bupati, had been under Mataram. They were useful to the Dutch as actors in a kind of political theater, but the power they had acquired stood in the way of rising groups on Java, the Western-educated nationalists on one hand and the traditional Muslim religious leaders on the other. In time, and in spite of some continuity in the powers for the priyayi bureaucracy, the regents were swept away by the Western-educated new bureaucrats and the military.

In Malaya, on the other hand, the sultans were able to survive, mainly because they gave up their power to a Western style of administration at lower levels. They were therefore no hindrance either to the colonial power or to the nationalist leadership after independence. As collective constitutional monarchs, the Malay sultans probably have more actual power in political affairs than most of their ancestors enjoyed. In both these cases, as in Bengal and central Asia, the European administrative choices were crucial to the course of later history, even after independence, but the outcome was not the one the Europeans had intended or predicted.

Further Reading

Becker, Seymour. *Russia's Protectorates in Central Asia: Bukhara and Khiva, 1865–1924* (Cambridge, MA: Harvard University Press, 1968).

Frykenberg, Robert Eric (ed.) *Land Control and Social Structure in Indian History* (Madison: University of Wisconsin Press, 1969).

Frykenberg, Robert Eric (ed.), *Land Tenure and Peasant in South Asia* (New Delhi: Orient Longman, 1977).

Kuitenbrouwer, Maarten, "Aristocracies Under Colonial Rule: North India and Java," in Bayly, C. A. and D. H. A. Kolff (eds.), *Two Colonial Empires: Comparative Essays on the History of India and Indonesia in the Nineteenth Century* (The Hague, Nijhoff, 1986), pp. 75–91.

Pierce, Richard A., *Russian Central Asia, 1867–1914: A Study in Colonial Rule* (Berkeley: University of California Press, 1960).

Steinberg, David Joel (ed.), *In Search of Southeast Asia: A Modern History,* revised ed. (Honolulu: University of Hawaii Press, 1987)

Sutherland, Heather, *The Making of a Bureaucratic Elite: the Colonial Transformation of the Javanese Priyayi* (Singapore: Heinemann Educational Books [Asia], 1979).

PART THREE

Conversion

The worldwide globalization of the past half-century has produced more intense cross-cultural contact than has occurred at any other time in history. In earlier periods, as today, much culture change has been an accidental by-product of contact between people with a different way of life, much of it unconscious. But culture change by intent, sometimes called conversion, has also been important. This includes religious conversion, but it is not limited to religion, and it can take place on the initiative of the cultural borrowers as well as that of cultural transmitters. It is a two-sided process in any event. Missionaries, including secular missionaries, have set out to persuade others to change their way of life, but they have usually succeeded only in part, and only when their audience wanted to hear what they had to say.

Culture change on the initiative of the borrowers is far more common. In recent centuries much of the initiative has come from non-Western modernizers, who had before them the threat of Western power and the lure of Western technological prowess. They were not, however, so much interested in imitating Western culture as they were anxious to participate in the benefits of high productivity and high consumption, which were the most visible aspects of the West of the early industrial age.

It is a common observation about culture change over recent centuries that Western Europe has been, along with Japan, among the most avid imitator of techniques from abroad. From a purely technical point of view, much of what the Europeans put together so successfully to create the industrial age was first borrowed from some other society. By the 1800s, the technical superiority of the West was visible to all, though it was not universally admired. This technological lead was one source of Europe's ability to conquer and establish its overseas empires, and the effort to escape the threat of European domination was a recurring theme in non-Western demands for modernization, especially in military technology.

Again, the term *modernization* as used it these essays does not mean copying the West; it may be driven in some instances by a desire to avoid the West, especially Western military power. *Modern,* by this definition is not a homogeneous entity, and the drive for modernization involves important choices among a number of possible roads to high productivity and high per capita consumption. The West, Japan, and the more recently industrialized countries of the western Pacific rim show important cultural differences, though they are all modern in the sense in which I am using the term.

The decisions people make, however, do not always distinguish between what is essential to achieve a modernizing goal and what is not. Some aspects that were first associated with the West seem to be essential, such as industrial technology and science, high rates of literacy and mass education, and a high degree of social mobility. Others are nonessential but are borrowed anyhow, such as the Japanese adoption of some of the more commercial Western aspects of Christmas, leaving aside the religious base. Some other elements of Western culture, such as American popular music and blue jeans, that are equally nonessential to modernization have spread worldwide in recent decades, even to places that have been relatively slow to modernize in other respects.

Cross-cultural borrowing has rarely resulted in a carbon copy of the original. When members of one society take over a desirable feature from an alien society, the innovation is pulled out of its original cultural context and fitted into a new one. When this takes place, it is either modified to suit its new setting or is itself modified in its new cultural environment. Usually both forms of modification take place to some degree.

The four chapters that follow deal with instances where people overseas, threatened in one way or another by the rise of Western power, chose to borrow from the West voluntarily and selectively, with a variety of different outcomes.

7

Christian Missions in East Africa

Islam, Christianity, and Buddhism have all played a major role in cultural convergence over the past two thousand years or so. It would be interesting, but far beyond the theme of these essays, to pursue the history of comparative proselytization, seeking to find why these three religions are so outstanding in their ability to acquire converts in foreign cultures. The answer would certainly be mixed, but a first approximation would be that the major religions of the modern world are those with a doctrinal basis that includes an effort to attract believers; proselytization at some level is a defining characteristic of the present world religions. On the other hand, the historical record contains far too much evidence of fruitless missionary effort for this to be the only explanation. Much religious change, perhaps most, must be explained as a response on the part of the converted.

The initiatives of Christian missionaries in the past century and a half were inevitably intertwined with the European conquests of that same period. The Christian message often appeared simultaneously with the victory of the Western military and the establishment of European empires. The way in which these interactions worked themselves out in East Africa generally and with the kingdom of Buganda specifically is the subject of this chapter. East Africa is not necessarily typical even of other parts of Africa, and Buganda was a special case, but developments in this small state illustrate the complexity of the social and political conditions within which cultural conversion took place.

The East African Setting

East Africa in 1850 was distant from the usual European spheres of influence. For some purposes, East Africa was on the way to India, but, of the European powers interested in the Indian Ocean, only Portugal even attempted a serious establishment on the tropical east coast, and the main Portuguese activity was by this time confined to Mozambique and the Zambezi valley to the south. Portugal had made an effort to fortify Mombasa on the present-day Kenya coast but had given up in the 1700s. On a map, the Red Sea appears to be a direct route for the passage from the Indian Ocean to the Mediterranean, but the winds blow from the north all year long in the northern part of the Red Sea, making it virtually useless in the age of sail. Shippers had long been accustomed to unload their cargoes at a midway port, such as Jiddah, for further transshipment to the Fertile Crescent by camel caravan. By the 1850s, however, steamers made it possible to shorten the time from India to Europe, using the Red Sea by way of Suez. With the opening of the Suez Canal in 1869, even transshipment across the isthmus of Suez was no longer necessary.

Before the 1800s, however, no European travelers had reached any part of the interior of the continent between Ethiopia on the north and the Zambezi valley on the south. The principal outsiders to come by sea were Arabs, who for centuries had an established trade diaspora reaching from southern Arabia and the Persian Gulf to the goldfields of present-day Zimbabwe. Arabs had found it convenient to establish a string of fortified towns from central Somalia along the coasts of Kenya and Tanzania as far as Sofala, near the present city of Beira in central Mozambique. Arab merchants also settled on offshore islands, such as Zanzibar, Pemba, and the Comoro Islands. Some of these settlements dated back to the 900s C.E., though they went through a period of special growth in the 1200s and 1300s, reaching a kind of apogee in the 1400s, just before the Portuguese arrival from around the Cape of Good Hope.

The Arab traders, however, did not attempt to rule over African territory, nor were the coastal cities normally ruled from Arabia. They existed principally for trade, but over the centuries a new Afro-Arab coastal culture came into existence. A new language developed, the ancestor of present-day Swahili, a word derived from an Arabic root

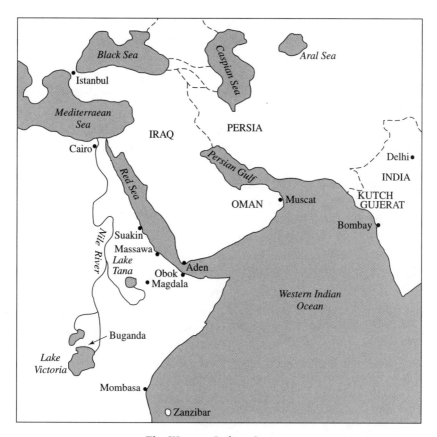

The Western Indian Ocean.

meaning coastal. Swahili is an African Bantu language, though it incorporates a wealth of loan words from Arabic, Portuguese, and English. The present Swahili-speaking people are, however, Muslim and thus identify with a foreign religion from the north, though they are in fact a community of mixed ethnic origin, settled on this coast over many generations. In present-day Swahili, local Afro-Arabs often call themselves Waarabu, while they call Arabs from Arabia Hadrami, from the Hadramaut region in southern Arabia to the east of Aden.

Before 1800, the trade of this coast with the outside world was mainly with Arabia, the Persian Gulf, and western India. One of the most important local products was mangrove poles to be used as house roof rafters along the relatively treeless coast of Arabia and the Gulf.

Another was mat bags for packing spices and other bulk commodities, ivory from the hinterland, and gold from what is now Zimbabwe, shipped down the Zambezi valley and transshipped at Kilwa for the passage north. Slaves were also an important export from the south. It was, in short, a developed commerce, handling cargoes of relatively high bulk and low value, alongside the gold and ivory.

Before the 1800s, this Afro-Arab trade diaspora was essentially seaborne. Goods from the interior were mainly carried by local traders, who ran their own trade diasporas to the coast. One route came down from central Kenya, another from what is now central Tanzania, a third from the vicinity of Lake Malawi, and a fourth from the Zimbabwe gold fields.

In the early 1800s, two important economic realignments took place. First, the price of ivory rose sharply, creating an increase in exports and pushing traders further into the interior. Second, cloves, a spice originally from Indonesia, were found to grow even better on the islands of Zanzibar and Pemba, and new clove plantations created a demand for outside labor, satisfied by an increase in the slave trade. This new trade drew some slaves from the mainland opposite Zanzibar, but it drew even more from further south, principally from the region of Lake Malawi. At first, most of the imported slaves served on the clove plantations, but with the passing of the decades, some were diverted to food production along the coast of present-day Kenya, and some were passed on to the Arabian mainland and the Persian Gulf.

These economic changes interacted with political changes. Up to this time, while the Afro-Arab trading towns were related nodes of a trade diaspora, they were not a trading-post empire under central authority. When, in the early 1800s, the British conquest of India was in full swing, the Presidency of Bombay in British India needed a friendly client state on the western shore of the Arabian Sea to help keep the peace and protect British interests. At the same time, the sultan of Muscat in Oman sought to increase his commercial advantage, using European naval technology to strengthen his position down the African coast, with the informal consent and support of Bombay. By 1835, Oman had a 74-gun ship, three frigates, two corvettes, and a brig, all of Western design, in addition to the armed dhows of local design – the most powerful non-European navy anywhere in the

Indian Ocean. This new navy could act as an informal extension of British power from its base in India, while at the same time its use of European naval technology allowed it to become a secondary empire anywhere its ships could go. Within a few decades, the Afro-Arab trade disapora was transformed into an Omani trading-post empire. By the 1830s, its coastal holdings were so important that the Sultan of Muscat moved his capital from Arabia to the island of Zanzibar, where the clove-producing slave plantations became an important non-Western offshoot of the European-dominated plantation complex.

Then, in the mid-1800s, some Zanzibari and Swahili traders initiated still another departure from past policy; they began to move into the interior with their own trade diasporas. Here a new element of secondary empire building appeared, when the Swahili traders introduced European firearms into the interior for the first time. Individual traders in the interior created their own spheres of secondary-imperial power, radiating outward from their trading centers, and, while they generally recognized the authority of the sultan of Zanzibar, the sultan's actual control beyond the coast was negligible. The Zanzibari and Swahili impact on East Africa mimicked some aspects of the secondary territorial empires elsewhere in Africa, as well as other aspects of overland trading-post empires of the kind Europeans had pioneered in Siberia and North America.

The degree and kind of European influence changed drastically over the 1800s. On the mainland, even the weak, informal influence that British diplomats exercised in Zanzibar disappeared. This was the century of the British shift from being the major slave traders on the world scene to abolishing their own slave trade and then attempting to suppress the slave trade of others. It was also the century of British predominance in the Indian Ocean, and Zanzibar was forced to bow to British pressure and reduce its legal slave trade. The powers of the British consul increased progressively, until, in 1890, Zanzibar became a formal British protectorate.

Missionary Alternatives

Christian missionaries who began to appear in the 1840s found a complex political scene on the East African mainland. African political authorities, once relatively isolated, now encountered Swahili traders from the coast with their guns and their demand for ivory and slaves. The Swahili incursion spread warfare and anarchy over large areas, with few islands of relative stability, and this left the missionary societies with two broad alternatives.

In some regions, in the absence of stable and powerful African states, missionaries created small secondary empires of their own. With no dependable source of law and order, they were moved to provide their own protection and in some cases recruited small armies, partly European and partly African. In other places, they simply equipped the mission stations with the latest European firearms, creating small circles of relative security capable of attracting a variety of refugees. These refugees, being uprooted, were among the first converts to Christianity.

Some missions also bought enslaved children whom they settled in self-supporting "orphanages" which were little more than slave plantations producing valuable products for sale. The fundamental difference was that the slave orphans were free to leave when they reached a certain age. From the point of view of religious conversion, these orphanages were an effective device to influence young people who had been uprooted and resettled in a new society. A second alternative was to work with stronger kingdoms where they existed, mainly in the region of the great lakes such as Victoria and Tanganyika. Some kingdoms, like Buganda and Bunyoro, had already armed themselves with muskets and had begun to build their own secondary empires even before the missionaries arrived. Missionaries were attracted by the sphere of relative security, where the African authorities were willing to accept and protect them, and they welcomed the opportunity to make converts without having to run a state on their own. The most attractive prospect was the opportunity to convert an important African king, which could lead on to a broad and general conversion from the top down.

The Kingdom of Buganda

The kingdom of Buganda, the core of the present-day Republic of Uganda, is a well-known and dramatic instance of interplay of European missionaries and local social and political forces. Present-day Uganda takes its name from a Swahili corruption of the word

KEBOBO, CHIEF OF CHAGWÉ.   MTESA, THE EMPEROR OF UGANDA.   CHAMBARANGO, THE CHIEF.

POKINO, THE PRIME MINISTER.

OTHER CHIEFS.

(*From a photograph by the Author.*)

[*Vol. I.*

2. Kabaka Musesa and his principal officials, drawing from Henry Morton Stanley, *Through the Dark Continent; or, The Source of the Nile, Around the Great Lakes of Equatorial Africa, and Down the Livingstone River to the Atlantic Ocean* (London: S. Low, Marston, Searle & Rivington, 1878), based on a photograph.

Buganda, but the pre-European Buganda was much smaller than the present republic of Uganda.[1] It covered only the area a hundred miles or so inland from the north shore of Lake Victoria, in a half-circle that ran west of the point where the Nile flows out of the lake. Within this small area, however, the population was very dense, with perhaps a total of one to two million people in the kingdom. The ruler, with the title of kabaka, Mutesa I (1857–1884) had recently taken the kingdom to one of its peak periods of political influence and military power (Fig. 2). In his reign, Buganda had already begun adopting muskets as its principal infantry weapon. The Ganda bought their guns from Swahili

[1] Both Kiswahili and Luganda are Bantu languages that use prefixes. The people of the kingdom of Buganda are Baganda, and the language is Luganda. English usage pemits the use of the root without prefix, as Ganda.

117

traders newly arrived from the coast, in return for ivory and slaves secured by using the guns. The guns, in turn, gave Buganda the capability of turning itself into a secondary empire.

Buganda's other important source of strength for empire building was its political constitution. Most African constitutions are based on the lineage, a group of people descended from a common ancestor. These lineages can be either patrilineal or matrilineal, or occasionally bilateral. In many African kingdoms, lineages were internally self-governing, and higher reaches of royal government tended to function as a place for conflict resolution between competing lineage groups.

In the past, the Ganda kingdom had functioned in this way, and the individual lineages in each village were joined together in thirty-odd clans, or larger kinship units, each with its own chief. This system posed a problem for a monarch; he could rule only through the clan chiefs, but they held their position though the lineage and therefore had a source of authority independent of the kabaka. A king might discipline them or remove them from office, but such action risked arousing broad resentment from the clan members.

The kabakas of Buganda had long since taken steps to remedy this source of royal weakness. By the 1700s, they were appointing chiefs from outside the hierarchy of kinship authority. Such chiefs, having been put in command by the kabaka, could be removed by the kabaka. These new-style chiefs were called *bakungu,* or client-chiefs.

By the 1870s, client-chiefs held most of the important offices, including the chief minister's office and the headship of provincial administration, which implied command over the lower reaches of the government. More important still, the kabaka also had a military force of semiprofessional warriors scattered through the country. Their officers were also appointed by the kabaka in the same way as the client-chiefs, and they served the kabaka as a makeweight against the remaining independent powers of the clan chiefs, and against any client-chief who might attempt to make his power more permanent than the king's gift.

Client-chiefs at the top level had authority to appoint subordinate chiefs in a hierarchy of command; in effect, they had client-chiefs of their own. These chiefs within the provincial administration controlled the allocation of land and therefore controlled the wealth of the country, based ultimately on the work of the peasantry, both slave and free.

The system provided an unusual concentration of power at the center of the kingdom, at the price of immense insecurity of tenure in the government service. A man might be chief minister one day and a peasant the next. A peasant might rise, if he knew the right people, to be an important chief overnight. Only the members of the royal clan, to which the kabaka belonged, had special rights by birth. This flexibility and insecurity tended to develop a certain style of political life, which put a premium on the qualities of intrigue, quickness, and adaptability in political maneuver, with ambitious men constantly having their eye on the main chance. At the kabaka's court in particular, a largish town of about 5,000 people, much of the population was caught up in an ongoing game of court intrigue.

The External Threat

Buganda had little to fear from its neighbors once it had access to guns. Its most powerful neighbor, Bunyoro, was also using imported firearms and building its own secondary empire, but its firepower was not a serious threat. By about 1870, the Ganda leadership was reasonably well informed about the sources of the guns. Swahili caravans had come up from the coast for several decades, bringing information about the world outside Africa, and, incidentally, engaging in the first effort to convert the Ganda to an outside religion, in this case Islam.

In the mid-1870s, other strangers appeared, this time from the north. They were European employees of the Egyptian government, on an expedition bent on extending the Egyptian secondary empire in the Sudan. Chaillé Long, an American in Egyptian service, visited Mutesa's capital and then withdrew to set up an Egyptian military post just beyond Buganda to the north.

No sooner had the Egyptian external threat appeared to the north, than another European explorer passed through Buganda. This was Henry Morton Stanley, an American newspaperman of Welsh origin, who was crossing Africa from east to west under the sponsorship of the *New York Herald* and the *Daily Telegraph* of London. Stanley was not yet working directly for Leopold of Belgium or the Congo Independent State, but he talked politics with Mutesa. In 1875, in a famous despatch to the *Daily Telegraph,* he reported that Mutesa was avidly interested in Christianity, and he challenged British missionary societies to respond to this opportunity. Whatever was actually said or understood through interpreters, Stanley no doubt gave his opinion that Britain was "top nation" in Europe. Whatever Mutesa's actual interest in Christianity, he was certainly interested in having European missionaries at his court to balance the threat of Muslim Egyptians to the north and Muslim Swahili to the east.

For British missionary societies, a mission to Buganda would have been a significant breach of the existing policy of advancing mission stations gradually inland from the coast. The route from the east coast to Buganda was roughly 800 miles, and it could be traveled only by caravans using head porterage. The longer route up the Nile was also possible, but this, too, was expensive. The country between the coast and Lake Victoria was politically fragmented, so that caravans had to defend themselves and sometimes to fight their way through. The cost of head porterage in any case was astronomical; if it were merely a matter of preaching the gospel, that could be done much more cheaply elsewhere. On the other hand, Stanley's report of Mutesa's interest suggested that Buganda would be an excellent opportunity to convert a whole population though royal support.

For whatever reason, an anonymous donor offered the Church Missionary Society (CMS) a gift of £ 6,500, on condition that it break its existing policy of incremental extension and place a mission station at Mutesa's court. The CMS also received an offer of assistance with more obvious political motives from Gordon Pasha, the English governor of the Equatorial province of Egypt, offering assistance if the CMS were to choose the Nile route. Gordon was acting for Egypt, but Egypt, like Zanzibar, was drifting into Britain's informal control. The central committee of the CMS decided to accept both offers. Its first missionaries arrived at Mutesa's court in 1877–some by way of Zanzibar and the east coast, some by way of the Nile with the assistance of Egyptian officials.

A second departure from mission policy followed shortly. The Catholic order of the White Fathers also became interested in Buganda. This order had been founded by Cardinal Lavigerie of Algiers, mainly to convert the Muslims of the Sahara and North Africa. It was, therefore, a special-purpose missionary society with little experience in East Africa, and its primary assignment was still unfinished in the north. Yet Lavigerie, too, decided to establish a mission station at the court of Mutesa of Buganda. The first White Fathers arrived in 1879, only two years after the arrival of the CMS.

The sudden appearance of these two missionary groups at this strategic and important point in the far interior of Africa raises some question about motives. In the late 1870s, the European conquest of Africa was not yet fully underway, but one is tempted to suspect government pressure, or the entering wedge of projected commercial development. In fact, the evidence of either commercial or direct governmental interference is very weak. Leopold of Belgium offered financial aid to the White Fathers, and he *did* have territorial ambitions in Africa, but the White Fathers turned him down at this point, fearing that his terms would give him too much control over mission policy. In the 1870s, the British government had a settled policy of not acquiring territory in East Africa and had recently repudiated the acts of men-on-the spot who had tried, and such influence as Britain had in Egypt at that time was shared with France. As to French government influence, Cardinal Lavigerie approached the government for assistance and received a flat refusal.

Commercial interest in Buganda was no greater. Buganda was far beyond the range of possible investment in commerce, plantations, or mines, and the costs of porterage were far too high for any product but one of high value relative to weight, such as ivory. A railway might have changed that, but in the 1890s, when the British government decided that a railroad was essential for strategic reasons, it failed to find private capital to build it. In the end, the government built the railroad at the expense of the British taxpayers and ran it at a loss.

It is more likely that the missionary societies, presented with the possibility of converting a major king, created their own pressure to move into Buganda. For the CMS, the move was tied to a conviction that missions should be self-supporting, self-governing, and self-propagating. A Christian kingdom would be an important beachhead from which Ganda Christians would move ahead to convert others, using the experience the CMS had gained with its effective use of African missionaries in West Africa.

Cardinal Lavigerie had somewhat different motives. He was personally ambitious and political, and he was a French patriot actively seeking to improve the strained relations between the papacy and the French Republic. He also hoped to use the White Fathers somewhere in the African lake region, for the sake of the church and France alike. These considerations seem to have lain behind his unsuccessful negotiations with Leopold of Belgium. While Lavigerie was unwilling to see the White Fathers as the religious arm of King Leopold's Congo scheme, he later accepted missionary jurisdiction over the eastern part of the Congo Independent State. An independent Christian and Catholic state in the heart of Africa, where the king would rule with the beneficent advice of the French missionaries, would meet many of his aspirations, and the White Fathers were well organized for such a role, better organized than the CMS. The White Fathers sent in a group of former papal *zouaves,* for example, to act as the officers of a private mission army to be recruited and trained in the interior for the defense of the missions – and any other Christian purpose that might come to hand.

Missions and Ganda Society

Matters must have looked very different from the Ganda perspective. Mutesa's outlook was certainly nothing like the simplistic view Stanley painted, of longing to learn more about Christianity after a short introductory description of that religion conveyed through an interpreter. Mutesa was a skillful politician who had succeeded by balancing the various kinds of chieftancy, also by balancing the interests of various local gods represented by their cult leaders, who in turn often had a connection to particular clans. The possibility of adding Christians to the balance to counteract the growing influence of Zanzibari Muslims was only a natural addition to the equation.

To Mutesa, the Christians offered technical knowledge and strategic insight about the threatening world beyond the African lake district. The missionaries' knowledge could be used for defensive modernization; the Ganda had already adopted firearms and remade their military organization. The missionaries were anxious to teach other important techniques the Ganda lacked, such as literacy. Islam offered similar advantages, but for Mutesa it was useful to have several sources of outside information and technology, and his longing for Christian knowledge varied in direct proportion to the Egyptian danger. That danger had been great in the mid-1870s, but in 1879, the Egyptians withdrew some distance down the Nile. In 1881, an anti-Egyptian revolt broke out in the Sudan, just south of the desert. A Muslim religious leader, Muhammed Ahmad, proclaimed himself mahdi or savior, and his forces cut off direct contact between Egypt and the Egyptian garrison in Equatoria, leaving it isolated under the command of a German mercenary.

After these events, the Christian missionaries in Buganda no longer had an advantage, but they were tolerated in case they might be needed again, and they were allowed to make such converts as they could. They were not successful at first, but Ganda curiosity was on their side. The courtiers surrounding the kabaka were used to looking for a chance to further their careers. Many, especially the young pages at the court and the young military officers, visited both missions to see what they had to offer of possible value in local politics. As long as Mutesa lived, nothing critical came of the religious competition at court, but in the mid-1880s, a more threatening situation developed. Leopold of Belgium became active in the Congo basin to the west. The Germans occupied the coast of Tanganyika to the southeast, and the British secured the Indian Ocean coast directly to the east. Furthermore, Zanzibari visits became more frequent, and the traders proselytized actively for Islam along with their commercial activity. Mutesa was old, and a struggle for power centering on the succession was predictable. Some client-chiefs and military officers lined up politically with the Catholic or the Protestant missions or with the Zanzibari, hoping to secure a source of firearms and information when the crisis came, though Mutesa in his last years still successfully played one faction against the rest.

When Mutesa died in 1884, the crisis began. Early in 1885, the succession passed to Mwanga, one of his many sons, a young man without the ability and the intelligence of his father. He lacked his father's control over the kingdom for other reasons as well, one of which was the growing prominence of firearms. Just as the possession of guns made it possible for Buganda to build a secondary empire, control of guns caused a major shift of power within Buganda itself. The monarchy bought the weapons from the coast, but it assigned them to special military formations, and Mwanga had difficulty keeping these companies of young men under his strict control. His policies increased his power as a personal despot, but simultaneously they increased the power of the military. Some factions within the military came to be associated with certain client-chiefs and with the converts to the three outside religious groups, but the major shift in power was away from the clan chiefs as a group and from the kabaka himself to the young leaders of the new military formations.

Mwanga increased his problems by making a number of errors, one of which was a mistaken appreciation of the international situation. He came to believe that Zanzibar was the strongest external power and therefore turned at first to the Muslim faction at the court. Homosexual practices became more common at court and for Mwanga personally, though opposed to Ganda ideas of morality as well as to those of Victorian Christianity. The new liberality also offended some men in ruling circles who had brought their young relatives to serve as pages in a court. These pages were also among those who turned to the missionaries for support and advice. When, in 1886, Mwanga sought sexual partners among this group, some resisted. Their resistance alarmed the kabaka, who arrested and burned to death about forty of the pages who were also "readers" at the missions. A number of Catholics among this group have been since canonized. The persecution did not completely alienate all Christians, and the Christian factions soon regained their earlier place at court, but it alarmed the young leaders of the military. In 1888, an alliance of Muslim and Christian religious factions seized the palace and sent Mwanga into exile.

He was to return, but his first exile introduced a complex, four-sided civil war, the factions being divided by religion as well by earlier political tensions surrounding the distribution of power in the Ganda kingdom. By this time, the Protestants and Catholics controlled about one thousand musketeers each; the Muslims had somewhat less, and followers of the old gods had fewer still. The war passed through stages of shifting alliances. First, the monotheists as a group defeated the traditionalists, then the Christians joined together against Islam, and finally the Protestants fought the Catholics. It was only at this stage, in the spring of 1892, that agents of a European power entered. The Imperial British East African Company sent in a small force of Sudanese troops under Captain Frederick Lugard, later one of the foremost proconsuls of British rule in Africa. His force was tiny, but he had a Maxim gun. This sealed the immediate military victory for the Protestant faction and prepared the way for British annexation of Buganda in 1893.

The Religious Revolution in Buganda

These events, from the arrival of the missionaries in 1877 to the British annexation, prepared the way for leaders of the Christian factions to become the dominant social and political voice in Buganda under British overrule. As of 1893, their position was not yet completely secure, but they were on the way to becoming a modernizing oligarchy with a dominant voice in Ganda affairs far into the next century, a phase of Ganda history that will be discussed in the next chapter. For the moment, the concern is with the interaction of Christian missionaries and Baganda that set the scene for the conversion that was perhaps the most spectacular and radical success story in the history of African Christianity. It is one of the prime cases in the literature seeking to explain why and how one of the world religions replaced a belief system of more limited geographical scope. Robin Horton argued, in papers that have become the classic treatment of African conversion, that the broadening scope of contact with the outside world prepared the way for the world religions. Many African religions feature deities associated with particular places, lineages, or functions, such as the control of smallpox or lightning. As societies move away from subsistence farming and come into contact with a broader intercommunicating zone, specialized or local deities tend to be less satisfactory, and people turn to an all-encompassing high god. Horton's explanation is useful in pointing up conditions that recur in many different places, but it has to be taken alongside other local causes. In the Ganda case, conversion occurred more rapidly and completely than among any other people in East Africa, at a period when East Africa in general was first entering into more intense contact with the intercommunicating zone of the Indian Ocean, followed by European colonial control.

In addition to these general circumstances, the role of missionaries in the British acquisition of Buganda is also the classic case in Africa history where missionary penetration preceded colonial rule and missionaries were largely responsible for the annexation of an African territory. There, more clearly than elsewhere, "the flag followed the cross." The Ganda case was also one of the few instances in Africa where Protestant and Catholic have fought one another in the name of religion. In other places, such as Northern Ireland, religious animosities express centuries-old social and political tensions. In Buganda, people fought each other in the name of a religion they had just joined.

These unusual features can be traced to the interaction of the Ganda political order with European missions at a unique time and place. Among the actors on this stage, the client-chiefs and military officers who joined the missions had motives that seem clear: their tenure in office and life itself were at the whim of a capricious ruler, and the missionaries had access to guns and other useful techniques, of which literacy was appealing. People at the Ganda court were already used to a competitive political life, where survival depended on whatever strategic advantage came their way. This is not to devalue their conversion to Christianity, but it was a case where self-interest and religious principle were mutually reinforcing.

In the perspective of time, it seems clear that Ganda political conditions were more important than the missionary initiatives. The missions entered in the hope of using favorable local political conditions. In the long run, they were to become important participants, though not the real leaders in Ganda political struggles. They were important agents in bringing Buganda into the larger outside world, but they were isolated in the smaller Ganda world. In the heart of Africa, they were so caught up in Ganda politics that it was hard for them to see far beyond their own work and the fortunes of their followers. They were too far beyond the area of European control to do other than to act according to the standards of African society and to respond with its responses.

To these outsiders, it appeared that the conversion of a few important people at the top would be reflected in mass conversions at lower levels, just as the powers of appointment under Mutesa ran from the client-chiefs through the lower orders of society. And so it worked out to some extent. Success at the top of Ganda society appeared to be definitive. If Protestants could control the kabaka, Catholic subchiefs were in danger of dismissal. If that happened, Catholic missionaries could imagine a rapid end to their dream of building "a fair Catholic kingdom in the heart of Africa," to quote one of them. Protestant missionaries, for their part, could imagine victory for the Catholic faction not as a temporary setback but as the destruction all their work.

Both sides worked hard, not only to help arm their followers but also to enlist European intervention in their own cause. In the end, the

British did intervene, but Lugard's military action on the Protestant side was not a move planned from London but only that of a man-on-the-spot with power to decide on his own, and his decision then became binding on future actors – like many other peripheral decisions in the decades of imperial advance. In fact, his military action on the Protestant side did not result in the winner-take-all solution that some missionaries feared.

After the British annexation and the creation of the Uganda Protectorate, the Protestants consolidated their position as the leading members of the modernizing oligarchy, but Catholics were not excluded, and the coming of English Catholic missionaries softened the implicit Anglo-French competition in the field of religion. More recently, however, aspects of the regime of Idi Amin represented the reemergence of some of the old Muslim resentments against the Christian dominance.

Further Reading

Hefner, Robert W. (ed.), *Conversion to Christianity: Historical and Anthropological Perspectives on a Great Transformation* (Berkeley: University of California Press, 1993).

Horton, Robin, "On the Rationality of Conversion," *Africa,* 45:108–141, 373–397 (1975).

Kimambo, I. A., "The East African Coast and Hinterland," in J. F. Ade Ajayi (ed.), *General History of Africa* (Paris: UNESCO, 1989), 6:234–269.

Kiwanuka, M. S. M. *Semakula, a History of Buganda: From the Foundation of the Kingdom to 1900* (New York: Africana, 1972).

Oliver, Roland, *The Missionary Factor in East Africa,* 2nd ed. (London: Oxford University Press, 1965).

Peel, J. D. Y,, "Conversion and Tradition in Ijebu and Buganda," *Past and Present,* no. 7, pp. 108–141 (1977).

Twaddle, Michael, *Kakungulu and the Creation of Uganda, 1868–1928* (London: James Currey, 1993).

Wright, Marcia, "East Africa, 1870–1905," in J. D. Fage and Roland Oliver, *The Cambridge History of Africa* (Cambridge, U.K.: Cambridge University Press, 1985), 6:539–589.

8

Varieties of Defensive Modernization

T he four essays that make up this section deal broadly with cultural conversion on the initiative of the borrowers. Even when Christian missionaries took the initiative, the decisions of local people were decisive, as in the case of the Ganda. Other Christian missions with a similar programs met very different conditions overseas and had a radically different measure of success. The Western threat, however, was most clearly identified as political and military, and non-Westerners most often responded by borrowing what they could of military and organizational technology. This chapter deals with a number of instances of defensive modernization, and it will also serve as a background for the more detailed consideration of modernization in Japan and Turkey in the two chapters than follow.

It is important, however, to go further back in time to earlier and fundamental patterns of world history that are broader than those involving the West and the rest of the world, and to begin near the beginning with the diffusion of agriculture, which not only marks the commencement of one of the principal eras in world history; but also raises important questions about the role of diffusion and independent invention in historical change.

The Diffusion of Agriculture

An old debate involves the relative importance of diffusion of knowledge as against independent invention. Both the Maya and the ancient Egyptians, for example, built pyramids. Did the Maya somehow or other learn from the Egyptians? The Egyptian pyramids were indubitably earlier in time, so that they might have been copied, and Maya and Egyptian pyramids both served ritual purposes. But artificial hills and mounds have built for so many different purposes by so many different people that they were no doubt reinvented many times over in human history. The different scale of the Maya and Egyptian pyramids and the different ritual purposes argues strongly against diffusion, but the problem recurs through history, and it can be illustrated by the development and diffusion of agriculture. (See map, page 130).

Most authorities now agree that agriculture began in at least seven independent centers over the period between 10,000 years B.P. and 4,000 years B.P. Research still continues, and other independent centers may be discovered. In any event, the degree of independence can be a problem. Between relatively nearby centers such as Mexico and the southern United States, stimulus diffusion might have been possible. That is, the knowledge that plants could be domesticated could pass by diffusion, even though the domestication of particular plants would take place independently, on the basis of the wild species available. But there is no evidence that stimulus diffusion did take place in this instance, and the possibility of stimulus diffusion between Afro-Eurasia and the Americas is remote. On the basis of present knowledge, it is safe to say that the domestication of plants and animals was independently invented in widely scattered parts of the world.

One notable fact about the data is that in the long run of human habitation on the earth, these independent centers should have appeared within a temporal range as narrow as about six millennia. Long before 10,000 years ago, *Homo Sapiens Sapiens* had moved out of Africa and come to live on all the major continents, but if plant domestication took place earlier, it has been lost to the historical record. Plant domestication, for that matter, is not as simple a process as might appear at first glance. Over the millennia, people have harvested certain wild grasses, controlled weeds, encouraged wild plants to multiply, or planted seeds, but that is not true domestication. To be domesticated in the technical sense, a plant or animal has to be at least a new variety, often a new species, that can no longer reproduce itself without human assistance.

Maize is a good example. The original wild maize was a grass in Mexico, *teosinte,* having a seed spike with a single row of kernels, each enclosed in a hard case. As the grain ripened, the spike shattered,

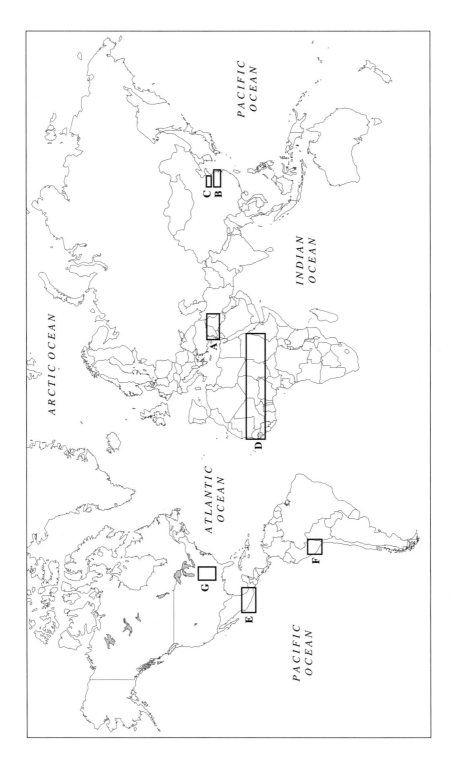

The invention of agriculture.

A. Fertile crescent beginning about 10,000 B.P. – sheep, goats, cattle, pigs, barley, emmer sheat, and einkorn wheat.

B. South China, in the Yangzi river corridor, about 8,500 B.P. – both long and short-grain rice, dogs, pigs, and water buffalo.

C. North China, yellow river valley, about 7,000 B.P. – two different species of millet, first domestication of chickens, and perhaps pigs simultaneously with the fertile crescent.

D. Sub-Saharan Africa, about 4,000 B.P. – Western Sudan, pearl millet and later, several sorghums and African rice.

E. Central Mexico, about 7,800 B.P. – maize, common beans (varieties of which are navy, kidney, black, and pinto), and squash (varieties of which are pumpkins, green, yellow, and scorn squash, zucchini, and marrow).

F. South-Central Andes, about 4,000 B.P. – llama, alpaca, guinea pig, potato, and quinoa.

G. Southeastern United States about 4,500 B.P. – some varieties of gourds, sunflowers, and marsh elders.

scattering the seeds and giving them an opportunity to produce a new plant each year. Maize seeds are heavier and less protected, and they do not scatter. An unattended cornfield will often produce a few volunteer stalks a second year, but without human care the plant would become extinct after only a few years. With wide variations and obvious exceptions, such as feral cats and dogs, the result would be the same for other domesticated plants and animals if left untended.

The most common explanation for the delay of plant domestication until just 10,000 years ago is that biological changes following the last Ice Age produced varieties of wild plants suitable for domestication in several parts of the world. It is also probable that population densities among hunters and foragers in several places made existing resources scarce enough to stimulate the development of agriculture.

The dates for the earliest agriculture shown in the map are later in time than the dates commonly cited in the earlier literature. During the 1980s, archaeological and botanical techniques for investigating early agriculture improved enormously. One new device was accelerator mass spectrometry, which can give a radiocarbon date from a very small sample of organic material. Earlier techniques required such a large sample that dating from a few seeds was impossible, and radiocarbon dates had to be established from those of associated organic material, a technique that was sometimes deceptive. Also in the 1980s, the scanning electron microscope became available for measuring seed characteristics, such as small differences in seed coatings that distinguish a wild seed from a domesticated seed of the same time period.

The list of domesticated plants and animals shown in the map includes almost no instances of possible repetitive invention. That is, while plants were domesticated independently several times, each plant or animal species was probably domesticated only once, and each agricultural center domesticated its own range of plants and animals.

The use of these domesticated species spread around the world through diffusion on the initiative of those who had the means to travel – by caravan across the silk road or by sea, carried by Polynesians or European mariners – but they were accepted or rejected by farmers who had a chance to use them. The successors of Columbus, for example, brought maize to Europe, but most Europeans rejected it at first, except as occasional feed for animals. The Ottoman Turks accepted it so readily as human food that maize is called "Turkish corn" in several European languages. Needless to say, those who had ships were also in a position to borrow crops, even from those who did not want to lend them. The Dutch carried coffee cultivation from Ethiopia to Java. Americans introduced pineapples from South America to Hawaii. British and Dutch moved wild cinchona from the eastern slopes of the Andes to make it a plantation crop in Ceylon and Indonesia, to the distress of Bolivians and Peruvians who had previously controlled the world's only source of quinine.

The Pace of Diffusion

The pace of diffusion depends mainly on population densities and the means of transportation. In the preagricultural period, diffusion was slow because people were sparsely settled and had little contact with strangers. A faster rate of diffusion followed almost automatically from denser populations and better means of transportation.

Within recent decades, scholars dealing with world history, have been moving toward a scheme for dividing human history into time periods, preagricultural up to about 10,000 B.P., agricultural spreading from its original centers, then an industrial period beginning about 1800 in Europe, and spreading as well. There is less agreement about how to subdivide the long agricultural period, but a beginning has been made, built on the pioneering work of historians such as William McNeill and Marshall Hodgson. One form of periodization is based on a combination of invention and diffusion. At several early centers, where agriculture made possible a rise of population, urban centers sprang up, leading to the first *civilizations,* a term that originally meant life in cities. Each of those early centers of relatively dense population and intercommunication became the center of a wider, intercommunicating zone. As population and intercommunication spread out from the original core areas, contact with the others increased by stages until in the past half century, intercommunication has become global, cheap, and virtually instantaneous.

Some authorities propose that a series of steps toward increasingly global communication should be taken to mark off the major subdivisions of the agricultural era. Opinions differ, but some of the steps are obvious and generally recognized. Shortly before the beginning of the Common era, the Han dynasty in China formed an empire in East Asia that has lasted in some form down to the present. The Greeks of the Hellenistic era created a cultural synthesis from Mesopotamian, Egyptian, and Mediterranean roots to create an equivalent intercommunicating zone centered on the eastern Mediterranean. A century or so before the common era, the silk road across Asia and monsoon navigation across the Indian Ocean and the South China Sea linked the major zones of the Afro-Eurasian land mass.

With the rise of Islam in the 800s, a single culture areas and religion bound together people from Morocco to Central Asia. It emerged as the single society having contact with all other Afro-Eurasian societies, borrowing from some and lending to others, and acting as the principal transmission agency for cultural diffusion. In this way, for example, the place notational system we call Arabic numbers moved from India to Europe. The seclusion of women came to be practiced from Christian Spain to Hindu India. Gunpowder and other Chinese inventions were known almost everywhere within a few centuries.

In time, the European maritime revolution between about 1425 and 1525 brought the previously isolated Americas into the world known to Europeans, and by the mid-1700s, Europe replaced the Muslim world as the central society with which the others had contact – in effect the core of the new order of intercommunication.

Nondiffusion

Knowledge about a possibly useful innovation, however, will not necessarily lead people to accept it. Religions sometimes spread rapidly, but they sometimes have faced each other across a frontier line for centuries without appreciable interchange. With the fall of the Roman Empire, the formerly unified Mediterranean basin split into three religiously defined zones, two forms of Christianity and Islam, and once established, the division remained relatively stable over centuries.

Such stabilized religious frontiers can also change suddenly. Among the Wolof of what is now Senegal, the first recorded Islamic ruler in the region died in 1040 c.e. Islam continued as the religion of merchants and royal courts, with little trickle-down to the main body of the peasantry, and this religious balance remained stable for nearly a thousand years. Then, quite suddenly between about 1800 and 1920, Islam became the religion of the vast majority, not only of the Wolof but of most other people of Senegambia.

Similar nonborrowing can also be found in technology, and here the explanation is more difficult. While it is difficult to argue successfully that one religion is better than another, technical devices are measurably good or bad according to their ability to perform their assigned tasks. Even so, their acceptance by others is not assured. One well-known example is the seeming refusal of the Romans to use stirrups. They knew about stirrups from their contact with Asian horsemen of the steppes, but they stuck with chariots in warfare and they rode horses without stirrups.

Other notorious examples involve the one-sided technological exchanges between China and the West. On the whole, before the present century the West borrowed intensively from China, but China borrowed very little from the West. By the 1700s, Western factories were turning out good imitations of Chinese silk and Chinese porcelain, but the Chinese were not turning out copies of Western sailing ships, which were demonstrably just as superior as Chinese porcelain.

Nor did the Chinese adopt the alphabet, or a phonetic syllabary, which would seem at first glance to be superior to a writing system built on thousands of individual characters. Part of the explanation is that the Chinese characters were valued because they were beautiful as well as useful, and they were intimately identified with many other aspects of Chinese culture. Each character carries its message not as a sound but as a concept, conveyed through complex combinations of other characters on which it is built, and can thus carry levels of meaning and suggestion that are impossible with an alphabet or syllabary. It also has the virtue of universality over a very large areas. People whose spoken language is not mutually intelligible can nevertheless communicate in writing, because the characters conveyed an idea, not a sound.

In the industrial age, however, the continued use of characters poses new problems. A Chinese dictionary is very hard to use, arranged as it is first according to a number of brush strokes in a character, then, secondarily, according to a set order of radicals, or basic forms for a character – more than two hundred of them. The problem of putting words on lists in a fixed order goes far beyond dictionaries, into many kinds of record keeping – think of a phone book based the number of strokes and the sequence of radicals. Computers can alphabetize, but they handle characters only with difficulty. The solution for certain kinds of communication in China and Taiwan is simply to write certain kinds of things in English. Whether, in the longer run, the alphabetical efficiency of computers will drive out the aesthetic advantage of the characters remains to be seen.

Cross-Cultural Borrowing Between the West and the World

Historians and other social scientists are concerned with finding general patterns of culture change, including acceptance, rejections, and reinterpretations of cultural borrowings. So far, though no one hypothesis seems to explain all these phenomena, a few broad generalizations stand out as useful. First, as these essays have noted several times, from the Middle Ages onward the West was enormously acquisitive in the field of technology. Western mariners arrived in Asia with ships whose design was borrowed partly from Asia, guided by astronomical and algebraic knowledge and magnetic compasses even more clearly

Asian in origin. But the West also innovated, incorporating borrowed technology in new ways. Borrowing and innovation went together; they are early signs of a technological emphasis in Western culture that was to flourish in the industrial age. Until the twentieth century, however, the West was uninterested in borrowing in certain other areas, such as non-Western religions. This particular religious intolerance was one aspect of a bundle of ideas that led Europeans and Americans to spend so much effort encouraging others to accept Christianity.

As a second generalization, most Asians before the 1700s were uninterested in Western technology, but, from the 1800s onward they began to borrow increasingly, though selectively, from Western technology and culture. Few wanted to become Westerners themselves, and this effort to modernize rarely meant simple imitation. Many admired the technology that made possible the high productivity and high consumption they saw in the West. Some accepted their own version of Christianity, though the majority rejected the Christian message that the West generously offered. They wanted the visible benefits of industrial technology, but they also wanted to preserve their own way of life, and for the most part, they took special care to preserve their own religion, whatever that might be.

Even before the full impact of the industrial age, non-Western societies had to take account of the Westerners as they appeared from the sea on the shores of every continent, offering trade and accompanied by missionaries offering Christianity. While Christian missions were not especially threatening, the opportunity to trade was often accompanied by a threat of force, and the Western military power became more ominous with the passing decades. Unless a non-Western state could defend itself, in time its whole way of life was threatened, yet self-defense required some imitation of the West. Military modernization was often the entering wedge, and it often called for further changes in spheres as diverse as social organization, education, and political life.

Japan and Turkey, the detailed examples of the next two chapters, are neither random nor typical. They are, however, two contrasting cases of defensive modernization: Japan was the earliest and most successful non-Western nation to industrialize, Turkey carried out a broad and revolutionary shift to Western norms across a wide range of the cultural spectrum. Meanwhile, it is worth looking at examples of defensive strategies in other settings, some of them still in the preindustrial age.

The Neo-Inca Resistance

The neo-Inca resistance to Spanish rule in Peru of the 1500s is significant because it occurred at such an early period in the history of European world conquest. It was a reaction among members of a society already defeated by alien conquerors and within the first decades after that defeat.

Most accounts of Latin American history tell the amazing story of a few hundred Spanish soldiers who marched into Tawantinsuyu, which the Europeans called the Inca Empire, and established one of the first of the European territorial empires overseas. The initial success owed far more to smallpox than it did to European military prowess, and weapons were less important than the element of strategic surprise; the people of Tawantinsuyu knew almost nothing about who the Spanish were, where they came from, or what they were likely to do. They came with cavalry into a country without horses and with cannon into a country without gunpowder.

At an early stage, the Spanish seized the person of the Inca, the head of a complex bureaucratic state, and they were able for a time to rule by giving orders in his name. When resistance emerged, it came too late to be effective, because the Spanish already controlled the apparatus of government. Some of the Peruvian nobility and their followers, however, fled into Vilcabamba, a frontier area between the high mountains and the tropical forest to the east of the Andes. There, they were close to the former capital of Cuzco, now occupied by the Spanish, but their stronghold was difficult to penetrate from the mountains. Machu Picchu was in this frontier region. In Vilcabamba, they set up an independent government, which they defended from the 1530s until 1572.

What they chose to preserve from their own culture and what they borrowed from the Spanish is an indicative early example of defensive modernization. They set out, first of all, to re-create the main bureaucratic structure of Tawantinsuyu, even though they now ruled a much smaller area. At the same time, they borrowed far more heavily from the Spanish than did other Quechua-speaking people who fell under

Spanish rule in these early decades. As might be expected, the neo-Inca state changed most rapidly to European military techniques, acquiring European arms and armor and breeding Europeans horses. This adaptation was all the more important, because they had no access to the manpower necessary for the mass infantry that had been the military strength of Tawantinsuyu. Because of depopulation from the early smallpox epidemics, the Spanish had not had to confront such armies, and after the initial defeat, the principal fighting involved Spanish factions fighting among themselves with only a few hundred men on each side.

The other principal area of borrowing is less expected. The Neo-Inca state also adopted the Spanish religion, and here, in fact, the Spanish and the Neo-Inca leaders worked together, each, perhaps, to serve their own ends. The Spanish sent missionaries into Vilcabamba as a way of trying to break the resistance and secure peaceful acceptance of Spanish rule. At the same time, the Indian resistance accepted the missionaries and used them as a source of information about the Spanish, about Spanish culture, and about Europe. In this way, they were able minimize the crucial Spanish advantage of strategic surprise. The use of missionaries as informants about Europe was, indeed, to recur in many phases of the confrontation between Europeans and the non-West – in pre-Tokugawa Japan, for example, in the missions of the Jesuits to the Yaqui valley of Mexico in the 1600s, or in the acceptance of Christianity in Buganda in the 1890s. In Peru of the mid-1500s, the people of the neo-Inca resistance became Christian well before the Christianization of the Peruvian highlands in general. Unlike central Mexico, where conversion was rapid in the 1500s, broad acceptance of Christianity in Peru dated only from the 1600s and even later. Religious conversion there came most rapidly to two groups, those who collaborated most closely with the Spanish and those who held out against them in Vilcabamba.

Westernization in Peter's Russia

The spread of Western culture into Russia and Ukraine began from the time Slavic eastern Europe joined Christendom during the centuries just before and after about 1000 C.E. The attachment was weak at first, and it was to Constantinople and Greek Christendom rather than to a Latin West. The Catholic – Orthodox division was to be remarkably long-lasting in eastern European history, and it still exists in the conflict between Orthodox Serbs and Catholic Croatians in the former Yugoslavia.

After the Ottoman capture of Constantinople in the mid-1400s, the Turks emerged as the political successors of the Byzantine empire, but Orthodox Christianity continued to function from its seat in Istanbul. The Muscovites and the Ottomans had much in common as fringe states beyond the land frontiers of Western Christendom but maintaining commercial and political relations with the West. As of the early 1600s, Muscovy, as a Christian country, had something in common with the West, but it remained a military backwater compared with either Western Europe or the Ottoman Empire. As of 1680, Russia was nevertheless expanding toward the east and south, down the valley of the Volga toward the Caspian Sea, just as Buganda of the 1880s, while also threatened from the outside, was building a secondary empire in its own neighborhood. The threat to Russia came from the superior military systems of Poland and then Sweden to its west, just as Mutesa's Buganda sensed danger from the Egyptians to the north and the Swahili from the Indian Ocean coast. Russia needed a better military system for its own protection, and in order to expand to the east and south, just as Buganda initially wanted Western guns for expansion as well as defense.

With military considerations principally in mind, Peter the Great, who ruled as czar from 1682 to 1725, began a conscious policy usually described as Westernization, though it can be recognized today as a planned modernization rather than simple imitation of the West. He and his followers were less concerned with making Russia like the West than with making it strong. Using the available Western model of military strength, they built an army powerful enough to stand off Sweden and went on to make Russia an important factor in the European state system for the first time. As elsewhere, military modernization could not easily be confined to strictly military pursuits, and Peter and his followers' reforms spread to other matters as well, some of them only peripheral to their own major interest.

Western Europeans laughed at the Russian Westernizers, just as they laughed at first when the Japanese set out to build a modern navy. Among other things, Peter tried to prohibit the wearing of beards. He issued a book of court etiquette designed to move Russian manners and court life toward the Western norms. He made changes in the alphabet, though not in the Russian language itself, but Western-language loan words began to slip into Russian from that time onward. His modernization program, however, did not include major religious change, as modernization had done in Vilcabamba and was to do again in Buganda two centuries later.

A second kind of spillover from military modernization changed the distribution of power in Russian society at large. Just as the new Russian army changed the balance of power in Europe, it made the czar stronger within Russia, in much the same way that muskets and missionary support made certain client-chiefs of Buganda stronger within the Ganda state. In Peter's Russia, the czar's enemies lost influence and the czar's friends gained in a realignment that continued far beyond his reign. Some Russians have chronically felt themselves overshadowed by western Europe, culturally and politically.

Modernizing Oligarchies in the Age of Imperialism: Buganda

Other societies faced a Western threat and responded with some form of defensive modernization. By the late 1800s, however, Western societies had already profited from nearly a century of industrialization, and the power differential between the West and others was greater that ever before. This power gap was at the heart of the age of imperialism, and, as the pace of European conquest increased, non-Western leaders everywhere had to confront the problem. Some, like those in Japan and Turkey, chose a form of defensive modernization that preserved the essence of their former way of life and, in the Japanese case, even enabled them to advance into the forefront of economic success.

The principal actors in these encounters were rarely single individuals, and the Westernizing achievements of Peter the Great, for example, were more representative of a group around the monarch than of Peter as an individual. Nor were the modernizing responses broadly based in these societies. Limited literacy and limited flow of information within almost any non-Western society limited possible responses to members of the élite, even to a particular group within the élite, who sometimes emerged as a new ruling and modernizing oligarchy.

We have already seen the early stages of defensive modernization of Buganda. During the Christian revolution of the 1880s and 1890s, the first important actor was Kabaka Mutesa, who helped to invite the missionaries into a society already in confrontation with outsiders – not European at first but Swahili traders from the east coast and the Egyptian secondary empire to the north. The aspects of exotic culture that most interested Ganda leadership at this point were arms and religion, those same aspects of Western culture that had most interested the resistance in Vilcabamba three centuries earlier. The Ganda, however, were able to use Western arms and Western religion to channel and limit European influence, in this case to postpone surrender but not to put it off altogether.

Even in Mutesa's reign, the military changes strengthened the office of kabaka at the expense of other élite groups. After Mutesa's death, power shifted from the titular kabaka to a group of client-chiefs, who used their military command and the external religions, Christianity and Islam, to advance their own interests. A decade of confusion followed, during which the official British annexation took place but without the establishment of a settled British government administration. The client-chiefs, with British help, then removed Kabaka Mwanga from power and established their own political supremacy over Ganda society. Not all the external dangers came from Europe; a rinderpest epidemic from southwest Asia killed most cattle, and a disastrous sleeping sickness epidemic swept through nearby parts of the Uganda Protectorate, though it was not so serious in Buganda itself.

It was not until after 1899 that the British established an actual administration for Buganda, and only later and more gradually over the rest of the Protectorate. By that time, the governor found the principal Christian client-chiefs in control of most of the country, protected by the influence of their missionary advisers, and the new Ganda oligarchs were now in a position to bargain from strength.

The result was a formal treaty, called the Uganda Agreement of 1900, which was a unique document in the British occupation of trop-

ical Africa. This formal agreement between the British governor and a
group of prominent client-chiefs laid out terms for the future government of Buganda. The new balance of power was largely dictated by
the interests and attitudes of the modernizing oligarchy, but the
understanding between the prominent client-chiefs and the British
was broader that the formal document. In time, some Ganda, mostly
drawn from the class of client-chiefs, were to act for the British administration in establishing British rule over the rest of the protectorate.
This process is sometimes called Ganda subimperialism, and non-
Ganda inhabitants of the Uganda Protectorate often thought of it as
Ganda rule with British connivance.

The Uganda Agreement is notable for its program of political modernization – and for both its achievements and its limitations. It preserved the integrity of the kingdom of Buganda and the office of
kabaka. The kabaka at that moment, Daude Chwa, was a minor. The
actual power within Buganda was to be exercised, under British overrule, by three regents, representing the most powerful religious factions among the client-chiefs.

While preserving the office of kabaka, it also ensured the future
political power of the client-chiefs by creating a representative council
of chiefs, called the Lukiiko, and it preserved their economic interests
by sweeping away the whole of the traditional system of land tenure. It
divided the valuable land of the kingdom among the principal client-
chiefs in fee-simple ownership, having care to represent all three religious factions – Protestant, Catholic, and Muslim. The largest share of
all went to Apolo Kagwa, the most prominent leader of the Protestant
faction.

As a revolution in land tenure, the Uganda Agreement echoes the
Permanent Settlement of Bengal. It created a landlord class vaguely
like that of Great Britain but totally unlike that of traditional Buganda
and still less like the land reforms that were projected and sometimes
carried out in areas of European settlement, such as the Australian
selection system or American homesteading. It honored British views
about representative government by setting up a council, but the
Lukiiko was not elected; it was rather like a Ganda House of Lords,
created at a time when the British Government was on the eve of
reducing the power of the Lords in Britain itself. The agreement was
clearly innovative, not so much by borrowing from the West as by rec-

ognizing and codifying in Western terms the revolutionary shifts in political power that had already taken place within Ganda society in recent decades.

The Uganda Agreement should not be interpreted as a move toward representative government with the possibility of increasing social mobility or the democratization of Ganda society. Nor should its establishment of fee-simple land ownership be interpreted as a move toward capitalist farming on the British model. The Ganda oligarchy borrowed from the West what was essential to their own goals but without evidence that these goals included setting up a modern or a Western style of society.

It was fashionable in recent decades, at the height of modernization theory, to oppose "traditional" to "modern," as though the only alternative were to hold things as they had been, or to go the way of the West. In Buganda, it is clear that the client-chiefs had overthrown many traditional forms in the course of their revolution, but that fact does did not make them ipso facto modernizers. They did not want to imitate Europe but to protect the new alignment of power, with Christianity and a few other borrowings from the West added. It could be argued that they used these Western cultural elements as a limited and defensive modernization, basically designed to protect the structure of Ganda society as it emerged shortly after 1900.

The constitutional settlement imbedded in the Uganda Agreement lasted for most of the colonial period, but that settlement was overthrown on the eve of independence by new men who claimed another route to modernization. They were mainly non-Ganda from other parts of the Uganda Protectorate, drawn mainly from non-chiefly classes who had risen in society with the help of Western education, which had given them new influence and new goals, though no more the goals of Western-style democracy than those of the Ganda oligarchs. They resented the old order represented by the Uganda Agreement, and they set out to overturn it. In 1962, Milton Obote came to power at the first president of an independent Uganda, partly with the support of a loosely anti-Ganda coalition.

In 1966, he led Uganda through a new constitutional crisis, in which he abolished the office of kabaka and the quasi-federal status of Buganda and increased his own personal power within the newly founded Republic of Uganda. Before he could translate a single electoral victory into a permanent hold on the presidency, he, too, was swept from power by a military revolt, leading to Idi Amin's dictatorship from 1972 to 1979. Even after Idi Amin's fall, the Ganda as a whole and the descendants of client-chiefs as a group were unable to recover the protected power they had had under the British. The drive for modernization fell into other hands and took other directions.

Modernizing Monarchies: Hawaii, Imerina, and Siam

Hawaii

Kamehameha (d. 1819), began his career as a minor political figure on the island of Hawaii. He began about 1790 to conquer his neighbors, not only on the big island but elsewhere in the Hawaiian chain, which he dominated by 1795. The key to his success was the recognition that European weapons could mean power for non-Europeans as well. He began buying muskets and light artillery, some of which he adapted for use on Polynesian double canoes.

Kamehameha's military success gained him the respect of European visitors, but western European and North Americans generally regarded Hawaii, as they had earlier regarded Muscovy, as a quaint, barbarian place. The new Hawaiian kingdom sought to Westernize appearances, in much the same way as Peter the Great had done in Russia a century and a half earlier. Appearances were especially important to gain the respect necessary for diplomatic recognition by the Western powers. Missionaries from America and Europe began to arrive in the 1820s, and their advice helped the monarchy to establish a Western-style political administration, essential to convince the Western powers that the monarchy could handle the islands' affairs. It was even more important to create a government apparatus that could actually govern. That administration was put in place during the long reign of Kamehameha III (1824 to 1854). Hawaii met several threatened annexations by one or another of the powers, but it stood them off, partly by modernizing the government administration and partly by rivalries among the Western powers, which helped to guarantee some measure of foreign support against whichever appeared most threatening at any given moment.

During the early 1800s, France and Britain had been the chief European rivals for influence in the islands, but American interest increased with the growth of North American whaling. After the United States annexed California in 1848, Hawaii was a logical stopping place on intercoastal voyages. Trade and contact with California increased, and with it American influence on the monarchy's affairs.

Meanwhile, exogenous events brought devastating changes to Hawaiian demography and society. Exotic diseases produced the same sweeping epidemics and population decline that had already occurred in the Americas. Elsewhere, the growth of the world economy and the end of the Atlantic slave trade was driving the plantation complex out of the Atlantic basin. Plantations reappeared in various forms in scattered places such as the Indian Ocean islands of Mauritius and Zanzibar, and in the Pacific, they took root in Queensland, Fiji, Peru, and Hawaii, among other places. In all of these places, growing sugarcane called for more labor than was available locally, which led to the importation of labor from overseas. In the twentieth century, the workers were no longer slaves but were indentured for a period of years, coerced to some degree from the poverty of their homelands. Some went home at the end of their indenture but many stayed on, and the balance of the Hawaiian population began to change. Native Hawaiians became a minority in a population largely descended from Japanese, Chinese, and Filipino immigrants and Portuguese immigrants from the Atlantic islands, along with descendants of missionaries, plantation managers, and commercial people from the United States and Europe.

By the 1890s, the native Hawaiians were still politically dominant under the constitutional monarchy, but the cultural and economic influence of Westerners was increasingly important. The culture of the Hawaiian upper class changed almost beyond recognition under missionary influence. 'Iolani Palace, the royal palace begun in the 1880s, illustrates the architectural style chosen by the Hawaiian monarchy, here illustrated flying the Hawaiian flag, which combined elements of the British and American national emblems (Fig. 3). The architectural style is not far different the one the British Raj used to symbolize its power in imperial Delhi at that same period. In the 1880s, the king of Hawaii, Kalakaua, became something of a world traveler, being welcomed as a monarch with full recognition by the international com-

3. 'Iolani Palace, Honolulu © 1993 The Friends of 'Iolani Palace.

munity on his royal visits to Japan, Britain, and the United States, among other countries (Fig. 4).

During the 1890s, a series of coups and countercoups signaled increasing outside influence on Hawaiian politics, some from foreign individuals, some from foreign governments. In the end, in 1898, after an intricate play of local and international political forces, the United States officially annexed Hawaii, and significantly, it was annexed as a territory, a status identical with that of existing mainland territories such as Arizona, New Mexico, or Alaska. This status opened the possibility, though not the promise, of ultimate statehood. When, only a few month later, the United States annexed Puerto Rico and the Philippines, they were only dependent possessions, not territories. The Philippines became independent even before Hawaii became a state in 1959, and the possibility of statehood for Puerto Rico is still undecided.

The history of the Hawaiian monarchy was a clear case of defensive modernization. Whether the defense was successful or not depends on

4. King Kalakaua of Hawaii (photo courtesy of the Bishop Museum, Honolulu).

one's point of view. From a material point of view, it brought Hawaii into the developed world by the end of the twentieth century. It is also clear that the islands' Polynesian culture, as it was in the 1790s, has changed beyond recognition, overlaid by the rich cultural diversity of present-day Hawaii.

Imerina

The monarchy of Imerina on Madagascar illustrates a similar effort at defensive modernization, but it was less successful than Hawaii, in spite of similar timing, missionary influence, and a Western annexation in the 1890s. European ships had visited the Malagasy coast since the early 1500s, and Europeans controlled and fortified some coastal points from time to time, but the densely settled central plateau had few contacts with Europeans or with the coast until the 1800s. The kingdom began in the central highlands, founded by Andrianapoinimerina (ruled circ 1783 to 1810), a local ruler of a small territory about thirty miles from Antananarivo, the later capital, who began by consolidating the territory of the Merina people of the central plateau and then extended his rule by conquering his neighbors until he had attained some claim to authority over most of the island. Like Kamehameha in Hawaii, his was an early secondary empire, based at least in part on muskets acquired from European slave traders. Missionaries began to come in the 1820s, transcribing the Malagasy language and teaching literacy, as they did in Hawaii.

The missionaries were successful with certain segments of the Malagasy upper classes, but the traditional religion remained strong among the masses and some of the nobility as well. In spite of alternation between rulers who seemed to be modernizing and others whom the missionaries called reactionary, the missionaries were proud of their success and the kingdom was officially Christian after 1869. The court adopted European fashions in clothing and Victorian style in architecture. The royal palace, or Manjakamiadana at Antananarivo, as reconstructed in the 1870s was the Malagasy equivalent the 'Iolani Palace, built in Honolulu about a decade later (Fig. 5). The Malagasy army also acquired modern weapons, including some repeating rifles and modern artillery; it wore uniforms and was trained by European officers. Superficially at least, this was one of

5. Manjakamiadana, the Royal Palace, Antananarivo.

most formidable examples of military modernization in the African region.

Underneath the surface symbols and overt Christianization, however, the changes in Imerina over the 1800s were not those that would provide a sure defense on the model of Japan or Hawaii. The Merina rulers enjoyed growing real incomes and consumed Western-style

149

goods, but their position was based on a vast increase in the incidence of forced labor, alongside overt slavery. They not only failed to modernize beyond adopting Christianity and superficial European fashions, they failed to build a kind of society and government administration that would perpetuate their own power. They lacked the kind of modern administration that made it possible for the Hawaiian monarchy to govern with some degree of efficiency, but, more important still, they failed to achieve any measure of popular support or even popular tolerance.

By the 1890s, Imerina faced confrontation with a European power. The Ethiopian Empire won a decisive battle against Italy at Adwa in 1896 and survived for another four decades. The Ganda oligarchs settled for the Uganda agreement. When, in 1895, France threatened to invade Imerina to force the queen to accept a French protectorate, the Merina oligarchs decided to fight. The French launched a major expedition, the largest they fielded anywhere in the conquest of tropical Africa, an expedition that suffered from near fatal mismanagement and terrible losses from disease.

A small surviving part of the French force nevertheless advanced on Antananarivo, but the modernized army of Imerina made only token resistance, and the monarchy's control of the country crumbled. Simultaneous revolts broke out in different regions for a variety of different causes, some in ethnic opposition to Merina rule, others anti-Christian, still others simple banditry. When the remains of the French army reached the capital, its commander forced the queen to accept a French protectorate, but the Imerina monarchy surrendered powers it no longer possessed. The French soon gave up the idea of a protectorate and annexed Madagascar as a French colony. Their actual conquest and occupation of the island was a gradual process over the next eight years, as they were forced to form a new government structure to replace the one that had collapsed.

Siam

Siam, by contrast, presents the case of a modernizing monarchy so successful in reforming its government administration and military establishment that it was able to escape European conquest. It went on to restructure government and society and became, as Thailand, one of the successful group of newly industrialized countries on the rim of East Asia. The present kings of Thailand are the direct descendants of the modernizing monarchs who began the process in the mid-1800s.

Siam was one of the group of mainland Southeast Asian empires centered on river valleys, a group that included Burma, Cambodia, and Vietnam. Their territorial extent was variable, as each reached out at times to establish its claims to the whole of the river basin and its highland fringes. The old Siamese capital at Ayudhya had been sacked by a Burmese army in 1767, but a new dynasty established its capital at Bangkok and began, from the 1780s, to reestablish a Siamese monarchy. In the mid-1800s, Mongkut, the king, recognized the threat of industrializing Europe and began to set Siam on the road toward military modernization, paving the way for his son, Chulalongkorn (ruled 1873 to 1910), to survive the same crisis of threatened Western annexation that caught up Hawaii and Imerina in the last decade of the century. Chulalongkorn is credited in Thailand today with the creation of modern Thai society (Figs. 6 and 7).

His accomplishment called for a certain amount of luck as well as genius and good planning on the part of a whole segment of the Siamese ruling class. One lucky element was geography, which gave Siam the opportunity to manipulate the rivalry between the French, who had already occupied parts of Indochina to the east, and the British in Malaya to the south and Burma to the west. Diplomatic success was not without a price in territorial concessions. Siam was forced to cede to France the provinces that are now Laos, and to Britain the four northernmost Malay states.

Chulalongkorn's success was also built on the political achievement of rallying a group of young men around his program. These men, including his twenty-seven brothers, were mainly from the old elite, but they were well educated and knowledgeable about the Western world, as he was himself. Gradually, from the mid-1880s, Chulalongkorn was able to create a government administration on a Western model, at both the central and the provincial level, borrowing from British examples in Burma and India and in effect using the kingship to create an administrative system similar to that created by the residents in the Malay states in the name of the titular sultans.

Chulalongkorn's accomplishments depended on the recognition that an effective defense force required more than new weapons. It

6. King Chulalongkorn of Siam in uniform (photo courtesy of the Royal Thai Embassy, Washington).

7. King Chulalongkorn of Siam in Siamese dress (photo courtesy of the Royal Thai Embassy, Washington).

required an effective power to tax and to govern and beyond that, a system of public education, all of which called for a profound modification of certain aspects of Siamese political life but did not involve traditional Thai Buddhism and its cultural roots. These changes almost inevitably carried with them aspects of Westernization in matters such as clothing and architecture. A new reception hall, the Chakri Mahprasad, at the royal palace, completed in 1882, was designed in an Italianate style by a British architect, though conservatives at court succeeded in adding some thoroughly Siamese spires to the finished building (Fig. 8). Chulalongkorn thus joined other modernizing monarchs in following the European architectural styles of his time, though with more touch of the local tradition than was found in the 'Iolani Palace or in the palace in Antananarivo.

In all these instances, the choice was not between Westernizing or holding on to one's own culture. The significant decision was among a range of options, of which modern weapons and military organization were the most obvious for self-defense. Weapons alone were not always enough, as the Imerina example illustrates. Other borrowing from the West, to create an effective government administration, for

8. Chakri Magaprasad, Grand Palace, Bangkok (photograph by the author).

example, was probably more important. Beyond that, was another, perhaps symbolic, range, including clothing styles and monumental architecture, which often seemed to be important signs of modernization but whose importance is hard to demonstrate in retrospect. Many options were open, and the choices made by other non-Western oligarchs in the second half of the 1800s are highlighted by the experience of Japan as described in the next chapter.

154

Further Reading

Brown, Mervyn, *A History of Madagascar* (London: Damien Tunnacliffe, 1995).

Daws, Gavan, *Shoal of Time: A History of the Hawaiian Islands* (Honolulu, University Press of Hawaii, 1968).

Kubler, George, "The Neo-Inca State (1537–1572)," *Hispanic American Historical Review,* 27:1289–1301 (1957).

Smith, Bruce D., *The Emergence of Agriculture* (New York: Scientific American Library, 1994)

Wyatt, David K., *Thailand: A Short History* (New Haven: Yale University Press, 1984).

9

Meiji Japan: Revolutionary Modernization

J apan is the first and most successful non-Western nation to achieve the high production and consumption pioneered by the West. Many historians used to regard the industrial revolution as a uniquely Western achievement and considered Japan's industrial success as a purely imitative borrowing of what the West had invented. Europe's comparative place in world history in the 1800s now seems less unique than historians thought only few decades ago. Historians of Japan have recently showed that much of the social and economic base of Japanese industrialization was already in place by the late 1700s.

The Tokugawa Heritage

The Western challenge was first of all military, but superior weapons were not necessarily available to Europeans only, as we have seen from the examples of secondary empires as diverse as those of Mutesa and Kamehameha. Japan first faced the threat of new military technology in the late 1500s, when the "gunpowder empires" were coming to power here and there throughout the world. Japan, too, adopted gunpowder weapons, but its military innovations included the use of massed, disciplined infantry, with or without guns, and the construction of castles capable of defense against artillery, changes parallel to similar innovations in Europe. The Europeans who appeared in Japan in that century, Christian missionaries and others, were no serious threat. In the early 1600s, the new military technology, only partly

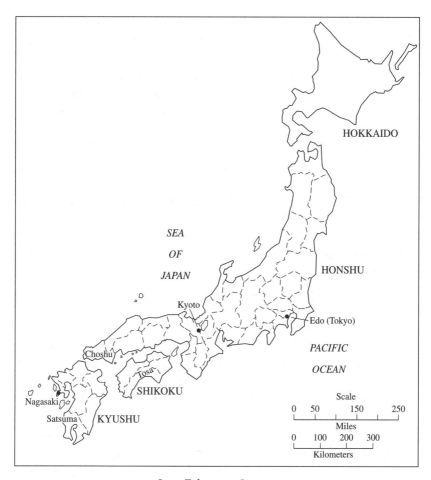

Late Tokugawa Japan.

borrowed from the outside, made possible the unification of Japan by the Tokugawa shogunate. New ways to organize military power led to the political unification of the islands, as they were to do two centuries later in Hawaii and Madagascar. The Tokugawa, however, followed up with the expulsion of foreign missionaries and a limitation of foreign trade to a few Dutch and Chinese, who were allowed to trade from bases near Nagasaki in the far southwest.

The Tokugawa brought Japan two and a half centuries of relative peace, both internally and externally. While they limited contact with foreigners, the Japanese knew something of the outside world and its affairs, and they were justifiably complacent for some time about their ability to keep the West at bay. That complacency, however, was shattered with the ease of the British victory in the Opium War of the early 1840s, which showed what British arms could achieve against the Chinese Empire. In the 1850s and 1860s, Japanese leadership suffered a series of further shocks as European powers and the United States forced an "open door" to world trade.

Until recent decades, historians, especially those outside Japan, tended to see Japanese modernization as a direct consequence of the arrival of an American fleet in Tokyo Bay in 1853, and it is true that remarkable changes in the Japanese economy followed during the second half of the nineteenth century. More recent historians, however, have examined important seeds of change in the Tokugawa period, dating back to the early 1600s.

For some centuries, Japan had a theoretical political unity under an emperor, an institution influenced by the Chinese example, but the emperor's real power was negligible. In the 1500s, Japan was divided into thousands of competing military and political units in a political system that was similar in some respects to European feudalism. Then, in the course of that century, Japan experienced a series of political and military changes equivalent to the rise of the national monarchies at the same period in Europe.

Political centralization was both a cause and a consequence of the military changes, as a succession of able military leaders gradually brought the country under their control. In 1603, one of these leaders, Tokugawa Ieyasu, obtained the title of shogun, or supreme military commander under the emperor, and the shogun soon made his office more powerful than that of the titular emperor and became the most important figure in Japan, founding the Tokugawa Shogunate. By the 1620s, Tokugawa successors had established their position as the genuine rulers with more real power than any emperor, past or present.

In theory, the Tokugawa regime was a military dictatorship, ruled by the *bakufu* (originally meaning camp), centered at the shogun's castle in Edo (now Tokyo). The actual power, however, was exercised through a set of institutions that were feudal in form and decentralized in practice, though the bakufu had more real power throughout the country than was available to the contemporary national monarchies in western Europe. Already in the 1580s, the shogun had introduced measures to systematize and control feudal disorder, such as a land survey that classified all land by its potential productivity in rice, measured in *koku* (about five bushels). Henceforth feudal domains were classified and taxed in terms of their assigned koku. Great lords, or *daimyo,* were those with more than 10,000 koku. Some of the greatest daimyo, such as the Tokugawa themselves, had other daimyo under them.

The number of daimyo fluctuated somewhat, but it was generally between 250 and 300. The domain of a particular daimyo, called a *han,* varied greatly in size and function. Some daimyo were directly associated with the Tokugawa family, and many of their holdings were concentrated in central Japan near Kyoto and Edo. Other holdings were scattered throughout the islands, and those least closely associated with the Tokugawa were called outer han, mainly located away from the center, in southwestern and northern Japan. They were a minority, being about one hundred in all, but they tended to be larger than those directly under the bakufu,

Each daimyo was served by a group of military retainers called *samurai,* a hereditary military class who were paid a regular salary of a fixed number of koku of rice, established by custom. Together with the daimyo, they constituted a class equivalent to the nobility and gentry of Europe, and they made up about 7 percent of the total population, supported mainly by the productive labor of other classes. The line between the political and military classes and the lower orders was legal, hereditary, and strictly maintained.

Among the lower classes, distinctions were also theoretically hereditary and legally defined, marking out peasants, artisans, and merchants in descending order. Actual distinctions between these lower levels were fluid and hard to maintain, and the real wealth, prestige, and political power within each class could vary greatly. Rich peasants and village leaders could be more powerful than many of the lowest samurai, and some merchants were very wealthy in spite of their low social status.

Although the emperor was the ceremonial head of state and the power theoretically in the hands of the bakufu and reached into every han, the practical authority of the bakufu was limited. Many daimyo acted as semi-independent rulers, particularly in the outer han. Tokugawa Japan was more nearly a federation of virtually independent

daimyo than a tightly controlled centralized state. The shogun had sufficient power to keep the peace but not enough to direct government
in the outer han in detail. Each han had its own standing army of
samurai, even though these armies were rarely called to active duty.
By the 1850s, the samurai had a social position and income based on
their military status, but their most important actual activity was
bureaucratic. Decentralization also left certain residual powers in the
hands of peasant village leadership, others in the hands of merchants
and other urban classes.

Social and economic change during the two and a half centuries of
Tokugawa rule was profound. Agricultural output approximately doubled between 1600 and 1850, while population increased by only
about 45 percent. Fewer people were needed to work the land and
urbanization increased, not only in Kyoto and Edo, but in the castle
towns that sprang up as the centers of the semi-independent han.
Japanese urbanization in the early 1800s was at much the same level
as that of early industrial Europe; Edo had more than a million people,
nearly twice the population of Paris. We have no adequate measure of
nonagricultural production, but urban crafts and rural cottage industries appear to have grown even faster than farm production. With
abundant resources for education, Japan was the most literate society
in Asia, and its literacy rate was probably higher than that of most of
western Europe. As of 1800, the Japanese standard of living was
roughly equal to that of Britain, and both island nations were better off
than their adjacent mainlands.

Historians have sometimes tried to account for the economic leadership of preindustrial Britain or of Japan by looking for a series of
causes foreshadowing industrial success. E. L. Jones has argued that
people normally try to add to their material wealth; when they succeed, the explanation is not so likely to be due to positive causes as to
the absence restraint by government or social superiors. In the case of
Japan, the two and a half centuries of relative peace were important.
So, too, was the balance of political power between the individual han
and the bakufu. Many historians have argued that in Europe the division into a number of competing national monarchies, with residual
power in the hands of the nobility, towns, and merchants, among others, was important for the rise of the West. An equivalent balance of
power occurred in Tokugawa Japan as well.

The Japanese Revolution

As a point of departure, it is worth emphasizing that the Japanese revolution of the 1860s and 1870s was as sweeping a social and political change as the French, Russian, or Mexican Revolutions in Western history. Its core event was the restoration in 1868 of the Meiji emperor and the end of the Tokugawa bakufu as the central government of Japan, but that restoration had paradoxical elements. Its leaders began with the reactionary slogan, "Restore the emperor; expel the barbarians," meaning the European traders and diplomats who were newly present in Japan. In fact, the restored Meiji emperor himself had little more power than his predecessors. Real power under the restoration was exercised by an oligarchic group of largely aristocratic origin, often, but not exclusively, from the outer han. This oligarchy revolutionized Japanese society from above, mainly by borrowing techniques and institutions from the barbarians they claimed to want to expel.

In the process, they destroyed the legal status and power of the daimyo and samurai, the class from which they themselves had come, and by the 1890s, they had achieved military parity with many European powers. By 1905, Japan was able to defeat the Russian Empire in a war that was not a defense against Western imperialism but a clash of Japanese and Russian imperial ambitions on the East Asian mainland.

Military Technology

Military technology was at the heart of Japanese modernization. Japan had an ancient military tradition, and the privileged samurai class was defined by its military function. Some Japanese had kept a watch on Western military affairs, even in the period when the bakufu was firmly in control and Japan was closed to all but a trickle of foreign trade. Already in the 1790s, Rin Shihei had written his famous book, whose title is usually translated as *Essay on the Military Problems of a Maritime State*. Knowledge of European technology was available through the Dutch post at Nagasaki, and the Japanese had used muskets and cannon for almost two centuries. They were not taken by surprise in quite the same way others were, who first encountered the

Europe in the decades of 1860 to 1910. They were nevertheless apathetic about the Western danger until the Chinese defeat in the Opium War of 1839–42.

That war was fought, on the British side, entirely by the naval forces of the Royal Navy and the East India Company, and the company was far ahead of the Royal Navy in modern weapons. It introduced for the first time low-draft iron steamers, mounting heavy cannon and rockets for use against shore fortifications as well as ships. These steamers were originally designed for use on the Indian rivers, but they were nevertheless capable of the long sea voyage around the Cape of Good Hope.

The economic centers of Chinese power were inland, not on the coast. Without an expeditionary force capable of moving inland, the British naval forces were comparatively ineffective. In the campaign of 1842, however, the steamers silenced the coastal batteries and sailed up the Yangzi, where they threatened to cut the important north-south link of the Grand Canal. Coastal forts were not vital to Chinese interests, but the Grand Canal was, and China was forced to surrender to British commercial demands and to cede the island of Hong Kong.

The lesson was not lost on the Japanese, at least in some circles. Defensive military modernization began almost immediately, though not at the central level of the bakufu. Each daimyo had its own military forces, and the most important response came from the larger outside han of the southwest, but others entered as well. In 1840, the daimyo of Mito set up a new iron foundry and gun factory on a Dutch model. Another han began making its own cannon as early as 1842, and it had a reverberatory furnace in operation by 1852, the year before the arrival of Commodore Perry.

The visit of the American fleet was a spectacular event for the Japanese, the first demonstration of Western naval power in Japanese waters. Though the fleet was only eight ships and the United States was far weaker than Britain in Asian waters, the visit was epoch-making, because in 1854, Japan signed with the Americans the first of a new series of treaties opening Japan to foreign trade. The American – Japanese treaty negotiated by Townsend Harris in 1858 was more important, and Japan was soon forced to extend its concessions to European foreigners in general. By the mid-1860s, significant, though resented, European communities had been established in Japanese ports, protected by their own guards and with treaty rights to shield them from Japanese law.

The period from 1853 to the restoration in 1868 was marked by serious internal readjustments in military and political power relationships within Japan. Each of several different groups of daimyo tried to strengthen its military and to jockey for power in a fluid political situation. During the first stage, the new weapons were principally in the hands of the outer han, though the bakufu and its allies were working toward their own military modernization.

The emperor had no significant military force of his own, so that he tended to become a figurehead for the opposition to the shogun. Political struggles of this period were contradictory, in any case. The bakufu of Edo had been forced to make concessions to the Westerners, while trying to build its own defense against the West. Some opposition groups accused the bakufu of making too many concessions, using the emperor as a nativist national symbol, while at the same time using Western technology to modernize their own forces. It was a period marked by a rise in aimless violence, led by factions that were ultimately pushed aside. By about 1865, both the bakufu and the important daimyo who supported the imperial court at Kyoto had much the same objective of defensive modernization – recruiting non-samurai as common soldiers, and giving them tactical training supplied by foreigners, many of them French. When the clash came in 1868, it was not so much for or against military modernization, or for or against emperor or shogun. The two sides were so similar that the brief but crucial fighting that ended the Tokugawa era was a struggle between competing military oligarchies seeking to control a new centralizing government, which would probably have sought to carry out similar policies, no matter which side won.

The term *restoration* is a misnomer. The government that began to transform Japan in 1868 was unlike anything Japan had previously known. Although it instituted revolutionary changes in the name of strengthening Japanese traditions, within a decade it wiped out the powers of the daimyo as well as the bakufu. The most important of the daimyo were pensioned off, and their economic position actually improved. Minor daimyo and the samurai class as a whole, however, lost the material support of the government and the legal distinction separating them from the rest of the population. In place of the decentralized power structure of the Tokugawa, with its semi-independent han, each with its entrenched rulers and its standing army, Japan was divided into 50 prefectures, each under the command of a prefect, appointed by the central government and removable by it.

Historians have sometimes sought to analyze these changes in class terms, with the upper samurai or lower samurai acting in their class interests. It seems simpler and more obvious to say that some groups from the old ruling class, many of them associated with the reforming military of the southwestern han, seized effective control of the Japanese government. They then created a new form of centralized government in the emperor's name, and in the process they created a new military power in the form of the national army, replacing, after a time, those of the han and the bakufu alike. As commanders of the new national army, the new oligarchy was in a position to take away the privileges of the old military aristocracy, from which they themselves had come.

In effect, they changed the locus of power in Japanese society by modernizing the army and navy and setting up a Western-style government administration to support it. As we have seen in other cases as various as Peter's Russia or Apolo Kagwa's Buganda, a change in military technology and the way military power is organized can change the locus of power in a society. In Japan, these changes fundamentally strengthened the government's powers by modernizing the military organization and government administration, but without changing the political process. The Meiji oligarchy ran its affairs in much the same way the bakufu had run Japan in the past, using thoroughly Japanese means of solving cases of group conflict. In time, Japan was to borrow more heavily from the West in the political process as well, but those changes only began with the formal granting of an imperial constitution in 1889, and many of the most important changes were delayed until after 1945.

The Military, Industrialization, and Social Change

The Japanese nobility, like the European, began as a military calling, but with its own traditions. The Western military tradition had a special emphasis on the horse. Knights fought mounted, while commoners fought on foot. The Japanese had cavalry as well, but the samurai's symbol of status was the sword, not the horse. Samurai had, indeed, by right and custom, the privilege of carrying two swords, a privilege denied to other classes, and this justified a particular samurai interest in weapons as an attribute of class. Both the Japanese and the European nobility looked down on other classes, but the Europeans disdained the technological aspects of warfare and thought of themselves as users of weapons, not their makers.

The European attitude had far-reaching implications for European military history. It led European armies in the beginning to turn the artillery over to civilians, and artillery was a low-prestige branch in most European armies into the 1800s. The same attitude toward the tools of battle led the Royal Navy to oppose the very idea of iron steamers. The British East India Company had to develop its iron steamers on the sly to avoid naval opposition. Similar attitudes toward weapons and their use led commanders brought up to admire the bravery of a cavalry charge to extend their view to the slaughter of men sent over the top against artillery and machine guns on the Western Front during the First World War.

In Japan, the military considered it appropriate for samurai to control the production of weapons rather than having that important task relegated to socially inferior merchants, urban craftsmen, or peasants. This attitude gave a particular direction to Japanese military modernization, compared with that elsewhere in the non-Western world. Worldwide, most efforts at defensive armament concentrated on securing Western weapons. The Japanese did this as well, but their effort extended beyond mere acquisition and use of the Western tools to manufacturing them on their own and improving the design where possible.

A similar attitude gave a special course and direction to Japanese industrialization. First of all, it set the order of priority. While Europe began to industrialize with light industry such as textiles and with labor-saving machinery for which small changes could be made with small investment by a merchant or craftsman, the Japanese began instead with the heaviest kind of industry and mining technology, for example, the metallurgy and foundries of the 1840s. The first Japanese silk mill was not built until 1870.

The new Japanese industries were built by the state for state purposes, which is to say, for military purposes. This practice began even before the restoration, when some daimyo set up their own munitions factories. Especially in the early stages, most of the bureaucracy in charge of the new industries was recruited from the class of samurai, and in the past samurai had run the government for the bakufu and the daimyo alike. Japanese merchants, however, were not entirely left out. A level of cooperation between the leaders of the Meiji oligarchy and men from mercantile-industrial callings went back to the pre-restoration era. It increased after the revolutionary social and legal changes of the 1870s, but the merchant class at first had a less important role in industrialization than the European bourgeoisie.

In early decades of the reform, the government participated in non-military enterprises as well. But in the 1880s, the government abandoned its investment in industries without clear military relevance. In a broad program that would now be called privatization, it began selling off mines, textile mills, and some railroads and steamships. As sometimes happened in later privatization, purchasers often had links to the ruling oligarchy and were able to buy at favorable prices. Some came from families who had supported the restoration; others were wealthy members of the merchant class, and in this way, some samurai and some merchants moved into a new class of industrial capitalists. The core of this group was a number of families known collectively as the Zaibatsu – combining the Mitsui, Mitsubishi, Sumitomo, and Yashuda – which have controlled a good share of Japanese industry ever since.

By the 1890s, a relatively stable pattern of industry-government relationships had developed, and it was to last far into the new century. It included three different industrial groups, distinguished by their relationship to the government. Some industries, considered to be of special importance to the military establishment, were kept under direct government control and operation. Another group of strategic importance but not directly involved with the manufacture of weapons were released to the Zaibatsu and other private individuals, though this sector of the economy was still under tight government control. Finally, some industries were founded by individual entrepreneurs who saw an opportunity to fit into the interstices of a modernizing economy. They were often the less mechanized, using more handicraft processes and traditional skills.

166

To outward appearances, Japan came to look like a modern capitalist state with Western forms of economic organization. The similarities were greatest in the realm of technology, while the institutions of management were only superficially Western. They bore names identifying them as banks, corporations, stock exchanges, and the like, but the surface impression of Japan as a carbon copy of a Western bourgeois capitalist society was deceptive. The reality was modern in the sense of movement toward high productivity and high consumption, but it was still Japanese in many methods of operation.

Political Westernization

The Meiji oligarchs began with military reform, and the reform of government administration shortly followed. The administrative system of the bakufu and daimyo was clearly unsuitable as a central government of the kind required to raise money and to exert genuine central control over the country. Political Westernization might well have stopped short with the reform of the military and government administration, but by the 1890s, the reforms included a written constitution, a cabinet, representative government, political parties, and much more – and only a quarter-century after the restoration of the emperor with its talk about a return to an ancient Japanese political system.

The class of young samurai and others who had seized power in the years immediately following 1868 were aging, but they still held the real power in the country. The Meiji oligarchy could have recruited new members and have gone on ruling in the name of traditionalism and the emperor, but in 1889, they decided to grant a Western-style constitution – or to have the emperor grant one, even though the Western-style formal constitution brought little real change in who exercised power within the Japanese state.

Several questions arise: Why change the outward form of government from an oligarchy ruling through a figurehead emperor to an oligarchy ruling through a paper cabinet and parliament? Why Westernize the outward appearance of government, unless you intend to Westernize the reality as well?

The participation of the military in this process of change was a crucial feature, but it was not unique to Japan. The military also played a substantial role in other places as distant and different as Buganda and the Ottoman Empire. The very demand fro defensive modernization often came from the military, but often from a minority among the military leadership – from those whose professional concerns alerted them, both to the dangers of Western military power and the opportunities that would accrue to those that copied it. That minority became the section of the military who put themselves in command of the new weapons and the new tactics, but their drive fro modernization of the military inevitably extended into other fields as well. The new weapons required new means of acquiring them, hence reorganization of the fiscal system to pay for them. This in itself brought new groups into the circle of power – industrialists, bureaucrats, the inner circle of capitalists. The samurai who were not close to the new centers of power lost their pensions and privileges in the course of the 1870s. Their old customs became outmoded; the new national army took their place, filled with drafted peasants and townsmen trained in the new weapons and new techniques. Those of the samurai who failed to make it into positions of command in the new order were unemployed.

The writing on the wall was clear by the mid-1870s, but one section of the samurai tried to stem the tide. After a scattering of armed revolts in the early seventies, in 1877 the lord of Satsuma, one of the main leaders of the restoration itself, turned to open rebellion based on the Satsuma army still in existence. It was a major insurrection that lasted eight months, with more than 100,000 troops engaged on both sides. It failed, in part because the militarized peasants defeated their social betters, but also because the daimyo of Satsuma could only claim the loyalty of samurai within his own han. Samurai elsewhere shared the general discontent of their group, but they lacked a national focus for effective organization.

Another alternative available to some of the old ruling class who had been excluded from power was to use ideological weapons borrowed from European politics. A Popular Rights Movement emerged in 1874–8, mainly led by men active in the restoration who now felt left out. They appealed to the ideas Western political philosophers going back to the Enlightenment – figures such as Rousseau or John Stuart Mill. Such ideas had a certain appeal as a form of fringe Westernization, but their popularity was limited.

Some of this opposition was genuinely convinced by writers like Mill that democracy was the proper goal for Japan, but most were liberal in the limited sense common in Europe in the 1800s, stopping well short of one man, one vote. The announcement of plans leading up to the constitution of 1889 was a form of concession to this liberal opposition drawn from the higher levels of society. Meanwhile, the oligarchy crushed opposition from the lower orders, and the disaffected aristocrats made little sustained effort to organize the peasants or the urban masses.

External Pressures

A second impetus toward political Westernization arose out of Japan's international position. As elsewhere, the fundamental goal of defensive modernization was protection in a hostile and aggressive world of Western empire building. Part of that goal could be met by improving the Japanese image abroad. Europeans and Americans tended to regard Japan, like other non-Western kingdoms, as quaint and barbarous at best, and that continued to the end of the century and beyond, even after the level of Japanese industrialization had passed that of many European countries – an attitude that led many Americans to dismiss the reality of the Japanese threat as late as 1941.

An early symbol of Western arrogance were the "unequal treaties" forced on Japan in the 1850s and 1860s. Among other things, they set limits on the import duties Japan might charge on Western goods and imposed Western consular representation with special legal jurisdiction over foreigners in Japan, provisions that hurt Japanese national pride. Japanese nationalism was growing in the late nineteenth century for the same reasons nationalism was growing in the West in an era of rapid economic growth and urbanization, as people were shaken loose from traditional and local ties and found new loyalties to the emperor or the nation to replace them.

The first way to satisfy the West that Japan was indeed a civilized power was to build a military force capable of opposing Western aggression, but it might also improve Japan's international status if it were to adopt a constitution that would look civilized to European opinion. This course was possible without doing too much violence to the reality of power and its distribution in Japanese society; Japan and Europe were not so far apart as they might have appeared in Western eyes. Japan had an oligarchy ruling in the name of the emperor;

Europe had several convenient oligarchic constitutions. The Prussian constitution was peculiarly appropriate; it retained the oligarchy in control while giving the appearance of representative government for the middle class. This model was the one Japan followed in a series of changes through the 1880s, leading to the final imperial constitution of 1889. It set up a representative assembly of two houses, the upper house mainly appointed from the class of daimyo, the lower elected by a restricted electorate consisting of less than 2 percent of the male population. The powers reserved to the emperor – in fact, to the oligarchs who had emerged with the restoration – continued to be so great that actual decision making was confined to them and their informal successors for decades to come.

The Constitution and the Military

In law, the constitution had been issued by the emperor and could only be changed by him. In fact, the formal document was never changed at all, but constitutional practice could and did evolve in ways that were to lead down to the Japanese militarism of the 1930s and 1940s. One constitutional practice had the effect of giving the military high command the right to dismiss any Japanese cabinet that failed to meet its approval. Beginning in 1898, a rule of the privy council – a nonrepresentative body – required that the posts of minister of war and minister of the navy be reserved for military officers of a specified high rank. This immediately limited the choice of any prime minister seeking to form a Government, but did more than that. The generals and admirals of the designated rank served under military discipline. They could take office only if their superiors gave permission. In office as well, they had to follow the orders of their military superiors. In this way, the ministers of war and navy acted at the direction of the closed corporation of the military, not for their civilian superiors, nor for the emperor, nor for the public. The military could even stop the formation of a government by refusing to supply an officer of the appropriate rank.

This is one example of the many ways Japanese political decision making combined some Western forms and Western-sounding official titles with practices that were still fundamentally derived from Japanese norms. The constitutional forms and practices of the early

170

Meiji restoration were swept away gradually over a half century and more, but Japanese traditions continued, incorporating Japanese values and beliefs about appropriate political behavior. The Western models, when used, were also reinterpreted to make them more congenial to Japanese culture. The result was not a Westernizing of Japanese political life, nor an unchanging continuation of earlier Japanese norms, but a series of new responses to changing conditions.

Modernizing Oligarchies in the Age of Imperialism

Japan stands in sharp contrast to the comparative lack of success of others who started down the road toward defensive modernization. In spite of the variety of outcomes, however, some common threads run through the experience of Japan and those of Buganda, Imerina, Hawaii, and Siam. The leadership in all of these countries had a necessarily confined circle of vision at a time when global intercommunication was limited. No one could have known or suspected what is obvious in retrospect, that the West was even then leading the world into a new era in human history. If they did suspect some such thing, there is no evidence that many wanted it for themselves. Most commonly, they began copying the military sources of Western power, in self-protection. Beyond that, they wanted to have for themselves some parts of the Western way of life that appeared to be attractive in the light of their own cultural heritage. The original Meiji leadership wanted to expel the barbarians, with no dream of making Japan into the kind of society it was to become at the end of the next century.

A comparison of Buganda and Japan nevertheless illustrates some common threads in their response to the perceived threat of the West. The leadership in both societies was originally alarmed by Western influence in the neighborhood – in the Ganda case, by the Zanzibari and Egyptian secondary empires, in the Japanese, by the attack on China in the Opium War. The first objective in both was defensive modernization, led by the part of the local aristocracy with ties to the military, the client-chiefs and the Meiji oligarchs. The result in either case was revolutionary change in the locus of power within the local society, incorporated in the Uganda Agreement and in the changes that followed the restoration in Japan. In both cases, military modernization led to local military superiority, permitting local imperialism

171

against less well armed neighbors, as with the Ganda secondary empire building as early as the 1880s and the Japanese empire building overseas beginning in the 1890s.

It is tempting to pile up parallels, and others could be found between Buganda, Japan, and the three non-Western kingdoms discussed in the last chapter. It is significant, however, that the response of the Ganda, who were overcome, and that of the Japanese, who came close to overtaking the United States in military power, have so much in common.

Further Reading

Hayami, Akira, "Japan in the Eighteenth Century: Demography and Economy," in Leonard Blussé and Femme Gaastra, *On the Eighteenth Century as a Category of Asian History; Van Leur in Retrospect* (Aldershot, U.K.; Ashgate, 1998).

Jansen, Marius (ed.), *The Emergency of Meiji Japan* (Cambridge, U.K.: Cambridge University Press, 1995)

Jones, E. L., *Growth Recurring: Economic Change in World History* (Oxford, Clarendon Press, 1988).

Macpherson, W. J., *The Economic Development of Japan 1868–1941* (Cambridge, U.K.: Cambridge University Press, 1987)

McClain, James L., John M. Merriman, and Ugawa Kaoru (eds.), *Edo and Paris: Urban Life and the State in the Early Modern Era* (Ithaca, NY: Cornell University Press, 1994).

Totman, Conrad, *Early Modern Japan* (Berkeley: University of California Press, 1993).

Reischauer, Edwin E., *The Japanese* (Cambridge, M.A: Harvard University Press, 1978).

10

Ottoman Reactions to the West

The Ottoman Empire and the Japanese Empire met the Western threat in vastly different circumstances. In the Muslim world, the Ottoman Empire was one of the three new Islamic centers in the Age of Three Empires, the others being the Mughals in India and the Safavids centered on Persia. From the 1300s, Ottoman territory was at the very borders of Christian Europe, and, in the 1400s and 1500s, it was southeast Europe that faced an Ottoman threat. In 1453, the Ottoman capture of Constantinople had destroyed what remained of the Byzantine Empire and put a Muslim empire in its place. Through the 1500s, the Turks were militarily equal to almost any Western power, often superior. On the world scene, the Ottoman Empire was one of the emerging gunpowder empires.

In the 1600s and after, the balance of military power gradually shifted toward the West. The Ottomans, like the Japanese, were not at first conscious of the power emerging in Europe, though signs were visible, at least in retrospect, even before the full industrialization of the 1800s. The Ottoman leadership, moreover, was well informed about Europe, though the cultural chauvinism common in the Muslim world of the time sometimes led them to discount the European threat. By the 1790s, however, a significant minority had become alarmed. In this, they were about a half-century ahead of Japan, where recognition of the Western danger did not reach an equivalent level until the events of the 1840s.

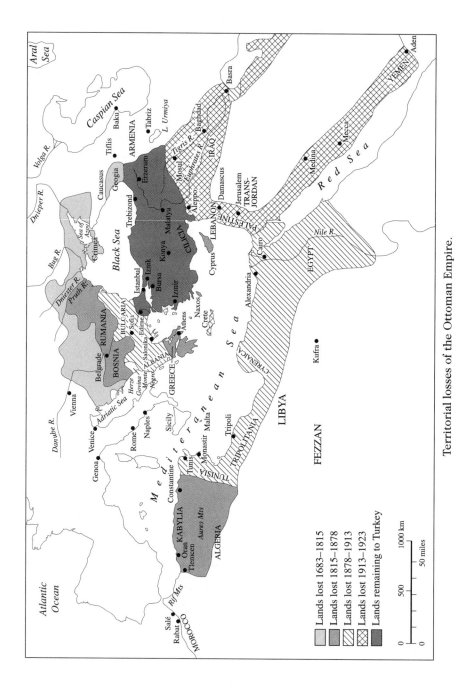

Territorial losses of the Ottoman Empire.

Lands lost 1683–1815
Lands lost 1815–1878
Lands lost 1878–1913
Lands lost 1913–1923
Lands remaining to Turkey

Ottoman Society and Culture

The Ottoman and Japanese Empires were alike in avoiding European conquest, but their modes of reaction were different. In either case, however, an effective response required something more than new weapons; it required a restructured social and political organization capable of organizing and equipping a kind of military force that could use the new weapons effectively. Most other non-Western societies failed to make that adjustment, and they consequently passed through a period of European rule.

The institutions that articulated and protected the Japanese and Ottoman ways of life were very different. Religion was more central to the Ottoman state than it was to Japan, or in Western Europe. In Europe, the Holy Roman Empire and the papacy had been at odds through most of the Middle Ages, and conflict between church and state was common elsewhere. The Christian injunction to "render unto Caesar what is Caesar's, and unto God, what is God's" implied that state and church performed different functions. For Muslim societies in general, law, the *shari'a,* had a religious, not secular origin and it made no such separation between church and state. The sultan was a legitimate ruler only because he protected the true religion and its laws. Secular and religious authorities quarreled, as they did in other societies, but no theoretical distinction existed between what was the sultan's and what was God's.

Ottoman society, furthermore, had no organized voice, equivalent to the European church, that could speak formally for religious interests. It had instead a class of Islamic teachers and men of learning, called the *ulema,* whose claim to authority rested on education rather than position in a bureaucratic order or ordination by superior religious authority. The position of the ulema varied within the Muslim world. In some states, the ulema were weaker than the church in Europe; in others, they were stronger.

The Ottoman Empire had institutionalized the role of religion more than many Islamic states. The Ottoman sultan stood at the top of two administrative hierarchies, one secular and one religious, each consisting of a separate body of officials. In the early days of the empire, the sultans had entrusted secular government to a class of slave-administrators who were the ruler's property, therefore free of family and other ties to the society they controlled. The judicial authority, however, was in the hands of the *qadis,* or judges, learned in Islamic law and hence drawn from the body of the ulema. This separate hierarchy of judicial – religious officials had its own head in the chief mufti or *Seyh-ul-Islam,* who was the supreme religious authority, with power to authorize the deposition of the sultan himself for a breach of the *Seriat,* as the shari's was known in Turkish.

In this way, the Ottomans had an institutionalized clergy, though not a priesthood in the Christian sense. It was nevertheless a body of men with religious and legal power, derived from the sultan's dual office as secular ruler and caliph, successor of Muhammed as leader of Muslims. In this way, the Ottoman ulema had more formal and legal power than their equivalents in many other Muslim kingdoms.

Like any other polity, the Ottomans strayed over time from the simplicity of early intentions. As the area under Ottoman control broadened, links with distant provinces became weaker, and they tended to become autonomous. An Ottoman dependency, such as the deylic of Algiers, could not be closely controlled from Istanbul, and the dey himself had only a loose and variable authority over his hinterland. Subordinate rulers, closer to home, were kept under more definite central control, but as in most preindustrial states, the actual power of the sultan or the central bureaucracy to issue orders and have them carried out was limited.

As elsewhere, the military played a particular role, because it had an independent source of power. The most important military units were the *janissaries,* the slave soldiers who constituted the standing army. They were recruited as children by purchase or as tribute, often from the fringes of the empire or beyond, and incorporated into an elite military force. Like other military forces before and since, they were often able to affect the course of government policy, sometimes making or unmaking rulers.

Another major center of power sometimes beyond the sultan's control were the *ayan,* a group that included provincial magnates, local "big men," quasi-feudal landholders, and tax farmers, some of whom had sufficient power to found local dynasties. They, the ulema, and the military all held power from sources independent of the sultan. They did not always obey orders, and they were difficult to remove from office. Even the central bureaucracy of slave-administrators, who were the sultan's property and could be appointed and removed at will, had its own bureaucratic inertia.

Another source of weakness that became increasingly important with the passage of time was the nationalities problem. All large states are to some degree multinational, but the Ottoman Empire was more diverse than most. In the 1600s and 1700s, the Ottoman state was more non-national than multinational. It was, of course, Turkish in the sense that Muslim Turks dominated the political structure and Turkish was the language of learning and administration, but most Ottoman subjects did not speak Turkish as their everyday language. Those who did speak Turkish did not identify themselves principally as Turks. Their primary mark of self-identification was their local community of farmers, nomads, or city-people – or Islam as the great brotherhood of believers.

As of the 1700s, the world view of the Ottoman ruling classes was a kind of hierarchy seen from the core area around Istanbul, and the heart of the empire was Rumelia on the western side of the straits, not Anatolia to the east. In their view, at the center of world affairs were Ottoman Muslims, believers who were also subjects of the Sultan, though Sunni Muslims who were not subjects were still considered as part of an in-group – brothers in religion if not allegiance.

Lower in the scale were fellow subjects who were not believers, and they constituted a large part of the Ottoman population. This group included the Armenian Christians concentrated to the east of Anatolia, the Greek Christians in the Balkans, a few Catholic Christians, and the Jewish community scattered throughout the empire. All of these religious minorities were organized as *millets,* recognized by the state and allowed to practice their religion at the price of higher taxation and other restrictions not placed on Muslims. The original head of the Greek Orthodox Church had been the archbishop of Constantinople, and the administrative center of Orthodox Christianity has continued to be in Istanbul down to the present.

Still lower on the scale were those who were both outside the empire and outside the religious pale. This group would include such neighbors as the Orthodox Christians to the north and the Frankish Christians to the west, but it also included, perhaps at a slightly higher level, the Shi'ite Muslims of Persia.

The Western Threat

From the 1400s onward, the Ottomans met the Christians of the Balkan peninsula across a frequently contested military frontier, and another area of contention was based on naval power in the Mediterranean. The 1500s had been a time of Ottoman advance; the 1600s were a century of stalemate on the Balkan frontier, with some retirement before Christian powers there and in the Mediterranean. The Ottomans retreated still further in the 1700s, but the basic integrity of the Ottoman Empire was not threatened until nearly the end of that century.

During all this period and in spite of frequent warfare, cultural exchange between Ottomans and the West ranged from watchful tolerance to benign contempt. The Christians had a long-standing horror of Islamic contamination, going back to the rise of Islam and intensifying with the Crusades. The Ottomans were more tolerant of religious difference, but the millet system combined permissiveness with an effort to seal off Christian and Jewish minorities into segregated communities.

The Christian-Ottoman border was, nevertheless, a military frontier, where both sides kept a close eye on their opponents and copied what seemed valuable, but borrowing was mainly limited to military techniques. Ottoman cultural conservatism led them to fall behind the West in other matters. Printing, for example, was forbidden to Ottoman Muslims until the 1700s, for fear of defiling the holy languages of Islam, Arabic and Turkish, though it was permitted for the millets to print in Hebrew, Greek, or other European languages. Even after it was permitted, printing in Turkish was not common until the 1800s.

Ottoman technology began to lag and especially to fall behind the European growth of economic potential, then in transition toward an industrial revolution. In the mid-1700s, these changes became obvious in relative military power, especially on the Balkan frontier, where the Austrians and others had, for a almost a century, been reconquering some of the captive Christian territories. The Ottomans were more alarmed, however, when they began to lose territory inhabited by Muslims. In the 1760s, the Russian advance from the north pushed down to the Black Sea, including the Crimea, whose Muslim Tatar rulers were at least theoretically under the suzerainty of Istanbul. In 1798, French armies invaded Egypt and, the following year, fought Ottoman armies in Syria. Only the intervention of British sea power saved the Ottomans from a major loss of some of their Arab provinces.

By this time, the Ottomans had already begun to respond. The Sultan Selim III (1789–1807), though personally conservative, recognized the growing European military lead. He and his advisors saw the need for a radical military reform backed by economic and fiscal reform, and in 1792 and 1793 they issued a set of regulations known collectively as The New Order. They were based on prior investigation of the military power of the West, not unlike Peter the Great's inquiries a century earlier. The central military feature of the New Order was a new corps of regular infantry, trained on European lines and separate from the old-style janissaries. It also included new military and naval academies, run mainly by French advisors, and radical reform of the fiscal administration, seeking more effective government in order to pay for the modernized military.

This effort had two significant consequences that were to recur in many later non-Western efforts at defensive modernization. First of all, it automatically brought a new group into power in Ottoman affairs. These were the new military officers, who, by virtue of their training, some of it gained the West, were professionally interested in borrowing Western military techniques, and, along with their learning about Western science and military technology, they often came to admire other things they saw in the West. The modernized officer corps became a secular and Westernizing element in Ottoman society, just as a similar generation of military innovators in Japan were the core of the modernizing movement in that society.

As a second and opposite consequence, the New Order was seen as a threat to the old order. The government need to raise taxes alienated those most able to pay. The fiscal reforms also threatened the ayan and tax collectors with increased pressure from the central government. More important still, the New Order threatened the military monopoly of the janissary officers, alienating still another important group. Finally, the military reforms were seen as borrowing from barbarian infidels, which could threaten Islam itself, thus alienating important elements within the ulema.

The crisis reproduced elements of Peter the Great's struggle to modernize the Russian military or of the Meiji oligarchs' efforts to modernize Japan, but this time the modernizers failed. The conservatives
joined forces in 1807 and overthrew Selim III, ending for the time
being military reform or any effective modernization.

The Nationalities Problem

In the course of time, the people of the millets experienced rising feelings of national identity. Beginning with the Greeks, the subject peoples began to think of themselves as national entities. The change may
have owed something to the slackening ties to locality or kinship,
which happened more broadly in the industrializing world of the
1800s, but the idea of belonging to a nation also spread from the West,
from France in particular in the era of the French Revolution, and
along with it the idea that nations have a right to self-government by
virtue of their nationhood.

The varied influence of nationalism will recur later in these essays,
but two of its many varieties should be mentioned in the Ottoman context. By and large, in west and central Europe, people who had lived
under a single state for several centuries came to have a common
experience that gave them a sense of solidarity. This is sometimes
called the state-nation type of nationalism, because the state came
first and created the nation over a period of time. Both Great Britain
and France are examples. Later, especially in central and eastern
Europe, people who had common language and some common historical experience tended, in the 1800s, to discover that they were a
nation. Some pushed this discovery into a political movement
demanding independent and sovereign government for whatever
national unit they identified for themselves. In this case, the sense of
nationality came first and the demand for a state followed, resulting in
a nation-state category of nationalism. Germany and Italy would be
prime examples of this type.

The Ottoman Empire showed a few signs that might have developed
a state-nation source of loyalty from its subjects, but in the longer run
the impetus failed and the kind of fractured nationalism that took hold
became infinitely subversive of the whole concept and structure of the
Ottoman state. That state was built, first of all, on religion and reli-

gious law, even though it did not insist that all subjects conform to the dominant religion. The millet system was designed to protect Islam by segregating dissident religious groups, but it gave those groups the common experience that made them think of themselves as nations. The result was incipient rebellion all along the fringes of Ottoman rule, and at some spots close to the center.

The Serbs rebelled even before the overthrow of Selim III. The Greeks followed after the end of the Napoleonic Wars and forced the Ottoman government, under some pressure from west European powers, to accept Greek independence. The Bulgars, too, discovered that they were a nation. So did the Armenians to the east of Anatolia. In time, even the Arabs, who were Muslim and therefore within the pale of the Ottoman system, were to discover a national identity.

Nationalism among the subject peoples was not the only sign of dissolution. Egypt broke away in the years after 1805 and became virtually independent. In 1830, France began the conquest of Algeria. Russians continued to attack from the north in a series of wars that brought the Ottoman Empire occasional help from the west European powers, as in the Crimean War, where Britain and France joined in its defense. But occasionally the Western powers also joined in taking slices of Turkey for themselves, as in 1878, when Britain took Cyprus, France was given permission to invade Tunisia, and the Russians gained compensating territory to the north.

The people of the millets were Christians or Jews, but otherwise hardly more Western in culture than the Turkish core culture of the Ottoman state. They were, however, the first to seize Westernization for their own purposes – not merely the idea of nationalism, though this was important, but by appealing to Western values and asking for Western aid in their revolts. The West appeared to them as an ally against their Ottoman rulers, and the appeal to a common religion was an effective source of sympathy in western Europe. The Christian and Jewish religions had, of course, come to Europe from the Middle East, but they were now domiciled in Europe, and Europeans thought of their remaining Middle Eastern practitioners as in some way like themselves. Balkan Christians also looked west for help, so that the drive for modernization on a west European model was far stronger among the millets than it was in dominant sectors of Ottoman society.

For the Ottoman state and its ruling class, effective modernization was difficult. They, like their opposite numbers in Japan, were sensitive to the fact that their apparent backwardness provoked Western disdain. But the core of their political and cultural identity was Islam, and that religion was imbedded in the particular division of authority within Ottoman society. Fundamental reforms such as those imposed on Japan by the Meiji oligarchy would have required even more complex revolutionary changes in Ottoman society, and those changes were slow to come.

Less radical changes did take place, however, and they were sufficient in the long run to save the Ottoman Empire from partition among the European powers. Military reforms were at the forefront. In 1826, Sultan Mohammed II engineered a revolt of the janissaries and then turned his new artillery against them. This massacre of the key forces of the old guard was followed by the elimination of the janissaries throughout the empire and their replacement by military on a Western model, which also brought Western-educated army officers into new positions of power.

These Western-trained officers helped make way for the introduction of Western science and Western education, at least for some of the élite. Many young men went to western Europe for their education, especially to Paris, and schools modeled on those of France were set up in the Ottoman Empire itself. Educational changes were gradual, but they had a growing influence on the whole of the ruling class from the 1790s into the early 1900s. In the end, these were probably the most subversive influence of all.

The modernization of government administration made significant progress from the middle 1800s onward. As in Japan over these same decades, the problems of political decision making were related to those of administration, but with notable differences. To meet the Western threat, the whole administrative structure was remade from the top down, essentially on the Western model. But these reforms themselves raised a new problem. They created for the sultan and those around him the possibility of using the new concentration of power in their own interest. The opposition accused the court of despotism, and with some reason. The central government did infringe on the traditional local powers of the ayan and threatened the special privileges of the millets, and, although new power for the state may have been necessary for self-defense, the problem of controlling the central power was unresolved.

As in Japan, one effort to solve this problem was to make the Ottoman state a constitutional monarchy. In 1876, a constitution was actually introduced, but the sultan abolished it after less than two years of sporadic operation, and its abolition had no serious political consequences. In fact, constitutionalism had little support outside the bureaucracy itself and a small group of reformers. The country at large was still conservative, still dominated by the ulema and by Islamic traditionalism. The reformers had reoriented much of the government administration, but they dared not try to reform religion, and they failed in their effort to tack a constitutional monarchy onto a conservative Islamic society.

Young Turks and the Failed Revolution

For the first three decades after the suppression of the constitution, from 1878 to 1908, the sultan ruled through ministries of his own choice. Abdul Hamid II (1876–1909) was not so much a traditionalist by conviction as a man who tried to save the Ottoman state as best he could. He saw it as his task to suppress both the modernizers and the dissident nationalities, but gradual modernization occurred in any case. The threat of Russia and the Balkan nationalists required a still more efficient bureaucracy and an army with still more officers with a Western-style education.

Men of this new generation became the focus of a revolutionary movement. They called themselves the Young Turks, the name itself echoing the nationalism common in central and western Europe. But this was not a revolution from below. The Young Turks were drawn from the highest ranks of Ottoman society, especially from the younger members of the officer corps. They were not revolutionaries in the sense of wanting to overturn Ottoman society – not, certainly, as radically at the Meiji oligarchs had done in Japan a few decades earlier. Their revolt aimed to be more effectively conservative through defensive modernization with a strong emphasis on defense, because they believed the sultan's despotism was ruining the country.

In 1908, the Young Turk revolt took the form of a military coup, without a strong popular following; the army was, in fact, the only effective power to oppose the sultan. Once in power, the Young Turks restored the constitution of 1876, which was not especially liberal in its actual workings. In effect, it set up a new oligarchy ruling through the sultan, which remained in power until the Ottoman defeat alongside Germany and Austria in the First World War.

The Young Turks' experience during their ten-year rule stands in notable contrast to that of the Japanese oligarchy only a few decades earlier. Both were drawn from the top military leadership of the country. Both wanted to modernize so as to preserve the society they knew. The Japanese oligarchy created a modern Japan. The Young Turks led the Ottoman Empire into a military defeat that effectively destroyed it.

One obvious explanation of the difference is that the Ottoman Empire chose the wrong side in an important European war, while Japan avoided war against any Western power until it was strong enough to win against Russia in 1905. But, aside from errors easily obvious in hindsight, the Ottoman Empire had special problems. It was a Muslim empire ruling over many non-Muslims. The Meiji reformers in Japan had no such nationalities problem to deal with.

The Young Turks' alternative course was to seek some modernization, but stopping short of measures that would change the fundamental Islamic character of the state. To do this provoked rebellion from the Christian millets, who were themselves Westernizing. By the logic of their choice, the Young Turks were drawn to repeat the policies of their predecessors. They suppressed opposition from the millets, attempted to suppress nationalist revolts, engaged in two Balkan wars, and entered a tangle of European diplomatic ties that led them into the First World War on the German side. It ended with a defeat that threatened the partition of the Empire.

It is hard, however, to envisage any course an Ottoman government of that time and place could have taken more wisely. The First World War began in the Balkans, in former Ottoman territory, and its origins involved precisely the problems of national and linguistic minorities that the Ottomans failed to solve. It is indicative that their successors in that part of the Balkans – first the Austro-Hungarian Empire and then the Republic of Yugoslavia and its successor states – have also failed to solve them.

The Political Setting After the Lost War

After 1918, the alternatives for disposing of the remnants of the Ottoman Empire depended on the military and diplomatic setting of the time. By the summer of 1918, the Germans were losing the war in western Europe, and the Ottoman defeat in the Middle East was even more imminent; the Arab provinces were already largely gone, and Allied armies were advancing in the Balkans and the Levant. In November, the Young Turk ministry fled into exile, and the sultan signed an armistice a few days before Germany did. A British naval force sailed into the Bosporus opposite Istanbul.

During the war, the Allies had made a variety of plans for the partition of Turkey, plans that shifted with the exigencies of the moment. One plan promised Russia a large piece of Ottoman territory when Russia was still in the war, but the Allies had no intention of keeping its promise after the Russian Revolution. They also made conflicting promises of parts of Anatolia to Greece and Italy and conflicting promises in the Levant to Arabs and to Zionist Jews. Behind the specific promises was a dominant attitude among the political classes of Britain, France, and Italy that considered Turkey not as a defeated but civilized enemy like Germany, but as a country to be treated as they had treated other non-Western kingdoms during the decades of high imperialism. Their clear intention was to partition most of the Ottoman Empire and to divide the rest into spheres of influence, which gave France, Britain, and Italy, respectively, large powers of informal empire over the remaining quasi-independent Ottoman state. There was even serious talk of putting the remaining fraction of Turkey under an American mandate from the League of Nations for a period of tutelage until it should be ready for self-government.

When the Ottoman government signed the armistice, most of its territory was not yet occupied by Allied armies. Without Turkish acquiescence, partition could not take place without more fighting. In May 1919, an Allied invasion of Anatolia began with the landing of a Greek expeditionary force under a naval escort supplied by Britain, France, and the United States. The Greeks intended to make this the beginning of a new Greek empire, which would occupy both sides of the Aegean as a kind of revived Byzantium replacing the Ottoman Empire.

In spite of the lost war and the signed armistice, these measures provoked a new resistance, not form the Ottoman government but from an unofficial Association for Defense, drawing its basic support from the Anatolian plateau and virtually independent of the Ottoman sultan in Istanbul, in much the same way that, during the Second World War, Charles De Gaulle organized a resistance movement independent of the official French government, which had surrendered.

From 1919 through most of 1922, this new government with its headquarters in Ankara fought the Greek invasion on one hand and the sultan and the surrender terms on the other. In 1923 it obtained a new settlement with the western Allies, the treaty of Lausanne, replacing the earlier peace treaty signed by the sultan, which the allies had been unable to enforce. In substance, the treaty of Lausanne gave the Ankara government the boundaries of modern Turkey and removed the provisions that would have put Turkey under informal control of foreign states.

This was a remarkable achievement for a defeated people of a country that the west Europeans considered so backward as to require Western tutelage in order to become capable of self-government. The military architect of the victory was Mustafa Kemal, who later called himself Atatürk, a man of great military ability. His military victories gave him and his associates enormous prestige, which enabled them to make sweeping decisions about the future course of Turkish history – the kind of choices that eluded Ottoman modernizers of the 1800s – a degree of freedom of action not unlike that enjoyed by the Meiji oligarchy in the 1870s.

In 1924, Mustafa Kemal proclaimed a constitution for a Turkish Republic, and within that framework he founded a new Republican People's Party, which governed Turkey as a one-party state from 1924 to 1945. Even after the party lost its one-party status, it remained in power until 1950, though Mustafa Kemal died in 1938. The staying power of the new regime made it possible for it, like the original Meiji leaders, to set the country on a new course, which was not easily changed even after they were gone from power.

The Problem of Nationality

A variety of alternatives faced the new leaders of the Turkish Republic. One of the first problems was find a viable national identity, and the present Turkish Republic is largely a result of the decisions Mustafa Kemal and his colleagues made, but they were not inevitable. Two alternatives were unlikely to appeal to the Kemalist leadership, but they were present nevertheless. One would have been to rework the notion of an Ottoman Empire and try to recapture some or all of the lost provinces in the Balkans or the Arab provinces to the southeast. A second might have been to try for the leadership of the Islamic world as a whole. The claim that the Ottoman sultan was the spiritual head of Muslims everywhere had been put forward in the prewar decades, based on the sultan's claim to be caliph and legitimate successor of Muhammed, but this was even further from Kemalist tendencies of thought.

A third but hardly more practical alternative would have been to accept the linguistic idea of nationality common in eastern Europe, and attempt to build Turkey into the center of a new Pan-Turanian empire. Several million Turkic-speaking peoples lived further east in territory that had been under Russia, and now that Russia was engaged in a postrevolutionary civil war, the

Western powers might have been willing to encourage Turkey to annex in the Caucasus and beyond. In the early 1920s, a former minister of war of the Young Turks' government actually went east in an attempt to lead Central Asian resistance to Soviet control.

A fourth alternative, and the one actually chosen, was to work with the territorial unit that was left, that is to accept the boundaries laid down by the treaty of Lausanne. This choice was more unexpected than might appear. It was a narrower concept than the Pan-Turanian idea, and narrower still than the all-Ottoman or Pan-Islamic solutions. West Europeans had long used the words Turk and Turkish for the Ottomans, but they did so because of their own identification of nationality with language. It was only recently that people in Anatolia had begun to identify themselves as Turks, a word formerly applied to Anatolians and suggesting unsophisticated peasants. The word Turk only began to take on favorable connotations within the Ottoman Empire after the Young Turks' rebellion of 1908. It was not used as the official name of the country in any law until 1921, and not definitively so until the Constitution of the Turkish Republic in 1924.

The Turkish entity that Mustafa Kemal had acquired appears, in retrospect, like a nation-state, but it also had some elements of nation building to be done, and its frontiers by no means defined all people who could claim to be Turks. After the First World War, there were significant population exchanges between Turkey and both Greece and Bulgaria, and leftover nationalities problems remained, involving Turks on Cyprus and non-Turkish Kurds within the Republic, to say nothing of the non-Turkish Muslim population in Albania and Bosnia left over from the period of Turkish rule.

Turkish Nation Building

The creation of Turkish nationalism was partly by intent and partly by accident. The state Mustafa Kemal took over had defeated the Greeks and the Allies, as well as the Ottoman sultan who had collaborated with them. The competing Ottoman state had just crowned a century of marginally effective military modernization with the disastrous defeat of 1918. But even during the wars of 1920–3, many people, perhaps most of the resistance fighters, thought they were fighting for the sultan, whom they considered to be a prisoner of the English.

Mustafa Kemal in Ankara was preparing the way for another concept of loyalty by passing a new series of fundamental laws through his assembly. These laws, among other things, vested sovereignty in the Turkish people. In 1922, in order to make this more palatable to the faithful, the assembly took the religious office of caliph away from the deposed sultan but vested it for a time in his cousin.

Next, the leaders of the revolution moved the capital from Istanbul to Ankara. The move was partly symbolic of the end of the Ottoman Empire, but it also removed the seat of government from a cosmopolitan center associated with past Ottoman and Byzantine splendors to a Turkish hill town. In 1924, as the formal moves were completed, the office of caliph was also abolished and Turkey became a completely secular state, organized as a republic with Mustafa Kemal as president.

It is unlikely that many people of influence would have tolerated these moves all at once, but they did tolerate them in stages. The sultan's apparent treason in collaborating with the British, against the background of Mustafa Kemal's military triumphs, made changes palatable that would otherwise have been very difficult.

The Problem of Religion

Among these changes, the shift from the concept of an Islamic state, where church and state are joined, was crucial. Mustafa Kemal's action was an early battle in the struggle between secularism and Islam, which was to recur throughout the Muslim world during the rest of the century. The abolition of the caliphate was only the most important outward symbol of the whole program that followed immediately in 1924 and 1925; the reorganization went on to abolish the office of the Seyh-ul-Islam, the ministry in charge of Muslim law, the separate religious schools and colleges for training members of the ulema, and the seriat courts where Muslim law was enforced.

These measures provoked the first and most serious armed revolt the modernizers faced, but this revolt did not come from the urban ulema, as might have been expected. The opposition came instead from the popular mystical piety of the countryside and was organized through the *tarikats,* derived from the Arabic word *tariqa* (plural *turuq*). These were the Islamic religious orders, the earliest founded in the later Middle Ages by mystics in search of a way around the aridity of a legalistic monotheism. They sought, instead, forms of worship that could give the individual a feeling of mystical contact with God. The turuq are found throughout the Muslim world, often in opposition to the more orthodox religion of the urban ulama. In Ottoman lands as elsewhere, the tarikats drew on many survivals of paganism, the worship of holy men or their relics, the veneration of charms, and a variety of magical practices.

The fact that these orders remained strong in the countryside, while the urban ulema had weakened in the face of government pressure, indicates how far the modernizing currents of the previous century had eroded the traditional religion of the urban upper classes without touching the popular religion of the countryside. The poorer urban population as well was often of rural origin and owed a personal allegiance to the leaders of a particular tarikat.

The revolt of 1925 not only came from the countryside, but it also combined ethnic and religious issues, and it provided Mustafa Kemal with the occasion to round up suspected reactionaries throughout the country. The leader on this occasion was the head of the Naksbendi religious order and also a Kurd, whose followers were largely drawn from the Kurdish populations of eastern Anatolia. The government suppressed this revolt with ease, and Mustafa Kemal went on to abolish the tarikats, in least in law, and enacted other measures that symbolically repudiated old belief and customs. One measure prohibited the wearing of the fez, the principal remaining sign of Muslim dress for men, where the urban classes were already accustomed to wearing Western-style clothing. Such superficial changes echo Peter the Great's prohibition of beards in Russia two centuries earlier and similar superficial changes in early Meiji Japan.

More significant measures followed in 1926, with the abolition of Muslim civil law and the substitution of a new code based on Swiss civil law. This change was fundamental, in law if not in popular beliefs and practices, and it affected the whole of family life, abolishing polygyny and moving toward Western norms for the position of women, though Switzerland of the 1920s was not in the forefront of women's rights.

In 1928, the modernizers followed up with the romanization of the Turkish alphabet. Up to this time, Turkish had been written with Arabic letters, since this was the language in which God had communicated the Koran through Muhammed. The European alphabet with its explicit vowels was actually better suited to Turkish than the Arabic was, but many at the time saw this as a secularizing measure as well; teaching Turkish children Western letters cut them off from the Arabic script and classical Arabic that had been the universal avenue to Pan-Islamic communication. But the Arabic alphabet did not fit the language people actually spoke, so that literary Turkish and spoken Turkish had been drifting apart. After the language reform, the new alphabet, combined with public education, led to increasing literacy and opened a new level of mass communication, an essential move toward an economy capable of high productivity and high consumption. In much the same way, the high level of Japanese literacy in the late Tokugawa period had been an important step toward modernization there.

By the beginning of the Great Depression, Mustafa Kemal's program of modernization had passed through its most radical phase. It did not succeed economically as rapidly as Japan did in the early Meiji era, but in other respects it made profound changes in Turkish society and culture, perhaps more fundamental changes than Japan underwent in an equivalent period of time. Mustafa Kemal set Turkey on a course that came close to making it a cultural part of Europe, just as Peter's earlier modernization had done in Russia. In both Japan and Turkey, modernization stopped short of full-scale Westernization, but Mustafa Kemal sought to move Turkey in a secular direction, with separation of church and state modeled on that of western Europe, though he himself remained a Muslim. He wanted a secular state, capable of guiding the moves toward industrialization. He was remarkably successful in creating a Turkish nationalism that could bring a sense of solidarity to the support of the republic, but Turkish politics a half century after his death still revolved to some degree around differences between Kemalist secularism and revived Islamist political sentiments. Nor will the nationalities problem Mustafa Kemal sought to solve be completely resolved as long an important elements of the Kurdish minority refuse to accept the legitimacy of their position within the Turkish Republic.

Further Reading

Göçek, Fatma Müge, *Rise of the Bourgeoisie, Demise of Empire: Ottoman Westernization and Social Change* (New York: Oxford University Press, 1996).

Kinross, Patrick Balfour, *A Biography of Mustafa Kemal, Father of Modern Turkey* (New York: Morrow, 1964).

Kazancigil, Ali, and Ergun Özbundun (eds.), *Atatürk: Founder of a Modern State* (London: Hurst, 1981).

Lewis, Bernard, *The Emergence of Modern Turkey,* rev. ed. (London: Oxford University Press, 1968).

Zürcher, Erik J., *Turkey: A Modern History* (London: I.B. Tauris, 1994).

PART FOUR

Independence and the Liquidation
of Empires

This final group of essays will be principally concerned with the 1950s through the 1970s, the central decades of the European withdrawal from political control of the non-Western world. The dramatic political changes, however, are only one phase in a longer process of culture change, which began much earlier and continued through the final quarter of the twentieth century. This account, however, will stop short near the point where the perspective of history gives way to the shorter-term (and potentially more myopic) view of current events.

The most dramatic change in these decades was the liquidation of empire. In less than a quarter-century, the Europeans gave up almost all of the overseas empires they had taken more than two centuries to acquire. European empires stopped growing after the early 1920s, when the League of Nations gave part of the former Ottoman Empire to Britain and France as mandated territories. Even earlier, there had been indications of the liquidation of empires to come. In 1917, Great Britain promised India independence, though only at some unspecified future date, and its actual achievement was postponed until after the end of the Second World War. In the first years of peace, India, Pakistan, and the Philippines became independent, and, once begun, the pace was rapid.

The homogenization of cultures the world over nevertheless continued. Nor was the direction of culture change principally from the West to the non-West; European and American cities have their sushi bars and Thai restaurants, just as Asian cities have American fast-food chains. Some American-appearing fast-food chains are, in fact,

Japanese. The continuing revolution, however, took off from a technology originally Western but now worldwide. It began with steamships and railroads, continued through cars and airplanes, and on to television, communication satellites, cheap computers, and the Internet.

These changes took place against the background of major events such as the Cold War, the Communist revolution in China, and the enormous acceleration in the pace of industrialization and globalization of the world economy. The economy we all live with now is increasingly worldwide, international, and interrelated. The connection is not merely through banking and stock markets and intercontinental flow of trade; new patterns of migration have brought substantial and growing minorities of non-Western origin into Europe and North America. These essays will not deal with these most recent and significant aspects of world history, but it is well to be conscious that they were already beginning during the decades when so much of the non-Western world again became independent.

11

Non-European Resistance and the European Withdrawal

The word *nationalism* is used to describe political opposition to foreign rule, but that term is as ambiguous as *imperialism* itself. In Europe, however, nationalism has a slightly different meaning as the sentiment of solidarity on the part of those who consider that they share a common cultural heritage, often including the goal of incorporating their nation in a sovereign state. At times the state came first and created a nation within its borders; at others, the group claiming to be a nation had had only an ephemeral political organization in the past. People's belief that they share a common culture is often subjective and transient, and the political goals that follow from it can be extremely diverse. Britain and North America in recent decades share far more elements of common culture than Italians or the Germans shared in the mid-1800s, yet German and Italian nationalism led to the formation of new national states, while sentiment in favor of the political reunification of Britain, Canada, and the United States is negligible. Clearly, something other than common history and culture are necessary to create a consequential nationalist movement.

In other circumstances, feelings of common culture, religion, language, and ethnic identity are a major cause of violence among neighbors. Nor are the causes of ethnic violence quite the same as those of political nationalism. Recent events in Northern Ireland and the former Yugoslavia bear this out, and the phenomenon it is not necessarily limited to Europe – witness the recent history of Israel and Palestine, Somalia and Sudan. Most European states before the 1700s were not ethnically homogeneous, and the idea that they should have ethnic unity was no stronger than it was in the Ottoman Empire. Ernest Gellner, among other authorities on nationalism, points out that in Europe the desire to have your nation incorporated in a state was weak before the dawn of the industrial era. Others have showed the relationship between nationalism and nascent industrialization in Japan and elsewhere.

But the role of national sentiment is ambiguous. Ethnic similarity does not necessarily lead to a demand for a nation-state – witness the lack of enthusiasm for the unification of the United States and Canada. Nor did the demand for independence from European rule often rest on feelings of ethnic identity. In the Balkans, to be sure, the Greeks and others who identified themselves as nations wanted national independence from the Ottoman Empire, but most movements for independence from European rule have wanted independence for whatever colonial state happened to exist. Only a few, such as Pakistan, have sought independence within newly defined borders. The colonial state and its successor state after independence did sometimes create a framework within which an ethnically homogeneous nation might begin to emerge, as we will see from the examples of Indonesia and Ghana.

The common denominator of nationalism in the non-West in the twentieth century has been the demand for international recognition of the independence of a state – most often the colonial state created by a European imperial power, rarely a precolonial political entity of any kind. The announced goal was most often to use the control of that state in order to secure something further – most often the material goals of high production and high consumption, not the reemergence of a nation, however defined.

Non-Western leaders of the independence movements nevertheless used the rhetoric of European nationalism, often borrowing from the Irish or the Greek nationalist movements. They adopted the term national for organizations such as the Indian National Congress (later the Congress Party) and the African National Congress (ANC) in South Africa. Both groups, however, favored an independent multiethnic state. Both have had a long record of opposition to ethnic or religious sources of solidarity. The Congress Party has appealed for support from both Muslims and Hindus. The ANC has consistently opposed ethnic subdivision, whether Afrikaner or Zulu.

Modernizing independence movements on the model of the Indian Congress Party and the ANC became, in time, the most successful of all the various kinds of political movements that have opposed European rule, but over the decades, political resistance has taken myriad forms. Resistance began in most cases as opposition to European conquest, then moved through a variety of protest movements taking many forms and pursuing many goals. Some of these movements met with limited success; others failed, but the most spectacular success came to the modernizing nationalist movements that gained control of a colonial state. Such states make up the vast majority of the United Nations today.

Primary Resistance

At its simplest, primary resistance was the effort of a polity to preserve its independence from the threat of European domination. In the age of European empires, wars of conquest most often ended with a European military victory followed by annexation of the vanquished. But the European takeover and the non-European resistance took many forms. Some annexation was peaceful, and the actual war of primary resistance followed later. In 1895, for example, Britain marched a small army from the Gold Coast colony into the kingdom of Asante. Asante surrendered without a fight and was annexed, and the king went into exile. Five years later, however, the Asante leadership was able to organize a war of independence, which Britain labeled a rebellion but which was, in reality, the war of primary resistance.

Much the same thing happened in present-day Zimbabwe. In 1890, Cecil Rhodes' British South Africa Company (BSA Co.) marched a military column into the politically fragmented territory of the Shona, north of the Boer republics and between the Limpopo and the Zambezi Rivers. Later, in 1893, company troops occupied the center of the Ndebele kingdom around Bulawayo. At first, the occupation was virtually unopposed, but the company's regime soon provoked African resistance among the Shona and the Ndebele alike. In 1896–7, both participated in a general uprising, the most serious African resistance the British were to encounter in Central Africa. The company called it a rebellion, and imperial troops were called in to suppress it.

197

Primary resistance often involved defensive modernization, which was successful in some cases, as in Japan or Siam; or it could be a rearguard action after the actual European conquest had taken place, as in Vilcabamba after the fall of the central government of Tawantinsuyu. In other cases, the former ruling class came to an understanding with the new rulers, which made it possible to preserve something of the their former identity, if not the full extent of their former power. Many of the Indian princely states are examples of varieties of compromise between local and imperial power, as is the protected status of the Malay sultans or the rights of the Ganda under the Uganda Agreement.

Most members of the United Nations today inherited the borders of a once-colonial state, not those of the precolonial entities it had incorporated, but a few exceptional territories came through the colonial period and maintained links with their precolonial identity if not their precise original territory. In Southeast Asia, Burma, Cambodia, and Vietnam are examples, though Malaysia and Indonesia are new creations. The borders of most states in sub-Saharan Africa are new, though Lesotho, Botswana, Swaziland, Rwanda, Burundi, and Zanzibar emerged from the colonial period with their old identity.

These present-day configurations are the result of a complex interplay of decision making by Europeans and non-Europeans alike; at the beginning and at the end of the colonial period there often occurred an opportunity for fluid change, which, when grasped, set the pattern for decades to come. Earlier chapters have discussed such moments in the history of Buganda, Malaysia, and Java. Sometimes the threat of effective resistance led to European concessions, as in Buganda. In other circumstances, the Europeans sought out allies to help them rule; the Malay States and Java are examples, though with different outcomes in those two cases.

It was sometimes in protectorates, such as Morocco or the Malay States, that the descendants of precolonial rulers kept a semblance of power into the postcolonial era – in Morocco, much of the reality as well. In most non-Western states, however, traditional authorities who emerged in control at independence were soon pushed aside by a new generation of modernizing nationalists. This sequence of events was most obvious in the victory of the Indian Congress Party over the recognized Native States. In Africa in the early decades of independence, traditional rulers fell from power in Tunisia, Egypt, Zanzibar, Ethiopia,

Rwanda, and Burundi. Successful primary resistance could sometimes preserve the precolonial identity through the colonial era; it rarely preserved precolonial rulers far beyond independence.

Colonial Resistance Movements

Between the failure of primary resistance and the victory of modernizing nationalism, a maze of resistance movements sprang up. They were led neither by the former rulers nor by the modernizing nationalists who emerged to control the postcolonial state. Today, from a postcolonial perspective, there is a tendency to view such movements with sympathy, simply because they opposed the imperialists, just as Europeans, at the height of their empire building, had a tendency to see their work overseas as a triumph of civilization. That judgment, too, was overly simple when it was not completely wrong. Many leaders of anticolonial protest movements were genuinely altruistic, pursuing their struggle for justice as they saw it. Others used opposition to the imperialists as a way to seek advantage for their class, family, or other special interest groups within their society, and some were simply opportunists.

These colonial protest movements were so various that they can only be approached through examples, with the warning that examples cannot represent all possibilities, nor can they be placed in a neat typology. Three types of protest, however, are chosen here to illustrate some of a much larger range of possible prenationalist opposition to European rule. One is ameliorative protest movements that are largely based on a desire to improve particular conditions. A second is state building to oppose Western takeover with more elaborate political structures. A third is nativist reaction, seeking to reject many aspects of European culture and influence.

Forms of Protest

Ameliorative Protest Movements

The broadest category of protest movements is not limited to the colonial world; it can be found anywhere people organize to better their conditions, and it includes political action, petitions, labor movements, strikes, demonstrations, and organized riots, among others. In a colonial situation, such movements almost always included anticolonial rhetoric, which could mask a great variety of actual aims.

In the 1890s in West Africa, for example, one such movement in the Gold Coast went by the name of Aborigines Rights Protective Society (ARPS), echoing the name of the humanitarian Aborigines Protection Society, active in Britain itself earlier in the century. In a region where the dominant agriculture was shifting cultivation, most land was necessarily fallow at any moment. It had been used in the past and would be used again, but meanwhile it had no obvious occupier and perhaps no definite owner in the Western sense of that term. From the beginning, the Gold Coast government had a problem of identifying an owner where several individuals or groups could hold certain rights to a particular plot. It was a recurrent problem for governments, as we have seen in Bengal, Central Asia, and elsewhere. The Gold Coast government proposed at one point to assign all unused land to the Crown, which is to say, to the colonial state. This proposal aroused a diverse opposition. Traditional chiefs could claim that the lands sought for the Crown were already the property of the Stool, the African equivalent, and this amounted to a claim that they themselves were proper custodians. Other possible claimants were the peasants who actually worked the land when the fallow period ended, though they were less likely to make their voices heard.

A number of the traditional chiefs organized their claims by working with African lawyers educated in Britain, and together they formed the ARPS. In the short run, the protest was effective. The ARPS leadership appealed to the British public over the head of the Gold Coast government. They sent a delegation to London and succeeded in modifying the proposed land legislation to protect their own rights to the land, but not those of the actual cultivators.

This movement was the first colony-wide protest movement to be politically effective in the Gold Coast, and it had long-term political importance as the beginning of the organized cooperation between traditional chiefs and the Western-educated colonial élite, leading, by the 1920s, to the formation of a National Congress of British West Africa, with branches in all four of the British West African colonies. In spite of the nationalist-sounding title, immediate independence was not an issue. Its demands concentrated on such matters as education, economic development, the promotion of an African press, African land rights, and judicial reform. These were reforms close to the African élite, not to the ordinary people, but they had modernizing objectives that were later to be grafted onto the independence movement.

Another kind of ameliorative movement developed in the 1950s among the Kikuyu of Kenya. The Europeans called it Mau Mau and characterized it as a reversion to African savagery. It did appeal to elements of traditional Kikuyu culture, but it was fundamentally a protest against the conditions imposed on the Kikuyu by the colonial regime, the most serious complaint growing out of the seizure of Kikuyu land to create estates for settlers from Europe. It was violent in a way the ARPS was not, with small guerrilla armies attacking African opponents as well as Europeans. It was a kind of independence movement, but it failed to capture support even of the majority of the Kikuyu and had little support from other Kenyan ethnic groups.

The British declared a state of emergency, brought in European troops, and crushed the movement. In the longer run, Mau Mau contributed to the victory of modernizing nationalism in Kenya by illustrating the depth of the dissatisfaction with the colonial regime, a lesson that had an important influence on British opinion and on that of Western-educated nationalists who were ultimately to take over the colonial state.

State Building to Oppose the West

This second category of resistance includes several efforts to create a new state in order to oppose European rule. It shares some elements of primary resistance and some elements of modernizing nationalism. None of these state-building efforts was truly successful, however, and historians have often neglected them for that reason. Significant efforts that end in failure, however, are nevertheless important evidence about the process of change in human societies, and these early attempts contained the seeds of the later independence movements.

Earlier chapters give examples of protective state building in other contexts. They included the neo-Inca resistance in Vilcabamba and the Yaqui adaptation of Jesuit village organization. Chan Santa Cruz was a new state with a background that was mainly Maya, but with Ladino overlays. None of these efforts secured international recognition, but all three produced at least a few decades of de facto independence from European rule.

Other non-Western societies responded in similar ways, but from other cultural points of departure. Two North African examples are related and significant. The first occurred during the French conquest of Algeria in the 1830s and 1840s. In North African Islamic societies of the mountains and deserts, kinship was an important element of political organization. Deep lineages were often identified by a first-named ancestor, as with the Aït Atta among the Moroccan Berbers and the Banu Muhammed of the Arabs, meaning the children of Atta or the children of Muhammed. These lineages were effective political units, often called tribes, though the term tribe is often incorrectly used of sub-Sahara ethnic groups that have only a common culture.

In precolonial Algeria, such kinship-based nomadic tribes competed politically and militarily with similar structures among sedentary Berbers and Arabs. They also competed with the authority claimed by the Turks from their urban centers such as Algiers and Oran. Sometimes the sultans of Morocco made similar claims to overlordship, and several religious authorities made crosscutting claims to loyalty and obedience. Among these, was the quasi-judicial role claimed by some descendants of the prophet Muhammed, and the heads of the Sufi religious orders, or turuq, exercised still another kind of authority.

In 1830, France began its North African conquests by occupying Algiers and deposing the dey, who had previously represented the distant authority of Istanbul. The deys had no regular administrative organization for governing the city's hinterland, only informal relations with various authorities who actually ruled there. The French, in accepting the Dey's surrender, inherited only his control over the city of Algiers; if they wished to rule the hinterland, they had to find way of imposing their authority there, which turned out to be a long process, politically and militarily, and was not completed until the 1860s.

One form of resistance the French encountered was a newly founded state in what was to become western Algeria. The core of this new power was the Sufi order of the Qadiriyya, the strongest tariqa in that region. Like some other orders in northwestern Africa, it not only had religious authority over its followers but a kind of political sovereignty as well. The Qadiriyya had, for example, a military following it could call upon in cases of conflict with tribal authorities or competing religious orders.

In 1834, a young man named 'Abd al-Qadir, after the founder of the Qadiriyya, became the local head of the order and began to extend its authority throughout western Algeria, fighting to extend its command over others in the region and sometimes fighting the French as well. By 1837, 'Abd al-Qadir was so successful that the French signed a treaty recognizing his sovereignty over a large, if scattered, territory. For a time, he was a more effective ruler over his territory than the dey had ever been. He had become, in effect, the head of a new state that had not existed in 1830 when the French first arrived.

Beginning in 1839, however, 'Abd al-Qadir was forced into a series of military confrontations with the French, leading to his final surrender in 1847. His new political creation emerged as the core element of primary resistance to the French. Though unsuccessful in the longer run, the administrative structures 'Abd al-Qadir had established to oppose the French became, on his defeat, the foundation of French administration of much of the interior.

A second state-building resistance movement emerged almost a century later in the Rif Mountains of northern Morocco. Though the sultan of Morocco had a more substantial government administration than the dey of Algiers, he suffered from similar weaknesses. Only a part of the territory he claimed was considered as government country, *bled al-makhsen*, under the actual administration of the sultan's officials. The remainder recognized the sultan's authority but was not under his firm control. These regions were classified as *bled-es-siba*, unadministered country.

In the years before the First World War, when France and Spain officially established their protectorates over Morocco, they effectively controlled only those areas the sultan had controlled in the past, limited to the bled al-Makhsen – mainly the principal cities and the plains along the Atlantic coast. For the bled es-siba, the remainder of central and southern Morocco, the French maintained what influence they could by recognizing, in the sultan's name, the authority of whoever was actually in control. The Spanish did the same in the north. They controlled the port cities such as Ceuta and Melilla, but the interior of the Rif Mountains was bled es-siba, and Spain had no more authority than the sultan had had in the past. Some of the bled es-siba in the far south drifted away altogether and became part of Spanish Sahara or French Mauritania.

The state-building effort in the Rif emerged from a maze of conflicts between the Europeans, the sultan, and dissident local authorities throughout the Moroccan empire. In began in the early 1920s, when 'Abd al-Krim emerged as a leader of the Aït Waryaghal (spelled in many different ways, because the Berber languages were written so variously in Arabic or Roman characters). The Rifian chain of mountains lies just south of the Mediterranean coast and had at that time a Berber-speaking population of about 600,000, divided among a number of tribes, though the Aït Waryaghal was the largest.

'Abd al-Krim was better prepared that most tribal leaders. He was educated in Tunisia in the Muslim tradition and later worked as a journalist and as judge for the Spanish authorities in northern Morocco. His background in European service was influential in forming the new Rifian state, which he called the Republic of the Rif. He took for himself the title of president, though he recognized the ultimate authority of the sultan should the sultan ever be free of French control. His point of departure was a tribal alliance, but he added an administrative structure modeled on that of the Moroccan makhzen. In effect, he established for the first time a central administration over part of what had been bled-es siba, with himself as president in place of the sultan. He also adopted Islamic modernism, represented by the order of the Salafiyya, which strongly opposed the influence of the older, more Sufi orders such as the Qadiriyya, and he claimed to stand above tribal loyalties, though he used them as a stepping stone. He began, in effect, as an ordinary representative of the dissidence of the bled es-siba and attempted to move in the direction of a modernizing nationalism.

He failed, but the Rif Republic of the 1920s nevertheless made an impressive defense. Fighting began in summer of 1921, when the Spanish authorities on the coast first sent military expeditions into the mountains. The Spanish had a force of about 30,000 men, against about 3,000 for the Rifians, but they lost the decisive battle, and another in 1924, leaving the Rifians in complete control of the mountain areas. In 1925, however, 'Abd al-Krim launched an attack toward Fez in the French zone, and this may have been his fatal error. The Europeans now came to realize that the Rifians were a not a mere dissident group of tribesmen who could safely be let go their own way. In the spring of 1926, France reinforced its Moroccan garrison by 400,000 men, while Spain increased its Moroccan force to about 100,000. With an army of a half-million men, approximately equal to the entire Rifian population, the Europeans could hardly fail against a Rifian army of less than 75,000. 'Abd al-Krim surrendered to the French in May 1926 and was sent into exile on the island of Réunion in the Indian Ocean.

In retrospect, the Rif War can be seen as relatively unimportant in itself, but it was nevertheless an important harbinger of the end of the age of European empires. In the 1950s, the modernizing nationalists of the Istiqlal party, acting in concert with Sultan Muhammed V, succeeded in gaining independence for the whole of Morocco. Like the Anglo-Boer War at the other end of Africa some decades earlier, the Rif War showed that the cost of gaining or holding empires against organized forces with modern weapons had increased enormously. In South Africa, Britain had to use an army of a half-million against a local force of about 65,000 because the Boers had secured the most recent European weapons, though their guerrilla tactics were important too, as they were in the Rif. But weapons counted there as well; by the last campaign against similar odds, the Spanish alone captured 220 machine guns, about 100 artillery pieces, and more than 6,000 rifles.

Nativist Reaction

Another category of colonial resistance movements is sometimes called nativist, sometimes revitalization movements, sometimes utopian reaction. These movements are diverse, but they are broadly distinguished by their aims, or most accurately, by what their aims were not. They did not seek to create new governmental forms capable of defensive modernization; they rarely sought modernization of any kind. Their main effort was to expel the barbarian Europeans, along with the influence of European culture in all aspects of life. Most failed, and they failed because they lacked the military and organizational technology that gave the Europeans their advantage.

In his book *Prophets of Rebellion,* Michael Adas has written a comparative history of five protest movements that fit this category.

They range from the Java War against the Dutch in 1825–30 and the anti-European movements in New Zealand in the 1860s to another in east central India at the century's end, still another in German East Africa in 1905–6, down to an anti-British rebellion in Burma in the 1930s. Many of the revolts in this series were difficult and expensive to suppress, but few seriously threatened European power, and none came close to establishing a viable state with the degree of international recognition received by the kingdom of Hawaii before its annexation.

Two other revolts in this category were, however, serious enough to alarm European opinion, at least in the short run. One was the Great Rebellion in the Ganges plains of India in 1857. This rebellion was serious because a large part of the Bengal army mutinied against its British officers, which gave the rebels command of a modern army of a European type. The military mutiny was simultaneous with civilian rebellions, which were particularly serious in the present-day state of Utar Pradesh occupying the Ganges plain downstream from Delhi. During its course, the rebellion picked up many and various sources of resentment against British rule, from princes and peasants, Muslims and Hindus, urban and rural. But the rebels failed to develop a central organization, and the movement had no common objective beyond a vague desire to restore the Mughal Empire.

The British rushed in massive reinforcements, and they kept the loyalty of the Indian troops in the armies of the two other presidencies, Bombay and Madras. Most critically, they kept the support of the Sikh forces from the recently annexed territories to the northwest. Almost everywhere in India, the British retained substantial support from important elements of the Indian population, especially in Punjab in the northwest and in Bengal proper around Calcutta, and by the end of 1858, they were successful in crushing the main rebel force. They took their losses seriously, however, and lessons they drew from the rebellion led to a systematic reorganization of British rule in India, including the formal abolition the Mughal Empire and the liquidation of the East India Company, ushering in a century of direct rule over British India in the name of the Crown.

The other spectacular movement was a web of linked events in China of the 1890s. Europeans called the affair the Boxer Rebellion, but it was not so much a rebellion as a popular uprising that was later taken up by antiforeign elements of the Chinese court. It became the last and largest war of resistance the Chinese Empire was to fight against the Europeans before its abolition in 1910.

In the 1890s, popular antiforeign sentiment had been growing for a half-century and more. At the local level, its organizational base was an ancient Chinese tradition of secret societies, in this particular case a society with a Chinese name the Europeans translated as the society of "righteous and harmonious fists," hence Boxers. The society appealed to ancient beliefs in the value of supernatural aid through religion and magic, combined with an equally old tradition of martial arts like kung fu and others that have spread so widely to the West in recent decades. The most active followers of the society were from the lower ranks of Chinese society, though the Boxers enjoyed a measure of tolerance and patronage from some highly placed members of the bureaucracy. In the end, the Boxer movement was taken up and accepted, or manipulated, by the court, leading to a formal Chinese declaration of war on foreigners.

The most active phase of Boxer activity began late in 1899, with a wave of antiforeign and anti-Christian violence, including widespread destruction of mission stations and the murder of Chinese Christians, especially in north China. Europeans there took refuge in defensible concessionary settlements, especially in Beijing and the port city of Tianjin, where they were besieged. After a period of confused fighting, an international military expedition, including Japanese, Indians, and Americans, relieved the Beijing legations and a measure of peace was restored. The Chinese army played an equivocal role throughout, some regional authorities maintaining peace in spite of the court's declaration of war. The Chinese court fled for a time to western China, leaving the foreigners free to sack and loot the Summer Palace, as they had done earlier in the century. Early in 1902, the court returned in Beijing, under the cover of the convenient fiction that the war had been only a popular rebellion.

The Boxer affair was in some respects similar to the Meiji restoration; both began with a cry for the support of dynasty and expulsion of the barbarians. Unlike the Meiji leadership, however, this movement had no program of modernization, defensive or otherwise. The foreign armies that suppressed it amounted to less than 50,000 men. In its military aspect, it was far weaker and less organized than the Indian rebellion of 1857, but it was similar in looking back to a former state of affairs, real or imagined. On a scale of variance from pragmatic to utopian, the Boxer affair was some distance from the pragmatic extreme but still some distance from the utopianism represented by millenarian movements that put their faith in the expectation of cosmic intervention, which never arrived. Movements of this type will be dealt with separately in the next chapter.

The Roots of the European Withdrawal

The withdrawal from empire has European as well as non-European origins. By any index of economic productivity, the West at the end of the Second World War was as powerful in comparison with the rest of the world as it had ever been. Yet the Europeans, after investing so much to conquer more than half the world, gave up their conquests in a few decades with few serious struggles.

An important part of the explanation was military. The West emerged from the Second World War more powerful than ever, but the comparative advantage it had enjoyed in the 1800s was gone forever. In the famous line of Hillaire Belloc, "Whatever happens, we have got/ The Maxim gun, and they have not," the final negative was significant, but it was temporary. British and French armies, made up mainly of African troops, conquered the whole of West Africa with forces that rarely counted more than 2,000 men for each. They had machine guns, and the opposition was mainly armed with muzzle-loaders, if they had any firearms at all. Three decades later, the opposition in the Rif also had machine guns, and they were only beaten when they were vastly outnumbered. A similar advantage for guerrilla opponents of modern armies was to continue into the wars of decolonization such as those of Algeria and Indo-China.

As late as the 1970s, the United States still had the power to win at the end of the Vietnam War, but the cost of victory was now much higher, and the value placed on the life of Western troops was higher than it had been in the period of empire building. The United States was not willing to pay that price. Even before the American experience in Vietnam, the French, Dutch, and British in similar circumstances had reached a similar conclusion.

But the political decision to withdraw without an all-out military effort also had roots in European opinion. Throughout the age of European empires, some critics in Europe had been opposed to having colonies in the first place, and in the politics of imperial advance, most central governments in Europe were overtly opposed to overseas annexation most of the time. Most annexations were manipulated by well-placed minorities, occasionally supported by nationalistic jingoism, and the low cost and ease of empire building always weighed in the balance.

Certain European countries had their own particular strands of anti-imperialist opinion. In France, there was a recurrent belief that France's true mission and national greatness lay it its role as leader of the European continent, as opposed to frittering away resources on distant imperial adventures. This opinion, often called continentalism, was especially strong from time to time on the political Right, especially after 1871, when the loss of Alsace and Lorraine to the new German state made some Frenchmen regard empire building overseas as little less than treason. A similar opinion was again prominent in the 1960s, when France came close to civil war over the settlement with Algeria. In this case, the Left was mainly for peace; the army and some of the Right wanted to maintain a French Algeria at almost any cost. It was Charles De Gaulle who rallied the continentalist sentiment, promising that France would cut its losses in Algeria in order to regain its proper role in the leadership of Europe.

Britain had another kind of political anti-imperialism based on its own historical experience, going back to the loss of the colonies that became the United States. After the first anger and disappointment, it was clear that the loss was not serious economically or strategically. By the mid-1800s, it appeared that Britain was better off buying in the cheapest market and selling in the dearest, regardless of political control. Resistance to the grant of self-government to Australia, Canada, and New Zealand weakened throughout the century, with the expectation that these settlement colonies should naturally drop from the mother tree as they became ripe for independence.

Pseudoscientific racism was so strong in the late 1800s that few expected India, Ceylon, or Nigeria to be prepared for independence in the near future, but they were included at a remarkably early date.

Indian self-government and ultimate independence were the declared aim of British policy from 1917. Tropical West Africa was added after 1945, though even the most optimistic expected the maturing process to take longer than it did.

Other currents of anti-imperialism were more general throughout Europe. When the costs of empire were recognized, a shifting minority in every imperial power objected to paying the price. On the political Left, economic objections were more specific and articulate. Even in the 1800s, currents of socialist pacifism had opposed military adventures. After 1902 and the appearance of J. A. Hobson's *Imperialism: A Study,* the link between capitalism and imperialism appeared in a new light, and European socialists were more than ever opposed to empire building.

Another kind of anti-imperialism went back to humanitarian links between Christian principles and government policy, and such links had been important in the British abolition of the slave trade and emancipation of the slaves. Similar sentiment moved the Belgian Parliament to take the Congo Independent State away from King Leopold and put it under the Belgian government. Humanitarian chords in German and Dutch opinion occasionally forced the reform of government polities in German Africa or the Netherlands Indies.

The rise and fall of pseudoscientific racism was a variable in European opinion that first contributed to the desire to build empires overseas and then to the willingness to liquidate them. In Europe of the 1800s, the belief in European cultural superiority increased with the growth of European industry, and racism rose along with cultural chauvinism. Between about 1890 and 1900, the racial superiority of Europeans was unquestioned, in Europe at least, and it was not completely accidental that this was the peak period of empire building overseas.

A dramatic change in European self-confidence came between the beginning of the First and the end of the Second World War. Military confidence began to be shaken as long ago as the Japanese defeat of Russia in 1905. The mass destruction of manpower in the First World War and the Holocaust during the Second raised doubts about Western moral superiority. The Great Depression raised still other doubts about the certainty of continued material progress, though a new kind of material optimism set in after about 1950.

The change in European mood was far broader than mere consideration of overseas empire, but its implications for empire were starkly represented by the change between the League of Nations Covenant of 1919 and the United Nations Charter of 1945. The League covenant was written at a time when the victors proclaimed "the self-determination of nations." It nevertheless turned over certain territories to the winning powers in trust as mandates, including the Germans colonies in Africa and Melanesia, plus the ex-Ottoman Arab provinces of Syria, Lebanon, and Iraq.

Countries accepting the mandate of the League of Nations promised to protect the "well-being and development" of the local people. But the promises were more significant for what was left out than for what was included. The subject people were to be prohibited from drinking alcoholic beverages and exempted from compulsory military service, and no other human or political rights were mentioned. Only the ex-Ottoman territories were explicitly to be prepared for independence, and even then without a set timetable.

By 1945, the Charter of the United Nations set up the Trusteeship Council, which adopted a clear goal of independence for all colonies in a limited period of time. It laid down ten years for Italian Somalia, for example. It recognized that all colonies might not be ready for immediate independence, and it had no real power to insist on independence everywhere; but the meaning of self-determination as a goal had altered dramatically.

Further Reading

Adas, Michael, *Prophets of Rebellion: Millenarian Protest Movements against the European Colonial Order* (Chapel Hill: University of North Carolina Press, 1979).

Bayly, C. A., *Indian Society and the Making of the British Empire* (Cambridge, U.K.: Cambridge University Press,. 1988).

Curtin, Philip D. (ed.), *Imperialism* (New York: Walker, 1971).

Gellner, Ernest, *Nations and Nationalism* (Ithaca, NY: Cornell University Press, 1983).

Kimble, David, *A Political History of Ghana 1850–1928* (Oxford: Clarendon Press, 1963).

Low, D. A., *Eclipse of Empire* (Cambridge, U.K.: Cambridge University Press, 1991).

Pennell, C. R., *A Country with a Government and a Flag: The Rif War in Morocco, 1921–26* (Wisbech, U.K.: Menas Press, 1986).

Rosberg, Carl, and John Nottingham, *The Myth of "Mau Mau": Nationalism in Kenya* (New York: Praeger, 1946).

12

Personal and Utopian Responses

Some reactions to the Western presence took overt and organized political form, but many of the most significant responses had little to do with politics. Some social and intellectual leaders in the non-West consciously considered the Western phenomenon and publicly outlined a program to deal with it. Other reactions were as personal and informal as the choice in the style of clothing or the language of public expression. In any case, the reaction to the Western presence was rarely a bipolar choice between local tradition on one hand and the West on the other. There was always room for innovation that would provide a number of alternatives.

A rich literature already deals with choices made by articulate non-Western leaders. Aside even from their own writings, biographers have dealt with figures such as Gandhi, Nehru, and similar outstanding people in other societies. Anthropologists and historians have also investigated the less documented responses of the less articulate, such as peasant intellectuals who sought to understand and to respond to conditions they confronted in a changing world.

Another, less common, approach, is the study of personal reactions to the Western impact through group biography. Leo Spitzer's *Lives in Between* has dealt comparatively with the permutations of race, religion, and class in culturally mixed societies. He traced three families through a number of generations in different parts of the world. One was the Sierra Leonean May family, descendants of slaves captured at sea and landed there by the British Navy in the early 1800s. By the late century, several of the Mays had become members of the Creole élite of that colony. A second example was the Rebouças family, Afro-

Brazilians who moved from slavery to a near élite status in Brazilian society. The third was the family of Stefan Zweig in Hapsburg Vienna, a Jewish family who sought acceptance in the dominant culture. In all three cases, family members found themselves making a group journey toward assimilation into the dominant élite, but with limited acceptance.

Frances Karttunen's *Between Two Worlds* represents still another approach to culture contact at the personal level. It is a biographical study of some twenty individuals who acted as guides, interpreters, or intermediaries between Westerners and others on the fringes of contact with the non-West. Several of her subjects are women, who are otherwise neglected by earlier historians. The best known of these are Doña Marina, who interpreted for Cortés in the Spanish conquest of Mexico, and Sacajawea, who accompanied Lewis and Clark to the Pacific in the early 1800s. Karttunen presents these and other, less familiar figures who assumed a similar role as cross-cultural interpreters, not mere figures of romance.

Personal aspects of cross-cultural interaction are also available through novels. Chinua Achebe's *Things Fall Apart,* set in eastern Nigeria at the beginning of the twentieth century, gives an intimate view of the individual caught between cultures in the early decades of colonial rule. Other African novelists and playwrights have taken up similar themes in other settings. Such personal accounts of ordinary people provide a valuable alternative to the study of mass behavior incorporated in political movements or to sophisticated statements by individuals who pass as the great men of their time and place.

Millennial Dreams

Conventional history, indeed, spends an inordinate amount of time recording the doings of people recognized as great men. It also records the doing of entities it recognizes as civilizations, at the expense of the barbarians beyond the frontier. Its grand narrative is often a success story, as recorded by the scribes of the winning side. The process of change in human societies, however, involves barbarians as well as civilized, women as well as men, losers as well as winners, and their affairs are also a significant part of the human experience. The rise of the West and the world's reaction to it are recent enough to leave clear footprints of human responses that are harder to trace for earlier times. At the end of the twentieth century, the success of modernizing nationalism is undoubted, but some ordinary people reacted to the West in ways that were less pragmatic and less fortunate.

One common reaction to overwhelming adversarial power was an appeal to supernatural aid. Most religions sanction some form of appeal to divine intervention, and such appeals in the face of Western power took many forms, from personal prayers to organized mass movements. Such mass movements often had *millennial* elements, though the term itself has a range of possible meanings. Its origins are various, but one of them goes back to early Christianity and other Middle Eastern religions, which hold that the world began with the creation and will end at some finite date in the future, when on the Day of Judgment God will make his will known. Many early Christians expected the day to come soon; some expected it at the millennium, a thousand years after the birth of Christ. For most later Christians, the immediacy of the expectation faded, and believers planned their lives in the expectation that things will go on as they have in the recent past.

From time to time, however, believers in many different religions have placed their expectation of drastic change in the near future, often with a date specified. Some such expectation of imminent change entered into many of the political movements discussed in the last chapter, notably those studied in Michael Adas's *Prophets of Rebellion*. Some millennial elements were present in the Indian rebellion of 1857, but they had been stronger in the nearly contemporaneous Taiping upheaval in China, and some continued in the anti-Christian Boxer movement in north China a half-century later. The strength of the millennial element varied greatly in the precision and predicted timing of the change to come and in whether the predicted salvation would come to all of humanity, to an identified group only, or simply to an individual.

Extreme Millennialism

Within this variety of millennial beliefs, it is possible to identify a family of extreme movements where the promise of other-worldly salvation applied to a large group and was expected here and now, or at least predictably soon. These movements can identified as extreme millennialism, but they were extreme only in their millennial expectations. In other respects, they could vary from passive to violent, but they predicted drastic change of a supernatural order, and soon, and they often called for specific behavior to attain the goal. These extreme millennial movements also have a set of recurring features common to many.[1]

The expected change in these beliefs was often total, sudden and complete – not a mere improvement but something very like perfection itself – perfection, that is, as the believers defined it. The imminence of the expected change was also important – well within the life-span of living people, and in this world, not the next. (Salvation in another world belongs to another family of beliefs with other causes and other consequences.) The expected revolution was also seen as part of the preordained course of history, but with supernatural causes, a plan formulated in advance by one or more gods. Finally, the salvation was to be collective, not individual, but the group to be saved was only a section, not all of humankind, a section identified as a social class, a body of believers, an ethnic group, or delimited in other ways.

Extreme millennial movements, in addition to these defining characteristics, had other elements that sometime occur. One was a tendency toward ethical dualism, a sharp distinction between those who were to profit from the change and those who to be the losers. Conflict was often seen as a struggle between good and evil, where the evil apparently triumphant at present would be overturned by the millennial miracle. Most movements also had a recognized prophet, who was not necessarily a single individual and could even be an absent leader, present only symbolically. The organizer, however, was rarely himself the prophet, his role was more often that of interpreting the prophecy of the millennium to come and organizing the response.

Millennial movements of this type originated among people who felt unusually deprived, often in a material way. Their relative deprivation, however, was sometimes subjective rather than actual or measurable.

---

[1] Many historians and social scientist have treated these phenomena in recent decades. My discussion is based largely the classic account of Yonina Talmon, "Millennarian Movements," *Archives europénnes de sociologie*, 7: 159–200 (1966).

Political revolutions rarely come from the lowest orders of society; the truly deprived usually lack the power to act effectively. Political revolutions more often come from the moderately well off who are not as well off as they think they should be. In much the same way, the relative deprivation of those who joined millennial movements was often measured against the circumstances of a real or imaginary past time.

Prophecies have tended to belong to one of two possible types. One type simply stated that the millennium is coming and called on people to be ready but called for no other action. The other called for action, often a sacrifice designed to bring about the predicted change. The action required was often antinomian, the ritualized performance of acts previously considered sinful or counterproductive, but hypernomianism, the insistence on especially strict ethical behavior, was also common.

When the millennial prophecy set an imminent date and that date arrived without the predicted change, an obvious crisis occurred. For the prophet and his or her followers, several solutions were possible. One was to reschedule the date, with a consequent loss of credibility after each failure, until the hope for the millennium faded into a symbolic faith in a distant future. Christians have generally handled millennial expectations in that way. Other millennial movements simply died out, and their followers sank back into their feelings of deprivation, ripe for another prophet, if one appeared. A third possibility has been for the leadership to turn from utopian dreams to seek more pragmatic solutions, ranging from various forms of political activism to violent rebellion. These general patterns, however, are best illustrated by individual examples.

The Ghost Dance

The Ghost Dance religion is the best known of the several millennial movements among North American Indians. In fact, it was not a single movement but two interconnected developments that spread out from a center in western Nevada. One occurred in 1870 and the following years and spread westward into California and southern Oregon. The other, which originated near the same area, is generally known as the Ghost Dance religion of 1890, though it began a little before that date and remnants lasted far into the next century. This later Ghost Dance

217

spread mainly eastward through the Great Basin and High Plains as far as the Missouri River.

This second movement has received most attention from Euro-Americans, partly because it was so widespread. By the mid-1880s, it also attracted the hostility of the United States Government, and the government's efforts to suppress it included the massacre at Wounded Knee and the death of the Sioux chief, Sitting Bull, the victor at the battle of the Little Big Horn. Partly as a result, it became the subject of a classic ethnographic study.[2]

The timing of the two movements closely followed Euro-American encroachment onto the High Plains and the Great Basin, a movement that began only after the mid-century. The pre-Columbian inhabitants had been sparsely settled hunters and foragers, living on the natural vegetation and hunting bison on foot. From the 1520s, the Spanish introduced cattle and horses to Mexico, some of which escaped. In the 1600s and 1700s, the Indians of the High Plains and Great Basin changed their material way of life in what is sometimes called the "horse revolution." They learned to tame the wild horses and to turn them to their own purposes, which made them vastly more efficient as buffalo hunters and more readily mobile as nomads or seminomads.

In time, they also began to suffer from the early impact of unfamiliar European diseases. It is impossible in retrospect to know how the damage from these imported pathogens and the benefit from the imported animals balanced each other. Some kind of balance apparently existed until about the 1840s, when the coming of Euro-American soldiers and settlers increased the mortality from imported diseases. Central Mexico had suffered the impact of these alien diseases in the 1500s and 1600s; by 1700, its Indian populations had begun to rise again. For the relatively isolated people of the High Plains and Great Basin, however, the population nadir was postponed until about the 1890s, more than two centuries later than that of central Mexico.

Disease was only the first of several ecological disasters. European hunters' firearms had long since killed off the buffalo east of the

---

[2] Mooney, James, "The Ghost-Dance Religion and the Sioux Outbreak of 1890," *Fourteenth Annual Report of the United States Bureau of Ethnology to the Secretary of the Smithsonian Institution, 1892–93. Part 2* (Washington, Government Printing Office, 1896), pp. 641–1136.

Mississippi, but an estimated one-third to one-half of the pre-Columbian buffalo population of North America were still alive as late as 1850. In the next half-century, the remaining wild buffalo were virtually exterminated, and the way of life of the horse-riding, buffalo-hunting Indians was destroyed, even before the full impact of advancing settlement and the loss of Indian lands in the decades after the American Civil War.

The original prophecy that led to the 1870 Ghost Dance movement came in the mid-1860s to Wodziwob, a Paviotso Indian in present-day western Nevada. While in a trance, he received the message that, if people would join together to perform a specific dance at regular intervals, dead Indians would return to life. Eternal life for all Indians and the death or disappearance of Europeans were often included in the promise. The dance itself was originally a Paviotso round dance, performed by a group who joined hands in a rotating circle, but, as the movement spread, both the millennial promise and the dance itself changed. In time, the movement died down, mainly because its promise was never realized.

The 1890 dance movement originated with another Paviotso prophet named Wovoka, the son of a follower of the earlier movement. Though the two movements were clearly connected, Wovoka's vision included a moral message as well. He urged people to love one another, to give up war and live in peace with the European settlers. If they obeyed his moral instruction as well as the ritual dance, the dead people and buffalo would return, and there would be no more sickness or old age. This millennial promise at first had no fixed date of fulfillment. The moral reforms were to be practiced over time, and the dance was to be performed at intervals of six weeks for five days each time. The return of the dead was to be miraculous, but it was to be an earned miracle. After an eclipse of the sun on January 1, 1889, Wovoka again went into a trance and predicted that the millennial change would to take place in the summer or fall of 1891.

As the movement spread to other ethnic groups, it kept its central promise of a return of the dead, though new prophets promised different events at different millennial dates. Some later versions took on a stronger antisettler aspect, predicting that a great catastrophe would sweep away the Europeans with landslides, whirlwinds, or floods, leaving the Indians unharmed. Regeneration would then again cover the plains with rich grass, horses, and buffalo. Others looked forward, instead, to a future day when the revival of the Indian dead would lead to an era of racial harmony for Indians and Europeans alike. Few leaders of the movement called for positive or violent action on the part of the believers – only a moral life, the ritual dancing, and nonviolent resistance to the American soldiers.

These doctrines spread far, but unevenly, and not everybody participated, even when the religion was widely accepted by a particular tribe. Some, notably the Navaho and other Athabascan peoples, whose religion included a profound fear of spirits, actively opposed the movement. The political position of a particular tribe as of the early 1890s influenced its acceptance or rejection of the new religion. The Navaho, for example, had recently reoccupied their former lands and were relatively secure. Many Apache, on the other hand, had already embarked on guerrilla warfare as their form of resistance to encroaching settlement.

The Sioux had just entered a moment of crisis in their dealings with the United States. A treaty of 1868 had given them all of South Dakota west of the Missouri River and some of that territory to the east as well. In 1889, however, an act of Congress reduced their land by more than half, split into five separate reservations, of which the Pine Ridge reservation was one. The loss of their land, together with the death of the buffalo, made their sense of deprivation especially severe. By the mid-1890s, about 40 percent of the population on the Pine Ridge reservation had converted to the Ghost Dance religion.

In December 1890, the final tragedy of the massacre at Wounded Knee began with the action of United States military and Indian agents, who rather than letting the Ghost Dance run its course in peace, brought in soldiers and tried to suppress it by force. The violence began with a small engagement, in which one of the police killed Sitting Bull. Peace was nevertheless about to be restored, including an arrangement for the Sioux to surrender their weapons at Wounded Knee, but in the course of the surrender, both sides panicked. The cavalry killed some 370 Indians, including many noncombatants.

The Ghost Dance religion continued for decades as a popular movement, losing some followers when the prophesied resurrection did not take place. But the religion survived far into the twentieth century, and, like other religions with millennial expectations, shifted from hope of imminent change to a more vague expression of faith that things could be made better in the future.

The Xhosa Cattle Killing

In the mid-1800s, the Xhosa people to the east of the Cape Colony in South Africa suffered from a crisis similar to that of the North American plains Indians. A combination of European military aggression over several decades, topped by an environmental disaster affecting their cattle, produced a situation equivalent to the death of the buffalo for the plains Indians. The Xhosa location was critical; they occupied the front line of Bantu-speaking people opposing the European advance from the west. Beyond them toward the Cape of Good Hope, the only African population was the Khoisan peoples, partly pastoralists and partly hunters and foragers, a sparse population in a region that was mainly semidesert. Neither the San nor the Khoikhoi were able to offer more than a weak resistance to the incoming Europeans. The Xhosa, more densely settled on better watered land, were an agricultural people, though livestock played an important part in their economy. They first encountered the Dutch settlers militarily in the 1770s. Over the decades that followed, they and the Boers settled down to a frontier conflict of raids and counterraids, punctuated by periods of open warfare.

The Xhosa gradually improved their defenses against the European threat, acquiring European guns in the process and learning to fight as mounted infantry, though they were never politically united, as the Zulu came to be in the early 1800s. The Xhosa as a whole were divided into a number of cultural subgroups, and even these were seldom united politically for long. Their most important political unit, often called a chiefdom, consisted of a leader, or chief, ruling over a group of kinsmen and clients, held together partly by kinship ties, partly by allegiance and common interest. In spite of political weakness, the Xhosa presented a relatively firm frontier against the Europeans, and in the 1840s, their resistance was a principal factor forcing the Boer expansion, often called the Great Trek, to take another route to the north, where the Boers soon established their supremacy in what was to become the Orange Free State and Transvaal.

The Europeans nevertheless gradually pushed back the Xhosa frontier in a series of wars, wining military victories in 1834, 1846–7, and again in 1850–3. This last war was especially bitter, with scorched-earth tactics on the part of the British and Xhosa guerrilla warfare within the regions already held by British troops. In 1853, the Cape Colony annexed the region west of the Kei River, leaving that to the east still disunited but independent of European rule. The Transkei, indeed, was able to keep its independence until the 1890s.

For the Xhosa, the greatest disaster of the early 1850s was not the loss of the war but the introduction into that part of Africa of a previously unknown cattle disease called lung sickness. The Xhosa escaped the disease problems of the Indians in the American West because their disease environment was already similar to that of Europe. The lung sickness was new, however, and like new human diseases, it came as a virgin-soil epidemic with very high death rates. It first appeared at Mossel Bay to the north in 1853, reaching the Xhosa on either side of the Kei in 1855, just after the military defeat. Lung disease affected almost all the cattle, and often it killed the great majority. Cattle were so important to the Xhosa economy that people began to die of starvation as well. An estimated 40,000 died, and another 40,000 fled as refugees into the Cape Colony in search of food and work.

Like the Indians of the Great Basin and the High Plains, they met the crisis by falling back on an adaptation of their traditional religion, in this case one that tended to explain evil in the world by the presence of witches or sorcerers, identified by professional diviners in times of stress. Xhosa culture also called for the sacrifice of cattle at important points in the life cycle, such as births, deaths, and initiations. Other Xhosa beliefs included the hope for some sort of resurrection or renewal of youth.

In the crisis of the mid-1850s, many Xhosa followed these traditional beliefs and concluded that their dying cattle had been polluted by some kind of group witchcraft. The ordinary remedy would have been sacrifice, and the sacrifice of some of the cattle that remained was one way of ensuring the health of cattle still unborn. These beliefs were not yet millennial, but prophets in the early 1850s predicted millennial miracles of various kinds. One, influenced by news about the Crimean War, envisioned the arrival of the Russians to drive away the British.

The prediction that caught on, however, began with a certain Mhlakaza, an important advisor to a chief of the Gcaleka located in the corner of Transkei closest to the Kei River and to the sea, hence on the frontier of the Cape Colony. Mhkalaza himself was not a prophet but an organizer. His niece, Ngonqawuse, had the vision and the message from the ancestors, telling the people to kill all the remaining cattle, to destroy all grain, and to plant none for the next year. The ancestors would then return from the dead and drive the Europeans into the sea; cattle would return to the earth and granaries would be miraculously refilled. Ngonqawuse predicted a series of dates for these events, beginning with August 1856 and stretching down to May 1857. Many people killed their cattle, but by 1856, most cattle were already dead of lung sickness. The crisis continued on either side of the Kei River, and, by the end that year, about two-thirds of the population were either dead of starvation or in flight.

The similarity to the Ghost Dance religion is striking. The dead were to live again. European enemies were to be destroyed though ritual preparation. The dead cattle or buffalo would return and flourish. Differences are striking as well. This time, the prophecy called for sacrifice, not just a ritual performance, and the religious background of the two cultures was enormously different. So was the degree of participation; it seems unlikely that even a bare majority among the Sioux danced, whereas the participants among the Xhosa were a majority estimated at 80 percent or more.

Jehovah's Witnesses

The cattle killing and the Ghost Dance religion arose in circumstances of intense relative deprivation, extending over decades. Not all millennial movements had that kind of background. The Jehovah's Witnesses began in western Pennsylvania in fairly prosperous times, and they have successfully retained a large following both in the United States and in Europe. They continued to make precise prophecies of the Second Coming up to a century after their original foundation. They had no experience of crosscultural conflict at the place of origin, but their doctrine spread widely to non-Western believers who did experience such conflict, especially in Africa.

The Witnesses were founded by Charles Taze Russell in the 1870s as a Bible study group with Adventist background. By the 1890s, the movement had spread and grown into the Watchtower Bible and Tract Society, with branches in many parts of the United States and Britain. Its doctrine in the early years was an intricate reading of the Scriptures, which, among other things, indicated that Christ had returned invisibly to earth in 1874. That date was the beginning of a "time of troubles," which was to lead to the end of the world in 1914, when the dead would return to corporeal form, giving believers an opportunity to convert them before the final judgment. After a whirl-wind conversion campaign, the converts would join the living believers to enter the heavenly city, while nonbelievers would drop into oblivion.

This doctrine obviously drew on elements in Protestant Christianity common in the United States in the 1800s, Seventh-Day Adventist among others. Some feelings of alienation from the rest of American society were present and continued, but such feelings were common enough among other sects, including the Shakers and others in America and elsewhere. It is hard to detect any intense sense of relative deprivation equivalent to that of the Ghost Dancers or the Xhosa. Millennialism in this instance seems to have grown more out of the literate Bible-reading Protestantism of middle America, which drew in turn on the strong millennialism of early Christianity.

On the other hand, the doctrine had elements that were transmutable for people of other cultural traditions. In southern Africa, the first carrier of the message was not a Watchtower missionary, nor even a genuine member of the sect, but a religious radical from New Zealand named Joseph Booth, who introduced some Watchtower literature into South Africa. It was Booth's influence on Elliot Kamwana that was to result in the spread of the doctrine to much of central and east Africa during the next century.

Kamwana was a migrant worker from Nyasaland (later Malawi), who returned to Nyasaland in 1908, at a period when people there were beginning to feel the impact of strict colonial control. The colonial government had only recently introduced the hut tax, a form of regressive taxation intended to tax each household so heavily that they would be unable to pay with the proceeds their own farms. The men would then be forced to take work on the European farms and plantations, which were spreading through the countryside, or to go to work in South Africa, as Kamwana himself had done.

Millennial prophecies had already been made in Nyasaland; a non-Christian priestess had predicted that the Europeans would disappear at the end of 1907, when Kamwana was still in South Africa. After he returned, he took advantage of the backlash of disappointment by making his own Christian-based prediction of the millennium to come in 1914. He made several thousand converts, but, when his prediction also failed to materialize, he followed the African priestess into exile.

Kamwana himself later reverted to a more orthodox, mission-based version of Christianity, but the movement expanded without the direct help of the original founders in the United States, who later disowned it and sent their own missionaries to Africa to expound a more orthodox version of the Watchtower beliefs.

Nyasaland remained a crucial center of the Africanized dispersion, because Nyasalanders spread widely as mine employees. They were sought after as clerks because of their Western education in mission schools, and they received higher pay and more stable employment than unskilled workers. The Watchtower religion became strong in the two Rhodesias (later Zambia and Zimbabwe) and was implicated in outbreaks of worker unrest at the mines of Northern Rhodesia beginning in 1917–19. As it spread, it absorbed aspects of African religions. Even the common name changed from the English Watchtower, to Ki-Tower to Kitawala and other variants.

As it spread, the emphasis on the millennial expectation decreased. In place of the ritual preparation of the Ghost Dance or the sacrifice of the Xhosa cattle killing, some branches of the movement turned to active anti-European agitation and helped to organize anti-European riots in Northern Rhodesia in the mid-1920s, followed by similar violent agitation in the Belgian Congo in 1931 and 1935.

After the Second World War, Kitawala had penetrated as far north as the French Congo under the new name Ki-Nsinga, and other offshoots turned up in Uganda. By then, it had traveled more than two thousand miles from its point of entry into Africa from the United States and more than a thousand miles from its secondary diffusion out of Nyasaland a half-century earlier. Offshoots of the movement later entered into the struggles for African independence. In 1961, some American newspapers published a report that fierce "Kikiwat tribesmen" had ambushed an Irish unit belonging to the United Nations expeditionary force sent out to prevent the secession of Katanga province of the former Belgian Congo.

This is not to say that the Africanized Watchtower movement lost its millennial drive completely. It still predicted a kind of millennium when the Europeans would be driven out of Africa, but the date was rarely precise and the expectation was allowed to dwindle. The movement retained the idea that to obey the colonial government was to obey the devil, even as the more orthodox Jehovah's Witnesses sometimes supported Christian disobedience to certain requirements of secular governments in Western countries.

Cargo Cults in Melanesia

In the southwest Pacific another family of millennial movements attracted attention during and after the Second World War. These are often called cargo cults from the pidgin word *cargo,* meaning imported goods of all kinds. The millennial expectations of many of these movements included the hope and belief that expensive gifts of European goods would arrive by sea or air, though the identity of the expected donors varied from one movement to another.

Cargo cults were most common in Melanesia, the conventional name for one of the three major cultural and linguistic divisions found in the Pacific islands. It included the large island of New Guinea and others to the east, the New Hebrides, the Solomons, and Fiji. The name came originally from the fact that the inhabitants have a darker skin color than other Pacific islanders, with a physical appearance similar to that of Australian aborigines. The neighboring Polynesians to the east are spread over an enormous area from Hawaii in the north to New Zealand to the south. The third division, Micronesia to the north, consists of scattered islands north of the equator, between Hawaii and the Philippines.

The European intrusion into Melanesia occurred late in comparison with other Pacific islands. Europeans rarely visited coastal New Guinea before the 1850s, and most formal annexations came only in the 1880s and 1890s. Even then, Europeans were slow to explore the interior of the larger islands, reaching the most out-of-the-way parts of highland New Guinea only after the Second World War. New Guinea and the rest of northwestern Melanesia were and are very sparsely populated, ten persons per square mile being a common measure.

When Europeans did arrive, they set up their colonial administrations mainly for strategic reasons, to prevent other Europeans from doing the same, rather than for the sake of expected economic benefits. They used the islands only for scattered coconut plantations, as a source of semicoerced labor largely employed elsewhere, and here and there for the exploitation of mineral resources. The few administrators ruled the native inhabitants mainly by supervising local subordinates recognized as chiefs. Such military or police forces as they required were almost entirely recruited locally, serving under European officers. Otherwise, the European presence consisted of a few plantation managers and a few missionaries, and the direct impact of Europe was small, after annexation as before.

The influence of the European presence on local culture was also paradoxical. In some ways, European influence was very limited; few of these Pacific islanders had access to European culture through education, and even fewer went beyond primary school. Few indeed were able to practice law or medicine or to serve the administration in senior posts. At the same time, the absence of young men for periods of migratory labor and the loss of land to plantations, followed by low-paid plantation jobs, shattered many of the older cultural traditions.

The introduction of exotic diseases was also important in coastal areas throughout the region, though not yet in isolated highlands, and it came a half-century or more later than it did in other Pacific areas such as New Zealand or Hawaii. The population nadir was even later than it was in the Great Basin of North America, occurring in the early decades after 1900.

Intense feelings of deprivation were common; Western goods were visible in European hands, but they were not available to Melanesians. These feelings were also influenced by the teachings of Christian missionaries, especially those elements of Christianity that spoke to their condition and were compatible with their previous beliefs. The Old Testament was influential, and the story of the Israelite captivity and escape from Egypt had a special appeal, as it did to the deprived elsewhere.

Millennarian themes in the New Testament also offered hope for the future, and millennarian hopes were implicit in many of the older religions throughout the region. Millennarian movements occurred in great variety throughout Melanesia, and coastal New Guinea can serve as a regional example. As early as 1857, missionaries in Dutch-occupied western New Guinea recorded a millennarian prophecy, based on a traditional legend about a messiah-like figure with the title of Mansren. His story was that of a miraculous old man, his wife, and his child, who traveled widely in the coastal areas performing a variety of miracles before they disappeared. The legend recounted their expected return, which would usher in a golden age. Old people would become young, the dead would return to life, harmony with nature would be restored, and the Europeans' demands for taxes and forced labor would disappear.

Several later prophets in western New Guinea evoked the Mansren legend but without firm millennial predictions. An occasional prophecy had anti-European overtones, and the administration took the prophet into custody. One prophet, arrested in 1911, kept some of his following until after his release from prison in 1916. Other prophets appeared in the interwar years, with occasional predictions that the day would come when large European steamships would bring cargo; another version held that factories to manufacture cargo would rise from the ground.

The Great Depression, followed by the outbreak of war in Europe and the German seizure of the Netherlands itself in 1940, brought economic hardship and political tension to the Dutch part of New Guinea. Prophets rose with greater frequency, and their prophesies took on more revolutionary anti-European overtones. Such movements were especially active on the north coast and the offshore islands such as Biak, though they split into a number of small uncoordinated groups, all looking out for the coming of the cargo. Their ritual preparation often included the use of European titles such as general, doctor, or radio operator.

When actual warfare came to Melanesia in 1942, the impact was immense. This backward area, which even the European conquerors had neglected up to this point, became for a few years an important battleground between some of the world's most powerful industrial nations. It had little intrinsic interest for the Japanese, but once they had captured the Philippines and Indonesia, it lay on the way to Australia and New Zealand, just as Burma lay on the way to India after

228

the easy seizure of the rest of Southeast Asia. It was in Burma and the Solomon Islands that the Allies were first able to make an effective stand against the Japanese advance. By chance, this brought on a major display of the most advanced types of military cargo available in the outer world.

For the people of coastal New Guinea, the Japanese invaders were first welcomed as enemies of their Dutch oppressors, but approval soon faded as the Japanese demands became even more onerous than the Dutch had been. Various groups of Papuans entered into the fighting, some against the Japanese, others against the Europeans, and some fought both sides at different times.

In 1944, the American occupation of Biak and the north coastal region brought an immense change in the scale of military activity. The Japanese force in the region had been less than 10,000 men, who were rapidly disarmed. The Americans made Hollandia a base for the movement north to the Philippines, and 400,000 American troops were stationed there by early 1944. During the last years of the war, an Allied force of more than a million men, with the ships and planes to carry them (including the author of this book), moved through nearby Manus Island. The local population had been about 25,000. This demonstration of the scale of cargo available in the outside world would have been impressive to anyone and certainly increased the millennial expectations, though different leaders specified them differently.

Some built storage places for the reception of the expected cargo and made other ritual preparations, but expectations and preparations tended to shift over time from utopian to pragmatic. Before the war, for example, the return of Mansren had been predicted and ritually prepared for. In the wartime fighting, Papuans had been accustomed to the use of force and had seen it used on a massive scale. Many still entertained millennial hopes, but they were now prepared to back up the hopes with a variety of political moves to further their interests.

The Melanesian regions that had the most intense experience with cargo in the hands of foreign soldiers were often those that added a pragmatic program to millennial hopes. In the Solomon Islands, for example, where the Americans and Australians had first fought the Japanese, late in 1945 a political movement called Massing Rule or Marching Rule emerged. It had nothing to do with Marxian rule, as opponents alleged at the time. The political side of the movement was an effort to set up government institutions with mixed European and Melanesian roots but separate from the colonial government. For a time, the Marching Rule leadership profited from Australian preoccupation elsewhere and became the actual government of some islands,

Alongside its pragmatic achievements, the movement held onto its predictions that the Americans who had passed through during the war would return with cargo, though in time such expectations were a mere sidelight. At first, the Australian colonial government branded the movement subversive and arrested the most prominent leaders, but it soon recognized that suppression was not worth the cost. In the early 1950s, Australia set up elected local government, which was a more effective backfire against Marching Rule's claims to independent authority. This was, indeed, the initial move toward independence for the Solomon Islands, declared in 1978.

Success or Failure?

Retrospective commentators disagree about the meaning and historical role of the more extreme millennial movements. Some of them had pragmatic as well as utopian aspects, but they all failed in one sense – the predicted millennium never arrived. One common assessment is to put them down as a form of social pathology, a mass paranoia that could lead nowhere. Such assessments would group them with recent American cults, such as that of the Branch Davidians outside Waco, Texas in the 1990s or the cult responsible for the Jonestown mass murders and suicides in the 1980s.

Other assessments emphasize the religious aspect of the millenial movements, and the hope for divine intervention has more in common with religion than it does with secular politics. Many religions help individuals overcome feelings of helplessness, and many of these movements, from the Ghost Dance religion to Jehovah's Witnesses, gave comfort to their followers, even after the millennium had failed to appear.

Whatever the retrospective assessments, such movements are significant to the understanding of change in human societies. Even though they were rarely successful in gaining some stated objectives, they illustrate some of the range of human responses to human problems. If pathological, they are nevertheless examples of responses to adversity. In this context, they belong somewhere in a continuum that stretches from criminal acts at one extreme, to admired and idealistic political revolutions like the American Revolution at the other.

Further Reading

Burridge, Kenelm, *Mambu: A Melanesian Millennium,* new ed. (Princeton: Princeton University Press, 1995), first published 1960.

Curtin, Philip D. (ed.), *Africa and the West: Intellectual Responses to European Culture* (Madison: University of Wisconsin Press, 1972).

Feierman, Steven, *Peasant Intellectuals: Anthropology and History in Tanzania* (Madison: University of Wisconsin Press, 1990).

Fields, Karen E., *Revival and Rebellion in Colonial Central Africa* (Princeton: Princeton University Press, 1985).

Karttunen, Frances, *Between Worlds: Interpreters, Guides, and Survivors* (New Brunswick, NJ: Rutgers Press, 1994).

Kehoe, Alice Beck, *The Ghost Dance: Ethnohistory and Revitalization* (Fort Worth, TX: Holt, Rinehart and Winston, 1989).

McHugh, Tom, *The Time of the Buffalo* (New York: Knopf, 1972).

Peires, Jeffrey B., *The Dead Will Arise: Nongqawuse and the Great Xhosa Cattle-Killing Movement of 1856–7* (Bloomington: University of Indiana Press, 1989).

Penton, M. James, *Apocalypse Delayed: The Story of Jehovah's Witnesses* (Toronto: Toronto University Press, 1985).

Spitzer, Leo, *Lives in Between: Assimilation and Marginality in Austria, Brazil, West Africa, 1780–1945* (Cambridge, U.K.: Cambridge University Press, 1989).

Thornton, Russell, *We Shall Live Again: The 1870 and 1890 Ghost Dance Movements as Demographic Revitalization* (Cambridge, U.K.: Cambridge University Press, 1986).

Worsley, Peter, *The Trumpet Shall Sound: A Study of "Cargo" Cults in Melanesia,* 2nd ed. (New York: Shocken Books, 1968).

13

The Search for Viable Independence: Indonesia

A t the end of the twentieth century, virtually all of the former colonial world has achieved the new status of recognized independence and membership in the United Nations. The paths to independence have varied, and the outcome now seems inevitable, but the nature of the independent unit was unpredictable in the beginning. Some countries became independent with nearly their precolonial boundaries as in the case of Morocco. Some became independent within the frontiers created by the colonial rulers – the next chapter deals with the example of Ghana. Still others seemed destined for independence in that form, and then broke apart, as British India broke into India, Pakistan, and Bangladesh. Some imperial federations subdivided almost without question, as French West Africa did; others remained as a unit, as Nigeria did, but only after a sharp civil war to decide the issue.

This chapter and the one that follows deal with ways in which two of these newly created nations sought, and succeeded in some measure, not merely to become independent but to do so as recognized nation-states with a measure of equality with others in the postcolonial international order. Indonesia and Ghana are very different places, almost a world apart, and their very viability is still in some respects in question. They illustrate, nevertheless, some of the ways in which the interaction of European rulers and local people over a relatively brief period succeeded in creating a new political society.

In Indonesia and Ghana, the course toward independence shows marked differences and some striking similarities. One similarity was superficial; both figured especially prominently in the news at the time of their independence – Indonesia in 1949, because was it was the first former colony in Southeast Asia to have its independence recognized, and only after a military struggle. It was also the largest of the emerging states of Southeast Asia, in geographical spread and population alike. Ghana was tiny in comparison, but it was prominent because it was one of the first newly independent states in sub-Saharan Africa. Both Indonesia and Ghana also attracted attention because of their charismatic leadership at that time. Sukarno in the Netherlands Indies and Kwame Nkrumah in the Gold Coast attracted worldwide attention, and both went on to rule an independent state until they were removed from power by the local military, Nkrumah in 1966 and Sukarno in 1967.

Another similarity was the early date of their independence movements, going back in both cases to a time before European rule was firmly in place. A detectable independence movement can be found in the Gold Coast in the 1870s. In Indonesia, the Java War of 1825–30 was an early and unsuccessful nationalist movement of sorts, whereas the Dutch conquest of the sultanate of Acheh began only in 1873 and dragged on in a long war that lasted more than a quarter-century, with the final resistance suppressed only in the 1910s. At the opposite end of present-day Indonesia, as late as the 1940s the Dutch had not yet explored much of the interior of western New Guinea. In 1969, indeed, when the Indonesian government took over the Dutch claims and named the territory Irian Jaya, the Europeans had still not established a regular administration over much of the interior. Indonesia of the 1970s thus included some of the first territory to fall to European rule and some areas where the Europeans still had only claims.

Cultural and Ecological Divisions

The whole East Indian archipelago had a form of linguistic unity in that most of the regions spoke Austronesian languages, though they were not mutually intelligible. Other members of that language family could be found as far east as Tahiti and Easter Island, north to Taiwan, and west to Madagascar. Cultural differences within that language family were immense; one of the most ancient and persistent was that between regions able to grow paddy rice and those that could not. Where wet rice can be grown, it is often possible to grow up to three

Indonesia.

crops a year on the same field year after year. The labor investment in the paddies and irrigation ditches is immense, but, in the wet-rice regions of Indonesia, the labor necessary to maintain it is well worth it. Agricultural population in wet-rice regions of Indonesia in the 1960s averaged about 190 people per square mile.

Agricultural populations in areas where wet-rice cultivation was not possible averaged only about ten people per square mile. These areas were generally tropical forest regions, where the soils are poor and most nutrients are locked in the tropical brush or forest vegetation. When farmers cut this vegetation and burn it, the ash returns the nutrients to the soil, making them temporarily available for cultivated plants. Within a very few years, these nutrients are used up or leached out, and the land must be allowed to return to brush or forest for a period of fallow before it can be cut and used again. This agricultural system, variously know as cut-and-burn, shifting cultivation, or swidden, limits the population level sustainable from agriculture alone, and some believe that the limit may be a low as twenty people per square mile. To exceed that limit may bring permanent and irreparable damage to the environment.

In Indonesia in the twentieth century, the paddy-rice area has been restricted to most of the island of Java, plus Bali and Lobok to the east. This is the fundamental reason why the Dutch regime focused on Java and treated the rest of the archipelago as the outer islands. In 1940, the total population of Java was about 40 million people, or 800 per square mile, while the outer islands contained only 18 million people, or 26 per square mile. Here and there, urban areas or permanent plantations with tree crops such as rubber have created pockets of dense population, but the swidden-paddy dichotomy is fundamental to many later and man-made cultural divisions.

At one time, historians depicted Southeast Asia as a region without a great civilization of its own, one that had over the centuries absorbed cultural influences from its neighbors, China to the north and the Indian subcontinent to the west. More recently, historians have come to recognize that Southeast Asians were interested in borrowing from the outside, as Europeans have done over the centuries, but they fitted their borrowings into vital local cultural traditions. In much the same way that Southeast Asia borrowed Buddhism or Islam, Europeans had borrowed Christianity from the Middle East, merging it with aspects of preexisting local religions, and Christianity continued to change in its new European home, just as borrowed religions continued to change in Southeast Asia. The Catholicism of East Timor is no longer precisely the Catholicism introduced by Dominican missionaries in the 1500s, nor is the Hinduism of Bali precisely that received from India even further back in time. The Islam introduced by traders from across the Bay of Bengal, mainly in the 1400s and 1500s, has also changed and accommodated indigenous religious ideas and practices and retained regional differences even within Southeast Asia.

Indian political traditions set the basic forms of kingship in many parts of Southeast Asia, but these forms were more significant and lasting in areas of wet-rice cultivation than where only swidden was possible. This fact left a continuing tension between the settled states of the plains and the mountain peoples on the fringes of Thailand, Burma, and Vietnam, a tension that has lasted to the present. In the islands, these royal traditions were strongest and most lasting in the wet-rice areas of Java and Bali. They involved elaborate courts and central bureaucracies, but with little penetration to the village level other than tax collection. On Java by the 1700s, the Dutch had already replaced the kings and ruled through the subordinate administration of the *regenten,* in effect adapting Javanese institutions for their own ends. It was far from creating a modern bureaucratic state, but it enabled the Dutch to rule Java more directly than they did the outer islands.

In the outer islands with their sparser populations, the Dutch East India Company and its successor, the Netherlands Indies, were often content with a still weaker form of indirect rule. This arrangement was politically useful as a divide-and-rule tactic, playing the outer islands against Java. This same tactic is evident in the way the Netherlands Indies organized its army in three segments, separate from the Netherlands army in Europe. One segment was recruited in Europe, in Germany and elsewhere as well as in Holland itself. A second part was recruited in Africa, originally by purchasing slaves, later with the permission of colonial powers such as Britain. Another, larger segment was recruited locally, officially designated as "Ambonese and other islanders" – that is to say, non-Javanese for the same reason that the Indian army after the rebellion of 1857 was mainly recruited from "martial races" who lived away from the centers of Indian population, including Gurkas from outside the sphere of direct British control.

The Role of Islam

In spite of enormous differences inherited from the past, forces for cultural homogenization had also been at work for centuries. The overlay, however incomplete, of political and religious influence from India had provided some degree of common political and religious culture through most of the wet-rice regions of Southeast Asia, including Indonesia.

In the 1400s and 1500s, Islam spread much more widely, and it often spread most rapidly in regions that been less touched by Indian culture. Bali, an exceptionally Indianized island, has retained its fundamental Hinduism up to the present, but more than 90 percent of the Indonesian population count themselves as Muslim. As a result, Indonesia is now the most populous Muslim country in the world, although the one most distant from Mecca.

As might be expected from the way other world religions spread, Indonesian Islam is neither a fixed and unified set of beliefs, nor are its beliefs identical with those of Muslims in Cairo or Baghdad. Indonesian Islam is divided first by a distinction between *abangan* and *santri*. People characterized as abangan tend to have roots in rural areas and to mix the formal tenets of Islam with a variety of Hindu and Buddhist beliefs, and others that have even deeper origins in the island religions. Santri, a comparatively small minority, are identified as those who take formal Islam more seriously and are more faithful to the commands of the Prophet. Santri are more commonly found in urban and commercial centers and in the coastal regions of Java. The abangan – santri distinction, though valuable, can also become an overemphasized dichotomy; Indonesian Islam is more nearly an array of mixed beliefs that are hard to characterize.

Some of the divisions within Indonesian Islam are also found elsewhere throughout the Muslim world. Sufi Muslim orders, the *turuq,* were present here as they were in Turkey or Morocco, providing believers with a more emotional religion than that of the urban 'ulama. At the same time, in the twentieth century, reformist Islam has spread through the Muslim world generally, seeking to purge Islam of non-

Muslim accretions, sometimes opposing the influence of the Sufi orders. In the Netherlands Indies, a reformist and modernizing order called Muhammadiyah has been especially important over the past century. It not only sought to bring the Islam of the Indies into line with beliefs and practices elsewhere; it was a part of the movement for Islamic modernization, which among other things, sought to accept the discoveries of modern science. It is indicative that some Indonesian nationalists, like 'Abd al-Krim in the Rif, sought support from Islamic modernist elements, though in very different political circumstances.

A Plural Society

While Dutch overrule was a common experience for all, the Netherlands Indies nevertheless remained a plural society with many different languages and cultures. Some were based on local cultural differences such as those between Minangkabau, Javanese, or Balinese. Other cultural minorities came from the outside, the largest and most important of which were the Chinese, making up about 3 percent of the Indies population in the 1930s. The Chinese themselves were culturally divided; the earliest immigrants had been almost exclusively Hokkienese from South China, bringing their own language, which was different from both Mandarin and Cantonese. They had long since become *peranakan,* or culturally mixed with local people; the vast majority of immigrants were men who took Javanese wives and often used Javanese rather than Hokkienese as their home language. The Dutch regime recognized them as a separate community and forced them to live under Dutch-appointed officials in special quarters in Javanese towns. Their contribution to Indies society, however, was far greater than their numbers would indicate. They were an urban, mercantile community, and their activities were crucial to the Indies economy.

Like alien merchant communities in many societies around the world, the Chinese were envied and feared by other segments of society, and this tension between the Chinese and others was to continue in Indonesia after independence. With the passing of time, however, the Chinese community was pulled in several new directions. Newly arrived immigrants reintroduced Chinese elements into peranakan culture. After the fall of the Chinese Empire in 1910, the Chinese community felt the appeal of Chinese nationalism. The victory of Chinese Communism in the 1940s brought new political pressures. Because of its relative wealth, the Chinese community could take better advantage than other Javanese of the Western education offered by Christian missionary schools. Thus, the older peranakan community was pulled simultaneously by the attractions of a changing Chinese homeland and closer contact with twentieth-century European culture.

The Dutch were still another alien segment in Indies society. On the eve of the Second World War, they made up only about 1 percent of the total population, but their wealth and power made them far more important. Their proportion was comparatively large for the colonial world, about that of the British community in Kenya, far greater than the British presence in Nigeria or India, but far less than the presence of Europeans in Algeria or South Africa.

Like the Chinese, the Dutch were internally divided. One group, equivalent to the peranakan Chinese, had come to make the Indies their home; others came out to the islands for a set number of years and returned to Europe at the end of the tour. Like the Chinese, the Dutch often arrived as single men, which gave rise to an important Eurasian community. Some Eurasians merged into broader East Indian society, but the great majority identified with their Dutch ancestry. They sought a Dutch education and emphasized their Dutch heritage, even though the Dutch from Europe tended to look down on them.

Cultural and Social Integration

Some aspects of cultural pluralism became more accentuated during his first half of the twentieth century, while others diminished. The Dutch presence provided a political framework within which many different forms of social, intellectual, and cultural integration took place. This amalgamation was partly an Indies version of the global homogenization of cultures taking place everywhere during the twentieth century, but some aspects were peculiar to the Netherlands Indies.

Language was a potential source of unity and disunity alike. Javanese was, of course, the language with the greatest number of speakers, and some minorities resented it for that reason alone. Dutch was the language of Western-style education, and it was commonly used by a growing body of government workers. From the early part of this century, however, the common trade language was peninsular Malay, even though it was home language for only a few people in the Netherlands Indies. It was useful because it was related to the major languages of all the islands, and being the home language for no larger part of the population, it was more neutral and acceptable than Javanese. In this respect, it resembled other successful trade languages that became the lingua franca over a large area, Swahili in East Africa, for example. Malay was already so widespread at the time of independence that the government simply declared it to be the national language and renamed it Indonesian.

Religion was another problem element in social and cultural integration. In the 1800s, the Dutch distrusted Islam as a possible rallying point for protest, but after the turn of the century, they shifted to encouragement in the belief that Islam was better than paganism, and they hoped to win over important Muslim clerics. They remained opposed to political pan-Islamic movements, but the mixture of encouragement and neutrality made it possible for Islam to spread into the less Muslim parts of the colony.

The Dutch also used Western-style education as a cultural weapon, designed to lure the better educated segments of society to a Western view of the world, not always specifically Christian, but secular rather than Islamic. On Java, where Western-style education was most readily available, many men from the petty nobility managed to enter a new élite of educated people. They tended to separate themselves from the values of their fathers and to demand the kind of social status that similar education gave to the Dutch themselves. They wanted, most of all, government jobs, and they were disillusioned when their education did not bring them the social mobility they thought they deserved.

These aspirations reflected an older Javanese tradition of rising in society through government service. In former times, the court provided the opportunity. Now it was the bureaucracy. Money counted for less among the Javanese élite than it did in the outer islands, where wealth was a normal way to power and status. The Chinese merchants on Java had money but not position. For some Javanese, education was a way to power through government, at first in the strong government the Dutch had begun to create, later through the modernizing bureaucracy of an independent Indonesia. In either case, they were not unfriendly to socialism.

Élite attitudes on the outer islands were mixed but different from those of the Javanese. The authority allowed them under forms of indirect rule had been greater than on Java, and the non-Javanese élites more often found it possible to use their control over the land to enter a variety of entrepreneurial activities of a kind left to the Chinese on Java. The contrast can be overdrawn, but the leadership on the outer islands was more interested in preserving its inherited political position and more interested in the ownership of property than in positions of command. Conflict between these attitudes often clouded relations between Indonesian regions, both before and after independence.

Peasant Discontents

The élites on Java and elsewhere were separated from the mass of the peasantry by substantial cultural differences as well as by status and wealth. Peasant discontent was recurrent and widespread, going far back into the precolonial period. Islamic leadership sometimes claimed the peasantry as its own, and nationalist leaders were to do the same. Communists sometimes tried to rally the peasantry; at other times, they depended more on the urban working class as their principal base. Neither tactic worked very well, nor do peasant movements figure as a sign of nascent nationalist discontent. Some peasant movements interacted with nationalist sentiments from the towns, but most were the kind of protest movement that was ubiquitous even before the emergence of modernizing nationalism. Even afterward, peasant movements were somewhat separate, with their roots and life in particular peasant communities.

One such movement began on Java in the 1880s, founded by an illiterate Javanese peasant named Surotiko Samin. Samin asked his followers to withdraw from the society around them and to refuse to pay taxes, perform work services for the state, or participate in Muslim prayer and marriage ceremonies. The government rounded up Samin and his chief lieutenants and exiled them from Java in 1907 and 1908, but the movement kept on, with an occasional flurry of activity

241

decades later. It was entirely nonviolent, without marked characteristics of a millenarian movement, and with no real significance for the nationalist movement.

Other peasant movements were millennial. They sometimes called up the Muslim idea of a mahdi, who would come to purify Islam, or more often, a pre-Muslim Javanese belief in the arrival of a "just prince" a *Ratu Adil,* who would establish a new kingdom with justice for all and prosperity without taxation or oppression. The earliest versions of this belief were associated with the interior Javanese courts and nobilities, but over time it spread to other orders of society. By the 1800s, a man of peasant origin would emerge from time to time to proclaim himself, or someone else, to be the Ratu Adil. There were many such movements, sometimes four or five in different parts of Java in a single year. Sometimes the millennial prophecy could take on antiforeign or anti-Dutch overtones. None of these movements provided effective opposition to the government, but they contained beliefs that could later be used to mobilize the peasantry for other and more modernizing ends.

The Rise of an Independence Movement

The independence movement in the Netherlands Indies that arose against this background was different from equivalent movements in Ghana or British India. The Dutch were more alarmed than the British by nationalist stirrings, and they were more rigorous in suppressing them. The significant element in the Netherlands Indies was the amalgamation of diverse movements and traditions; the millennial Ratu Adil theme could join Muslim religious loyalties, modern nationalism, and the international communist movement of the interwar period. The result bore some resemblance to the millennial movements in Melanesia, but it was also a particular and unique outgrowth of the Javanese cultural and social setting.

The Indonesian nationalist movement began in a manner typical of the times. Cultural associations proliferated in the first decade of the twentieth century, often with names such as Young Java or Young Celebes, recalling the European nationalism of Young Ireland or the Young Turks. At the next stage, in 1912, Western-educated intellectuals founded a Western-style political party, the Indies Party. It appealed mainly to the Eurasian minority and died out after a short time, but it was the first organization to identity itself with the Netherlands Indies as a political entity.

The first large-scale movement had a different base. It began as Sarekat Dagang Islam, or Muslim Trading Association, but it soon became called Sarekat Islam, simply Muslim Association. The title was indicative; the early membership was drawn from Javanese merchants who sought joint action against their Chinese competitors. The reference to Islam was principally to identify commercial interests that were neither Chinese nor European.

Sarekat Islam began by organizing boycotts of Chinese merchants, but it then broadened its activity and drew in a larger membership. From its foundation in 1912, it rose to nearly 400,000 members in two years, dropped off slightly, and then rose against to about 500,000 in 1918, about 10 percent from outside Java. A charismatic leader, Umar Said Tjokroaminoto, was instrumental in the change of direction, playing down the anti-Chinese element and introducing the promise of a better life through political independence. His large following in a society still comparatively untouched by mass education came in part because he seemed to fulfill the prophecies of a Ratu Adil.

After 1918, Sarekat Islam lost support, partly because it had no achievements to show, but also because of new political currents in the early 1920s, marked by the initial successes of the Russian Revolution; one part of Sarekat Islam detached itself in 1920 to found the Indies Communist Party (PKI) and join the Soviet International. The majority drifted toward a more moderate socialism, retaining its Islamic identity, and Tjokroaminoto accommodated these new political tendencies by claiming that the true Ratu Adil would come, not in human form but in the form of socialism.

But Sarekat Islam had already begun to fall apart. From 1919, the Dutch colonial government began overt suppression, arresting some of the more radical leaders, but that action was hardly necessary. Struggles broke out within individual branches, chiefly between the more religious leadership and those who leaned toward the PKI. When the PKI won, as it often did, the peasantry departed and the religious leadership drifted off to organizations such as the Muhammadiyah. For a time, the PKI was left as the main descendant of the mass movement, but it too became divided. In 1926–7, when one of its segments tried to stage a violent revolution in western Java and parts of Sumatra, the government quickly used the revolt as grounds for rounding up the leaders and smashing the party once and for all.

Also in 1927, Sukarno appeared on the scene as a significant nationalist leader. He had been a follower of Tjokroaminoto and was married for a time to his daughter. He now founded the Indies National Party (PNI), regaining some of the appeal of the early Sarekat Islam. Sukarno was an excellent orator who could reach the peasantry, and he was noted for what some describe as a special indirection or fuzziness of thought, admired in the Javanese tradition, which made it possible for him to attract people of very diverse opinions, and he was also adept at manipulating the symbols of the "just prince". His own thought developed during the 1930s in the aim of creating a synthesis of nationalism, Marxism, and Islam. He, like other nationalist leaders of the time, spent much of the prewar decade in jail or in exile.

Before the Second World War, several diverse tendencies of opposition to Dutch rule had come into existence, too disunited to be identified as broad Indies national sentiment, and there is small evidence that people generally believed they belonged to an Indonesian nation. The Japanese invasion was to change the situation dramatically.

The Japanese Occupation

The Japanese occupation began in March 1942, as part of the broader conquest of Southeast Asia. It ended equally suddenly after the Japanese surrender in August 1945. In the occupation years, the Japanese unintentionally set the scene for the Indonesian Revolution of 1945–50, and it was then that a potential Indonesian nation came into existence. Formal independence can be dated from the renunciation of Dutch claims in December 1949.

Japanese wartime propaganda claimed an anti-imperialist mission, but their occupation proved to be a simply a substitution of control by one industrial power for control by another. The long-term Japanese aims for Indonesia were shifting and uncertain, but their short-term goal was to use the islands and their resources as a stepping stone to victory in the war against the Western Allies.

The Japanese regime was actually more oppressive than the Dutch. They sent as many as 300,000 peasants to work as forced laborers

near the battle fronts in New Guinea and the Southeast Asian mainland, from which few returned. They interned the Dutch, removed
Eurasians from administrative posts, and filled the highest offices with
Japanese. Since they could not spare enough skilled manpower to staff
a whole new administration, they filled most subordinate posts with
Indonesians who had some Western education. These were from the
same urban groups that had often been involved in the nationalist
movements and as before, they were also somewhat removed from the
mass of the population. The most prominent were Sukarno and
Mohammed Hatta, who had been active nationalists in the prewar
decades and who now came out publicly for the Japanese as a way of
promoting the nationalist cause.

The Japanese also departed from the military policy of the
Netherlands Indies and other colonial powers. They recruited a well
trained and well armed military force of about 65,000, serving under
Indonesian officers except at the highest levels. The officer corps was
drawn from the same urban and educated echelons that staffed the
civilian bureaucracy. These civilian and military leaders who emerged
during the occupation were to step forward on the Japanese surrender
to become the nucleus of whatever government emerged. Otherwise,
the Japanese regime affected different social groups in different ways.
The old élites generally moved down in power and prestige, the
Western-educated moved up, Eurasians moved down, the Dutch
moved both down and out, and the peasants moved down economically but not otherwise.

As the Japanese regime collapsed, these changes had important consequences. Those whom the Japanese pushed down wanted to regain
their position. Those whom the Japanese pushed up wanted to preserve their gains, and they knew they would lose out if the Dutch
returned. In this situation a return to the old status quo was virtually
impossible. And this would have been true whether or not there had
been a prewar independence movement.

The End of the War and the Pemuda Movement

When the Japanese Empire surrendered, the Allied reconquest of
Southeast Asia had barely begun. The Japanese army of occupation
was still in place, but the Japanese were not anxious to fight in what

was no longer their quarrel. Sukarno and Hatta proclaimed independence for the Republic of Indonesia with a paper constitution and began to create an Indonesian government before the Dutch could return in force. In the first brief phases, the new republic made a clean sweep. Sukarno took over some units of the force the Japanese had organized to form a new Indonesian army and began to accept the surrender of the Japanese, capturing their arms in the process.

In September 1945, the British, who had the only nearby Allied force, landed in Indonesia to accept the surrender of the Japanese garrison, acting in theory for the Netherlands. The Dutch government, having spent the war in exile in Britain, was only then in the process of regaining control of the Netherlands itself. Ironically, the Allied troops included Indians, who found themselves fighting the Indonesian Republic at the very moment Britain was organizing the transfer of power in India itself.

The Republic of Indonesia under the older generation of urban nationalists was not only overcome by the Allied invasion; it was overtaken by new revolutionary Indonesian movements from below. Especially in the period between September 1945 and the summer of 1946, most of Java and Sumatra fell into a period of confused fighting among various contenders, usually lumped together as the *pemuda* movement. Pemuda means youth, but it was not a youth movement in the ordinary Western sense. The pemuda is a phase in the male Javanese life cycle, consisting of instruction and purification in preparation for adulthood. At this time of crisis, instead of withdrawing from the world these young activists set out in a variety of different directions, often fighting against whatever forces the republic could muster, against the Allied invaders, or occasionally against the Japanese, who mainly acted only in self-defense.

The core of pemuda activity was on Java and Sumatra. Sometimes, civil war broke out between conflicting pemuda forces, of which there were hundreds in Indonesia at the time. In Acheh, in northern Sumatra, the war turned into an attack led by Muslim religious leaders on the petty aristocratic families that had formerly dominated the region. In the East coast residency of Sumatra, the movement has been called a social revolution, actually a form of peasants' revolt, where mobs under local communist leadership attacked the wealthy and any who lived in a Western style.

Elsewhere, some Eurasians attempted to take the Dutch side in an effort to regain their past privileges.

By mid-1946, a sort of government was restored in most areas, and the republic appeared to be in control. The Dutch now took over from their British stand-ins, trying to reestablish their imperial position, at first through diplomacy, seeking to play off the outer islands against Java. By 1947, when that diplomatic effort had failed, they shifted to an all-out military attack on Java, and they won. They captured Sukarno and Hatta and most of the island, but the military victory was not enough. In the end, the unpopularity of the war in Holland, plus international pressure from the emerging superpowers, defeated their effort to reestablish contol in spite of victory in the field. The Netherlands recognized the independence of Indonesia in December 1949. The puppet governments they had set up in South Sulawesi and parts of Sumatra soon fell to military attack by the Indonesian Republic.

The political outcome was a victory for the urban, secular leaders who had guided the nationalist movement since the 1920s. The important shift during the eight years of war and revolution was the percolation of nationalist and religious politics into the mass of the population, who were previously untouched by larger political issues. Most people now recognized that they were Indonesian, though it was mainly change in focus without altering the social and political difference that had existed all along. The conflicts between Java and the outer islands continued, and so did ethnic conflicts. The fighting in the revolutionary years sometimes sharpened the religious difference between the santri and the abangan in Javanese villages, and fierce disputes about the future of the country continued to be fought out even while the war against the Dutch was still in progress. In 1948, for example, elements of the PKI and others from the left wing of the nationalist movement revolted against the republic at Madiun in east Java, and the republic suppressed the revolt by force of arms.

Indonesian Politics After Independence

Indonesia began its political life under an oligarchy, which nevertheless respected democratic forms. There were no elections at first, but in 1945, the republican leaders organized the Central National

Committee (KNIP), initiating a form of political participation by representative leaders. The principal leaders were a quadrumvirate made up of Sukarno, Sutan Sjharir, Mohammed Hatta, and Amir Sjarifuddin. Within that framework, cabinets rose and fell, political alliances were made and broken, and a form of parliamentary political life went on.

In 1955, the first elections were contested by the political parties already active. These parties were different from the usual pattern of a political spectrum ranging from radical to conservative or from left to right. There were actually two different kinds of parties, those mainly concerned with religious issues and those mainly concerned with sociopolitical issues. Representatives of Muslim opinion, such as those who had joined Sarekat Islam, were now divided between two parties. One, Masjumi, had come to represent the by now conservative modernist Islamic circles that had belonged to the Muhammadiyah. A second and larger Muslim party was known as *Nahdatul Ulama,* usually translated as the Muslim Teachers Party. It stood for Islamic fundamentalism, with the goal of making Indonesia into a Muslim state. As the name suggests, the core of the movement was the class of village intellectuals and clerics. The two major Muslim parties together carried 43 percent of the big-party vote in the election of 1955, giving abundant evidence that Islam was still an important political force.

Meanwhile, the more secular-minded were attracted to parties representing secular solutions to Indonesia's problems – the Communists (PKI), Socialists (PSI), and Sukarno's Nationalists (PNI). The secular parties together held a slight majority in the 1955 election, with the largest vote going to the PNI and Sukarno, though he won only a minority overall. His major support was on Java, the center of Dutch power and the center of the revolution. The PKI's showing was more surprising. It had rebelled against the republic in 1948, after which the party was disgraced and some of its old-time leadership were shot, but the party was not suppressed. It remained in Parliament and still had a quarter of the big-party vote in the 1955 elections.

Politics and the Military

Another important political factor, in Indonesia as in most postcolonial countries, was the military. Most newly independent regimes began with whatever defense force the colonial power had seen fit to create. For security, colonial powers often recruited their armies from people on the fringes, as the Dutch had recruited "Ambonese and other islanders" in preference to Javanese. During the Japanese occupation, however, these forces were disbanded, and the Japanese recruited the new defense force mainly on Java. This force provided the initial core of the new Indonesian army, but most of the army as it emerged in the early 1950s was organized by young men who had been associated with the pemuda movement. The result was a seeming reversal of the familiar pattern of the professional military going into politics; the Indonesian military were political to begin with, and it was their political interests that took them into the military.

As a result, the army was political force in a particular way. In the mid-1940s it was first of all a youth movement, led by men who were mostly under thirty. The republican leadership as a whole, including Sukarno and the leaders of the PKI, belonged to another generation, some of whom had been in political life since the days of Sarekat Islam, and were drawn from the Dutch-educated class with an urban base. The military, by contrast, were mainly drawn from the Javanese small towns, with rarely more than a secondary education, and they knew little Dutch. In religion, they tended to be Muslims, but abangan, not santri. And, since most of the fighting was on Java, they tended to be Javanese and not outer islanders.

Guided Democracy

The move toward democracy began and ended with the election of 1955, though parliamentary struggles continued for a few years, parallel to other struggles within the politicized army. No faction dominated the assembly; civilian control over the army was weak, and the high command had only loose control over regional commanders.

Late in 1956, a number of local commanders on Sumatra and again on South Sulawesi took over the local government as a protest against Javanese domination. The crisis deepened in 1958, when the Masjumi and the PSI joined to form a revolutionary government based in West Sumatra. A short civil war followed, and the central government won easily, though some guerrilla activity occurred as late as 1961. These events led to the virtual suppression of both the Masjumi and the Socialists.

In 1959 Sukarno abolished the constitution and instituted a regime he called *Guided Democracy,* and he tried to unite the country behind a new ideology he called *Nasakom,* linking nationalism, Islam, and communism. Political power now belonged mainly to Sukarno's PNI, with growing influence from PKI. In fact, it was a tripartite alliance of strange bedfellows, uniting the two major socioeconomic parties with the support of the army.

Sukarno tried to build support for his government with aggressive foreign policy, which included the expropriation of all Dutch property, the annexation of West Irian (initially under Dutch control), an unsuccessful attack on Malaysian territory on Borneo, an entente with the People's Republic of China, and resignation from the United Nations. His move to the left encouraged the growth of the PKI under D.N. Aidit, but it did not unite the country. It tended to alienate the aristocratic groups in the outer islands, the army, and a good many of the old-line PNI people, who still regarded the PKI as potential rebels, who might use force to establish their sole control of the government. In addition, Sukarno was now in his sixties, which provoked background struggles for power in the event of his death.

The Coup and Countercoup of 1965

Toward the end of 1965, two rival groups were preparing for armed conflict. An anticommunist group was led by General Nasution, the minister of war. Simultaneously, the PKI under Aidit was also preparing a coup or a countercoup, depending on circumstances. The PKI struck first, killed some six opposition generals, and briefly captured Jakarta and Yogyakarta. The army then struck back. It may not have intended genocide, but that is what followed. The slaughter began with the army's counterattack on the PKI and its followers, but others joined in. In the ensuing carnage, people turned their fury on any long-standing enemies who came to hand.

The initial cause of the violence appears to have been a growing conviction among the officer corps that they were in danger of their own lives if the PKI took power. They certainly feared for their jobs. Many of the older social and personal tensions that had been building under the independence movement were still evident in the guerrilla warfare that sprang up. The army was the main perpetrator, but the Nahdatul

Ulama had its own militia on Java and was responsible for many killings. Muhammadiyah also joined in with a fatwah declaring the elimination of PKI to be a religious duty, though it is hard to isolate the religious element from other possible motives. To be santri, for example, could also indicate village leadership roles, and abangan could be taken to be not only irreligious but possible communists. The original coup occurred on September 30, 1965. Within two months, Aidit was dead and the revolt was over, but the mass murders continued into January 1966.

The numbers killed were reported variously, but the total seems in retrospect to be about 800,000 dead in central and east Java and 100,000 each in Bali and Sumatra, or a total of about one million. The successful military incarcerated another group of somewhat more than one million in concentration camps on remote islands. A few hundred were still in prison as late as 1995, though 1,353,000 were officially reported released by 1992.

Many questions are still unanswered, such as the role of the United States government, though it is clear that American diplomats in Jakarta were in close touch with the new army command under General Suharto. Some reports said that an initial list of people to be killed was assembled by the American embassy. Certainly, the American government and press were generally in favor of the coup, and the U.S. government made no protest against the killings. At that period, it was preparing its military intervention in Vietnam.

The new government under Suharto represented the military, especially the generation that had led the pemuda movement. General Suharto allowed Sukarno to continue as president with only the trappings of office and under virtual house arrest. It was only on March 12, 1967 that the army felt strong enough finally to remove him as president.

General Suharto was 46 when he took office, therefore in his early twenties when the revolution began. He retained power as leader of a military oligarchy until 1998, when popular unrest forced him to resign. During these decades, the military introduced its own brand of guided democracy, which it called the New Order. It suppressed the PKI and some other political movements, but the PNI continued to function. The new government even permitted elections for representatives with limited powers. The elections, even though controlled, served as a useful way of keeping the government informed and giving the people an impression that their views were heard. The military, indeed, set up its own party, the Joint Secretariat of Functional Groups, called Golkar.

Many of the stresses and strains that had troubled Indonesia throughout the century were still present, but for at least three decades the modernizing oligarchy of aging revolutionaries provided a moderately stable regime and period of successful economic growth. In many other respects Indonesia failed to achieve the hopes many shared in the first decades of independence. It achieved a measure of per capita economic growth, but the gains were unevenly distributed. Its human rights record was marred by the political genocide of the 1960s, and the promise of democratic government, always in the background, was never a reality. For all the spotty record, the territory the Dutch had put together as the Netherlands Indies managed to become, as Indonesia, a more viable national state than many would have dared to predict in 1945.

Further Reading

Reid, Anthony, *Indonesian National Revolution, 1945–50* (Hawthorn, Australia: Longman, 1974).

Reid, Anthony, *The Last Stand of Asian Autonomies: Responses to Modernity in the Diverse States of Southeast Asia and Korea, 1750–1900* (London: Macmillan, 1997).

Steinberg, David Joel, *In Search of Southeast Asia: A Modern History,* rev. ed. (Honolulu: University of Hawaii Press, 1987).

Dahn, Bernhard, *History of Indonesia in the Twentieth Century* (New York: Praeger, 1971).

14

Paths to Viable Independence: Ghana

The process of nation building in Ghana was very different from that of Indonesia and probably more successful. Ghana is unlike Indonesia in many respects. The two countries are on nearly opposite sides of the globe. Their cultures have little in common. Though both are tropical, all of the Gold Coast hinterland that became Ghana is a region of shifting cultivation, with no wet-rice areas capable of sustaining a dense population. The territory of Indonesia is diverse and scattered over a vast area, with a population at independence of about 85 million, against 6 million for Ghana. Yet, for all of these differences, their historical experience has much in common.

Both regions first met Europeans in the guise of trading-post empires. The Portuguese fort at Elmina on the Gold Coast was begun in 1481, and Columbus visited there before he went on to discover America. The Dutch base at Batavia on Java was established in 1619, more than a century later. The move from trade enclaves to territorial empire, however, had much the same timing for the Gold Coast and the Netherlands Indies. In spite of an earlier Dutch overrule on Java, their conquest of northern Sumatra occurred simultaneously with the British seizure of Asante and its hinterland in the 1890s. In Ghana and the Netherlands Indies alike, anticolonial protest movements appeared even before the conquest was complete, and both countries gained formal independence in the 1950s.

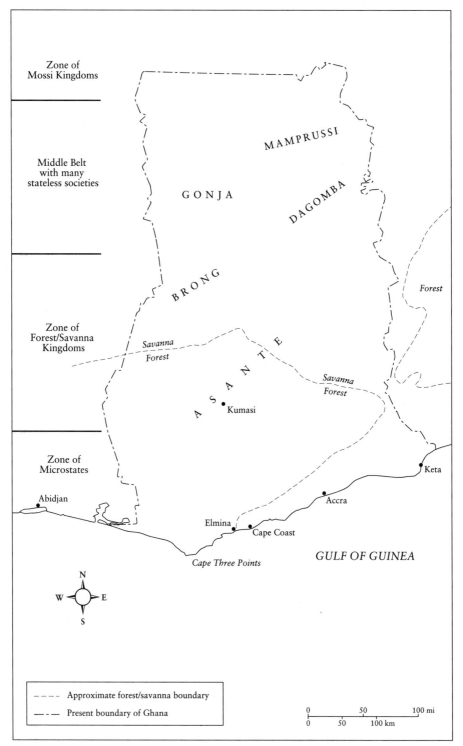

Zone of
Mossi Kingdoms

Middle Belt
with many
stateless societies

Zone of
Forest/Savanna
Kingdoms

Zone of
Microstates

MAMPRUSSI

G O N J A

DAGOMBA

B R O N G

Forest

Savanna
Forest

Savanna
Forest

A S A N T E

Kumasi

Keta

Abidjan

Accra

Elmina

Cape Coast

Cape Three Points

GULF OF GUINEA

N
W — E
S

- - - - Approximate forest/savanna boundary
— · — Present boundary of Ghana

0   50   100 mi
0   50   100 km

Ghana: vegetation zones and precolonial polities.

254

Territory and People

It is often said that African boundaries are artificial, created by the colonial powers during the scramble for Africa. This is partly true, but the boundaries laid down by agreement among Europeans have tended to remain in place up to the present. For that matter, many other boundaries are equally artificial; the boundaries often came first, and a sense of national identity grew up within them. This was true of Indonesia, as it was of Ghana – and of the United States.

The territory that came to be Ghana was made up of four different kinds of precolonial polity, arranged as a rough layer cake, with parallel layers stretching east to west along the Gulf of Guinea. As the British advanced from the coast into the hinterland, they incorporated part of each new zone in turn as a political subdivision of the Gold Coast, though treating each in turn somewhat differently (See map, page 254).

The first of these zones was that of the microstates south of Asante, where Europeans presence had long been limited to the trading forts, and sovereignty over these forts was ambiguous. Most of the European trading firms paid a form of rent or subsidy to the nearby African rulers. The first clear case of territorial annexation came only in 1874, when Great Britain annexed the belt of trading states along the coast, giving the Gold Coast Colony its first official existence.

To use the term *state* in this context is a problem for African history. Colonial rulers and outsiders sometimes used the term *tribe,* but that usage is clearly pejorative, and without precise meaning in any case. State on the other hand, suggests a more elaborate government than existed anywhere before the beginning of the industrial age. Kingdom may be a more accurate term, but these units were so small that they are sometimes called microstates. The number of these units differed with the political fortunes of individual polities. There were perhaps 40 in the 1500s, and with some consolidation over time, the number was reduced to about 20 in the early 1800s. These had much in common culturally, though a major linguistic division separated the broadly Akan culture area to the west and center from the Ga and Adangme culture areas in Accra and its hinterland eastward to the Volta River.

These small kingdoms had an active commerce long before the Europeans arrived from the sea. The coastal people exchanged salt and fish from the ocean for textiles and other products of the interior. From the 1480s, contact with Europe by sea increased the volume of north-south trade, but it continued to be entirely in African hands. Unlike the Dutch in Batavia, Europeans exerted little political control over the hinterland. They controlled only the trade castles and a number of unfortified trading posts. The forts were not mainly for protection from Africans but from other Europeans, whose raids were a potential threat, since a large part of the trade was in gold.

By the 1700s, the Europeans had built some twenty-five stone forts along the Gold Coast, an average of one every ten miles, not counting a number of unfortified or lightly fortified out-stations. The number seems extravagant, but each European power wanted protected access to as many as possible of the paths leading into the interior. The Portuguese were the first to arrive but dropped out after a time, to be replaced by interspersed posts managed by Dutch, British, Danes, and occasionally others.

The zone representing the second layer began about thirty to fifty miles inland. It was a region of somewhat larger kingdoms, located partly in the forest belt and partly beyond it in the southern savanna. Before about 1600, they had been as small as the coastal kingdoms. By the early 1800s, political consolidation had made Asante the largest of this group, but others, for example Denkyira in the west and Akwamu in the east, had also been absorbing their smaller neighbors before they, in turn, were absorbed by Asante. Asante, like the coastal kingdoms, was essentially Akan in culture. By the early 1800s, however, Asante power extended well beyond the Akan culture area, eastward across the Volta River and northward until it reached in some instances beyond the present frontier of Ghana.

The region north of Asante proper formed the third layer, more complex and varied than the first two. The natural vegetation, even in northern Asante, changes from tropical forest into savanna or open woodland. In Nigeria next door, this region is sometimes called the "middle belt" between the rain forest to the south and the full savanna to the north. In the case of Ghana, however, the region equivalent to the Nigerian north lay mainly across the frontier in Burkina Faso. Like the Nigerian middle belts, the Ghanaian north tended to be more sparsely populated, politically fragmented, and ethnically diverse than its neighboring regions to the north and south. In included some stateless societies, which survived into the twentieth century; the Tallensi would be the classic example. They are classified as stateless because they had no centralized political authority, not because they lacked political authority altogether. Instead, political institutions were based on kinship, with an intricate balance between lineages and shifting responsibilities for settling conflict, rather than having conflicts resolved by some kind of central judicial figure. The web of these kinship relations stretched out from a single village to a sequence of other isolated villages, so that there was often no clear territorial limit to the extent of these relationships.

Finally, to the north of the middle belt was a zone of more substantial savanna kingdoms, which stretched from the Atlantic to Lake Chad and beyond. The people to the north of Ghana were dominantly Mossi in culture, centered in present-day Burkina Faso, though their influence often extended to the south of the present frontier.

Political Consolidation in the Interior

None of these societies – coastal, forest, or savanna – was static. Part of the political consolidation that had been going on for centuries was the product of developing trade routes. The Akan goldfields in the south were a source of monetary metal exported very broadly, reaching North Africa and Europe even before European mariners reached the coast. People called Juula, which is simply the Mande word for merchant, had for several centuries been establishing their political dominance in the region north and west of Asante. They introduced Islam to the area. Other horse-mounted Mande used the Juula route of entry to advance into present-day northern Ghana, where they established the kingdom of Gonja. Still other cavalrymen, this time non-Muslim, entered the region from the north and northeast, founding other small kingdoms associated with the Mossi kingdoms in present-day Burkina Faso.

The most crucial changes, however, were not political. Trade brought knowledge of other societies and other ways of doing things. It brought Islam and with it literacy. Muslim scholars not only spread their religion, but they were useful, even to non-Muslim rulers, as scribes and officials. By the 1700s, Muslim traders sometimes appeared on the coast, and Islam gained converts as far south as Asante.

Political consolidation was not only an episode of conquest and overrule. The rise of Asante is the most spectacular example of a process that can be called precolonial nation building. Asante began as one of the numerous Akan microstates of the forest zone and its savanna fringe. These kingdoms tended to have a quasi-elective chieftancy, based on a constitutional balance between a series of lineages, expressed through a distribution of political power between a chief, a council of important men, the queen mother, and the body of commoners. There were also slaves, though they held no significant political power beyond that delegated to them by their masters. The office of the king was partly religious, since he was charged with intercession between living people and their departed ancestors, whose spirits were symbolically represented by the carved wooden stool upon which the king sat at ceremonial occasions. A new stool was made for each reign, and the stools of past monarchs were preserved in the stool house, equivalent to a royal museum preserving the crown of each past monarch. The articulating core of legitimacy was kinship and the union of the present with the past through the ancestors, who were the particular representatives of each lineage and each kingdom in the general world of spirits.

It was hard to join these tiny kingdoms together when each king represented the ancestors of a particular group. In the late 1600s, however, a king of Kumasi, or Kumasehene, and his advisors devised a symbol of a wider unity. This was a golden stool, which theoretically descended from heaven and represented the ancestors of all people within a new kingdom then being formed out of a military alliance. This state was Asante, and the king of Kumasi became the Asantehene, or king of the whole confederation as it then was. The Asantehene, however, did not sit on the golden stool. Because it represented the whole people rather than an individual ruler, it was displayed on a stool of its own.

In 1700, Asante defeated Denkyira and became the most important consolidated state of the forest belt, with a general council as well as a general military and judicial system, but leaving each of the incorporated kingdoms – now become provinces – its own identity and symbols of kinship and loyalty. Asante expansion continued into the mid-1800s, but the conquered territories were treated in a number of different ways. Some that were Akan in culture joined as integral parts of the Asante kingdom. Several of the coastal Akan microstates were also annexed in theory, but they were not integral parts of the Asante state. They were mainly left to run their own affairs, and they were not asked to contribute to Asante armies on campaign. In a sense, they were protectorates. Asante also conquered several kingdoms to the north, beyond the region of Akan culture, but it treated them still differently. It forced them to recognize their subordination and to pay tribute, but otherwise it allowed them to run their internal affairs. These subordinate northern territories included such major kingdoms as Gonja and Dagomba.

Over this century and a half of expansion, Asante created a new administrative structure, including titled posts controlled by the Asantehene but having authority over subordinate kingdoms. The political system was rudimentary by European standards of the time, but some authorities have seen it as the beginning of a bureaucracy.

Political Consolidation on the Coast

In the early 1800s, a similar pattern of political consolidation took place among the coastal microstates, mainly in response to the threat of Asante expansion. They turned to the European forts for assistance, although, in earlier centuries when the slave trade flourished, the coastal forts had been very lightly manned and were no match for their African neighbors. Their commanders were nevertheless inevitably involved in the political affairs of the region. With the abolition of the British slave trade in 1809, there was little reason to maintain fortified coastal points, but they nevertheless persisted and became more than ever involved in local quarrels. In 1824–6, the British entered an anti-Asante alliance of coastal states, and a British governor was killed in combat against Asante forces.

The initiative for this alliance was African, but a series of British governors acquiesced, ostensibly to protect the security of trade. By the 1830s, a British governor began to settle disputes among the Fante peoples around Cape Coast Castle, the principal British post. Then, beginning in 1844, he formalized this influence by signing a series of treaties, called bonds. These provided legal cover for a relationship that was growing informally, sometimes called a judicial protectorate. British officials gained the authority to try certain cases involving the rulers or subjects of different microstates, but the cases were tried under African, not English law, a reversal of the extraterritorial jurisdiction that Europeans often demanded elsewhere, as in the Ottoman Empire or the Chinese treaty posts.

In 1850 the British bought the Danish forts, but by the late 1860s, the British themselves began planning to evacuate all their posts with the threat of Asante power still in the background. With this uncertainty, one initiative for political consolidation came from Western-educated Africans, who had already begun to appear in various capacities around the forts. An educated Eurafrican served as acting governor in the 1840s, and others were high in the administration. One of the leaders of the consolidation was Dr. J. A. B. Horton, who had been born further east in what was to become Nigeria, captured as a slave, recaptured at sea by the British, educated in England, and was now a regular member of the British Army Medical Service stationed on the Gold Coast.

Horton and his friends sponsored a new form of political confederation embracing all the microstates in the central and western Gold Coast south of Asante. The plan retained the traditional rulers but balanced their authority against other powers assigned to the Western-educated intelligentsia. In retrospect, this plan for a Fante confederation can be recognized as a variety of modernizing nationalism, advocated before the Gold Coast Colony was actually founded.

The British officials in the forts were neutral at first, and the new state, known as the Mankessim Confederation after its capital town, came briefly into existence and began to set up a rudimentary administration. British policy changed, however, in the early 1870s, when Britain not only decided to retain the forts but began negotiations to purchase of the Dutch forts as well. In 1873 Asante once again invaded the coastal kingdoms and occupied much of the territory right down to the forts themselves. The British responded by a lightning invasion of Asante, which advanced to Kumasi, burned the capital, and then withdrew. Britain then moved to protect its future position by unilateral annexation of all of the coastal kingdoms in the hinterland of the coastal forts and south of Asante, creating the Gold Coast Colony. It was the first clear and unequivocal claim to European sovereignty outside the forts themselves. Political consolidation that had previously been undertaken on African initiative passed to that of the Europeans.

Competitive Annexation and the Establishment
of Boundaries

In the conventional view of African political geography, the Europeans drew their colonial frontiers in ignorance of African reality, and this was sometimes the case. The British on the Gold Coast, however, began by annexing whole African kingdoms, much as Asante had done in the past, and in 1895 the British added Asante itself as a unit. North of Asante, European rivalries were more important in determining where boundaries were drawn. The French were pushing north from the Ivory Coast on the west, and the Germans were moving north from Togo to the east. As a result, whereas boundaries of the southern Gold Coast had been established by agreement, however involuntary, between the British and African authorities, the northern boundaries were established by agreement between the British and other Europeans. Africans learned the result after the fact.

In spite of the intervention of European diplomacy, more than half of the people of Ghana are Akan in culture and speak closely related languages, but other Akan-speaking kingdoms in the present Côte d'Ivoire had avoided Asante control, so that about a quarter of all the Akan peoples are actually outside of Ghana. The Ga and Adangme peoples of the Accra region, on the other hand, are entirely within Ghana.

The Ewe people, on the eastern frontier to the north of Accra, were never a political unit, though they have strong cultural ties and have sometimes supported a claim that they should all be included in a single modern state. They were nevertheless first divided between the Gold Coast and German Togoland. Then in 1919, Togo was split into separate French and British mandates under the League of Nations, and British Togoland became part of Ghana. Today, about two-thirds of all Ewe live in Ghana, though the other third became the dominant ethnic group in the independent Togo, successor of the French mandate. North of Asante, most of the kingdoms of Gonja and Dagomba ended up as part of Ghana, and several small ethnic groups are entirely within Ghana, though the Mossi and Mamprusi of the far north form part of cultural groupings now centered in Burkina Faso.

The majority of Ghanaians thus are Akan in culture. The ancestors of present-day Ghanaians had more in common culturally than the

261

ancestors of present-day French had when they were first annexed to the French monarchy. Asante was clearly a nation with traditions of historical unity, and these persist as an aspect of Ghanaian political life. The dominance of Akan culture in Ghana is not far different from that of Java in Indonesia, though the resulting political strains between the Akan and the rest have been far less serious than those between Java and the outer islands.

British Policy and Political Modernization

British attitudes toward the cultures of tropical Africa began to change sharply about the 1880s. Before that, and especially in the decades from the 1830s through the 1870s, most British observers took it for granted that Africa should be "civilized," and that civilization would spread, not by British rule but by the less direct influence of missionaries and commercial contact. While some kind of British presence in the coastal forts was taken for granted, few advocated or foresaw the kind of conquest and annexation that was to take place in the last decades of the century.

By the 1890s, when Britain annexed Asante and the Northern Territories, these assumptions had changed dramatically. The British no longer looked with favor on Africans in high office in the colonies. They foresaw a future of quasi-permanent trusteeship, which they were to exercise over people they thought of as inferior to themselves. They began systematically to exclude African doctors from the West African medical service, to restrict the appointment of Africans to senior grades in the civil service, and to distrust Africans who were beginning to play a role in colonial politics, especially the qualified lawyers returned from education in Britain to practice before the colonial courts. The new ideal of trusteeship was not opposed to modernization for tropical Africa or for the Gold Coast, but it was based on the belief that improvements in the immediate future would be reached more surely with British officials in charge and Africans in an inferior position.

It was hard to turn back all the gains Africans had made in the Gold Coast Colony, but it was possible to deal more firmly with the newly annexed territories. They were not made a part of the Colony but organized separately as Ashanti, the Northern Territories, and British

Togoland. The new territories were organized as "protectorates," where British law did not necessarily prevail. Their inhabitants lacked the rights of British subjects and were only "British-protected persons," and that distinction could be significant. Such imperial legislation as the 1833 act emancipating slaves in the British Empire applied only to colonies, not to protectorates. Trial by jury was also prohibited for a time in the new territories, for fear of "trouble making" by British-trained African lawyers.

Throughout the decades from the 1890s into the 1920s, the policy of Indirect Rule (with initial capitals) was broadly seen in Britain as the best way to govern African colonies. It was cheap to rule through the chiefs, but advocates of Indirect Rule in this period urged it on other grounds as well, deeply influenced by the European racism of that period. The argument that Africans should be governed "in their own way" was not mere cultural relativism. Few British, if any, believed that the African way was as good as the British way, but many, if not most, believed that it was appropriate for people of inferior racial status.

As a result of these new attitudes in the era of trusteeship, the spread of Western styles of government was virtually frozen from about 1895 until after the Second World War. In spite of representative elections in the Colony, democratic government was not extended to Ashanti, the Northern Territories, or Togo until 1946, less than ten years before independence.

Education

In spite of the neglect of any preparation for self-government, the British administration contributed to nation building in other, unforeseen ways. One crucial decision involved language policy. Several alternatives were available. Education could be in the home language of students, a mixture of home language and English, or English from the outset. It could also be in an African language other than the home language of the students. Swahili served in this way in Kenya and Tanzania, even though it was the home language of only a tiny minority. Bazaar Malay became Indonesian in much the same way. Malay served Indonesia well, but some authorities on African language policy built their ideas on racist assumptions. They considered that African languages, though inferior to English, were better suited to the racial status of Africans. One official even suggested that primary education in the Gold Coast should be in Hausa, the principal language of northern Nigeria and totally unrelated linguistically to any Gold Coast language.

Fortunately for the Gold Coast, the decision was made for English as the language of education, including the important missionary schools, and English opened up the wealth of knowledge available in the world beyond Africa. English became the sole language of administration and the language of command for the Gold Coast Regiment. Colonial officials, furthermore, were not strongly encouraged to learn Twi, the most widely spoken Akan language. A different policy was often adopted elsewhere in British Africa, where officials were expected to show a level of competence in an African language. Swahili was the language of command for the King's African Rifles in East Africa, and administrators in Northern Nigeria had to know some Hausa, sometimes Fulani as well.

The policy of encouraging Africans to develop "in their own way" was in fact a contradiction; few administrators really approved of the African way. In spite of lip service to the African way, government offices and British businesses and missions employed only people who knew how to do things in the British way. The exclusive employment of British expatriates would have been prohibitively expensive, so that Africans were inevitably trained to do the work. This created a practical need for more schools, including secondary schools. Secondary schools were often boarding schools that brought together people from different regions, and as in Britain, school experience forged networks of friendship and cooperation. Even outside such old-boy networks, the uniform language of education brought increasing numbers into contact, no matter what their ethnic background; it was this educated élite that initiated the independence movement. By the 1930s, this élite had enough in common to constitute a rudimentary nation, even though it was still limited to a small part of the population.

Possible Frameworks for Independence

Ghana became independent within the boundaries of the Gold Coast Colony and attached protectorates, but that choice was not inevitable.

People can choose which of several possible nations they feel they belong to. Just as the political leaders in the Ottoman Empire had a choice between an Ottoman identity, an Islamic identity, and the Turkish identity that finally emerged as the present Turkish Republic, political leaders in the Gold Coast had a similar range of choices, and a variety of different feelings of solidarity were present and have continued, changing through time.

Racial stereotypes in most European attitudes toward sub-Saharan Africa were one factor determining a choice of identity. One African response was to seek solidarity with others subject to similar slurs, linking all people of sub-Saharan Africa and the diaspora, and the Pan-Africanism that arose from this source continues to be an effective appeal in some circumstances. The goal of a United States of Africa, however, has never been strong. A possible unit based on British West Africa surfaced briefly in the 1920s as a kind of federation of Gambia, Sierra Leone, the Gold Coast, and Nigeria, but this idea lost its appeal as the actual time of independence approached.

Units smaller than the present-day Ghana have also been possibilities. A breakdown into the constituent territories of the Colony proper, Ashanti, British Togoland, and the Northern Territories, was theoretically possible. A pan-Akan movement, seeking to unite people of Akan culture in Côte d'Ivoire and the Gold Coast, was also possible, but no such movement emerged. The only claims for extending nationhood beyond the Gold Coast frontiers was a pan-Ewe movement to unite people divided between British and French mandates, but even that movement was weak. The strongest movement with an ethnic base within the Gold Coast was the National Liberation Movement to restore the Asante kingdom. It flourished only briefly in the mid-1950s, though Asante loyalty can still be a political force.

Kwame Nkrumah is often quoted as saying: "Seek ye first the political kingdom, and all else shall be added unto you." This statement is often interpreted to mean that Africans should first seek independence within whatever political boundaries the Europeans recognized and to work for other goals within this framework. African political geography has been quite stable since independence, unusually so given the often noted lack of "natural frontiers." But the Gold Coast of the early 1950s was on its way to becoming a viable independent state, partly because it was a long-term natural region and partly because of political and economic integration over the past half-century.

Integration: Geographical and Economic

The region the Europeans called the Gold Coast was physically distinct in ways that are not immediately apparent. It took its name from the Akan goldfields, which supplied gold for export by sea as early as the 1480s. The goldfields had attracted merchants from the north even earlier, so maritime contact opened up commercial relations extending from the Gulf of Guinea to the Sahara fringe and beyond.

The Gold Coast was physically distinct for another reason. The east-west coast of the Gulf of Guinea has prevailing winds and current from the west, and most of it is marked by a steeply shelving beach and a strong surf, making it difficult to land. Along the Gold Coast, however, a series of rocky headlands provide a comparatively safe landing place on the leeward side of each. At a few points such as Elmina, the headland sheltered a cove, which made the landing from surf boats easier still. Fortifications on the rocky headlands could protect landing places. This fact, in combination with the need to protect gold awaiting shipment, encouraged the Europeans to build the dense array of fortifications that was unmatched elsewhere in tropical West Africa. To the east and west of the Gold Coast, landing was more difficult, but lagoons often lay parallel to the coast only a few miles inland. Here and there, significant openings to the sea, such as those at Lagos and later Abidjan, would became major ports.

The Gold Coast had no equivalent natural harbor, but in 1898 the British administration began building an artificial harbor at Takoradi to serve as the base for a railroad, which reached Kumasi in 1919 and was later extended to Accra. Motor roads later supplemented and extended the rail links to the principal shipping point at Takoradi, and the roads deteriorated as they approached the colonial boundaries All were designed to pull the movement of goods and people into the colonial network, just as language and education created a parallel framework for intellectual life.

Economic growth moved through a succession of export crops. In the mid-1800s, the chief export had been palm products, which were still 44 percent of exports in 1891, with wild rubber at 30 percent.

Both products came from the forests of the interior, and African merchants organized their shipment to the coast, where European firms bought them and bulked them for export.

Twenty years later, gold and cocoa had replaced rubber and palm products. By 1911, new mining technology brought the value of gold to 30 percent of total exports, while the value of cocoa exports reached 46 percent. The two decades ending in 1911 were the boom decades of the Gold Coast entry into the world economy, in which estimated per capita income doubled. It would take a half-century, until 1960, for per capita income to double again.

Much of the capital for the increased gold production was European, but Africans supplied the capital and commercial skills for the trade in rubber and palm products, extended in time to cocoa as well. Many of the active traders began with a base in coastal cities such as Cape Coast or Accra, but some came from interior towns in Ashanti. Whatever their initial base, African merchants worked increasingly in a commercial setting that tended to expand beyond a local region toward the colonial boundaries.

This broadening field of economic integration may be seen in the history of cocoa cultivation. This was an American crop, unknown in the Gold Coast before the 1890s, when it was introduced from the offshore island of Bioko, then a Spanish colony. It then spread through the forested regions of the Gold Coast almost entirely on the initiative of African farmers. By 1920, the Gold Coast had become the largest producer of cocoa for the world market.

The spread of cocoa is an entrepreneurial success story. One center was the Akwapim ridge, inland from Accra. Akwapim farmers were already involved in cash-crop farming, and responding to the market opportunity, they shifted quickly to planting cocoa. Cocoa is a tree crop, which takes some years from planting to production, but, once in production, it paid handsomely, giving the farmer capital to expand. Where suitable land was not available nearby, the first generation of cocoa farmers tended set out new cocoa farms at a distance on land secured from the local chief. Within a few decades, the original cocoa entrepreneurs from Akwapim had farms scattered through the forest zone, as cocoa growing spread to the west and north. Much the same system was established in other early centers of cocoa production such as Ashanti. Within a few decades, the entrepreneurial range of cocoa farmers had grown, like that of African merchants, far beyond the range of their precolonial political unit.

Cocoa was limited to the forest belt, but it drew people into a broader and more integrated agricultural economy. As the increase in cocoa growing led to a labor shortage in the forest zone, it drew people in from the north, especially at harvest time. The savanna country north of the forest has a six-month dry season, when little agricultural work is possible, and this slack time coincided with the cocoa harvest. Northerners then began to move south for a few months of wage labor, but what began as a seasonal move could stretch into years, and migrants, who were single men at first, began to bring families. In time, the lure of the cocoa region drew people from beyond the Gold Coast frontier, from present-day Burkina Faso and other French colonies. The migratory patterns that began early in the century and continued over many decades helped to integrate the people of the Northern Territories into the centers of economic development in the forest belt and the coast.

Political Action

Signs of modernizing nationalism can be detected even before Britain established the Gold Coast Colony in 1874 – at least as far back and the projected Mankessim confederation and continuing to the end of the century and beyond – but it was confined to a small group of Western-educated Africans. Newspapers, published in English under African editors, began to appear. African lawyers and doctors, trained in Britain, joined the older élite groups of merchants and traditional chiefs.

These groups were not in close touch with the villagers of the countryside, but they could sometimes influence the colonial government. Even though most members of the Legislative Council were government officials, a small minority were appointed unofficial members, so that the council could act as a kind of local parliament with limited powers. The three principal towns on the coast also had elected municipal governments whose powers were also limited, but they too acted as a forum for colonial politics.

On occasion, local élite groups could also appeal effectively to the central government in London, as they did in the 1890s by organizing the Aborigines Rights Protective Society. The occasion was a land controversy brought on by the effort of the colonial government to declare its title to idle lands. A group of traditional chiefs and African lawyers responded in the name of African rights. The issue was not so much one of the Africans' right to the land as the chiefs' right to sell off stool lands to concession hunters. The rights of the African peasant occupier of the land hardly entered the controversy, but the outcome showed that traditional chiefs and African lawyers, acting together, could influence government policies.

The élite groups all across British West Africa had more interests in common with similar groups in other British colonies than they had with the peasantry of the hinterland. The National Congress of British West Africa, founded in 1920, with branches in all four British colonies, was not nationalist in the sense of demanding independence, but it served the interests of a modernizing élite. Its program called for a West African Court of Appeals, abolition of racial discrimination in the civil service, and establishment of a West African University – issues that appealed to the Western-educated minority and were appropriate to an all-West African framework, though they said little about the interests of a broader public in any individual colony. At first, the traditional chiefs and the Western-educated worked together. They were often relatives. By the 1920s, however, cooperation between the two groups began to break down as new colonial policies entered the picture, supporting the claims of the chiefs to speak for the people at large and denying the similar claims of the urban educated classes.

The new constitution of 1925, which was to last till 1946, represented the high noon of British policy for the Gold Coast. Though it was not a large step forward, it did more for educated Africans than early colonial governments had done. It tripled the number of higher government posts open to Africans, though that was to be the last increase before the Second World War. For the Colony proper, where people had the status of British subjects, a Provincial Councils of Chiefs sat as a kind of House of Lords in each of the provinces, and the Provincial Councils chose six of their number to represent them in the Legislative Council. African voters in each of the three large towns that already had elected municipal governments were allowed to elect a member of the Legislative Council. Otherwise, local government was in the hands of the chiefs, in the Colony as elsewhere. Ashanti, Togo, and the Northern Territories were not even represented in the Legislative Council.

This policy represented a variant of the tactics the Dutch followed in Indonesia in these same decades, based on a similar fear of the Western-educated and their demands for a role in the colonial government. The goal of British policy was the stability of Indirect Rule, assigning local authority to the chiefs, as the Dutch did to the regents. The chiefs were to function as the visible government, with British overrule only in the background. The Gold Coast government, however, was more benign than the Dutch in Indonesia, perhaps because of the lesser threat of violent revolt. The Gold Coast still had no mass movements such as Sarekat Islam and nothing equivalent to the Communist revolt of 1926 on Java. Yet, in spite of government intentions and in spite of the Great Depression, the number and influence of the educated Africans increased during the interwar years. The vast majority of the educated in the Gold Coast had no more than an elementary education, but it was enough to qualify them for employment in the European sector of business and governments.

The principal evidence of opposition rising from below the élite level came from two sources. One was an incipient antiaristocratic movement at a very local level. Most Akan chieftancies had a constitutional procedure for removing chiefs from offices on the initiative of commoners. The process, called *destoolment,* continued under British overrule and was used far more frequently during the interwar decades than it had been in the past. Commoners were also generally more active in stool politics than they had been, though this activity expressed local resentments rather than a demand for independence.

The second kind of organized opposition was directed not against the colonial government but against price fixing by the European firms exporting cocoa. Like the prices of other primary products in the depression years, the price of cocoa dropped faster and further than the prices of the manufactured goods the Gold Coast imported. The number of European firms exporting cocoa was only about fifteen to twenty, and they could easily arrange among themselves the prices they would offer in Africa. They made open agreements every few years, and African growers had little recourse, though they occasionally tried a hold-up, or refusal to sell at less than a higher, competitive price, but most such efforts were local and ineffectual.

When, in the summer of 1937, the export firms again agreed to fix prices, farmers unions, some traditional chiefs, and a variety of others organized a hold-up for the Gold Coast Colony and Ashanti and Togo as well. They were successful in withholding virtually the entire crop, and they followed the hold-up with a boycott against the offending firms. In April 1938 the European firms surrendered and agreed to buy the cocoa crop at a competitive price.

At the time, the Gold Coast had more than 100,000 individual cocoa farmers. Effective organization of such a large number for common action was not only a victory on an economic issue but also an indicator for the future, even though a decade was to pass before similar organization was to take political form as an independence movement.

The War and the Coming of Independence

As everywhere else in the world, the Second World War accelerated the pace of change in some matters, retarded it in others, and deflected the direction of change in still others. West Africa was little involved in direct military action. Only the French territories under the Vichy French government were indirectly controlled by the Axis powers, and they were no considerable threat to their British-controlled neighbors as long as Allied navies controlled the sea lanes. West African troops, however, participated in the war overseas in East Africa and Burma. Along with the rest of British West Africa, the Gold Coast passed through the usual wartime pattern of conscription, dislocation, and shortages of consumer goods.

With the end of the war, generalized discontent increased and took on a new tone. War veterans returning from experience abroad lent a new perspective. The availability of cheap short-wave radios made it possible for even the most distant and illiterate villages to have a wealth of information about the outside world, and from a variety of sources. The rapid transition toward independence in India and Pakistan was known, and so were the emerging nationalist revolutions in Southeast Asia.

Two competing nationalist parties appeared in the Gold Coast. The United Gold Coast Convention (UGCC), under J. B. Danquah, represented the older generation of élite leaders, who expected to be allowed to take over the colonial government in due course, as the Congress Party was doing in India. The Convention People's Party (CPP) was a more radical movement organized by Kwame Nkrumah and associates to contest the position of the UGCC, based on broader popular support from all classes.

Meanwhile, the British Government in the late 1940s had already decided on a course of action for the West African colonies. It planned to concede independence in the foreseeable future, but with a period of delay to negotiate details and to promote a form of independence that would be in Britain's interest. Serious riots first broke out in Gold Coast towns in 1948. Kwame Nkrumah was jailed briefly in 1950, but the CPP emerged victorious over the UGCC in the first popular elections, and Nkrumah was freed from jail to become His Majesty's Chief Minister.

Through all these changes during the crisis decade from 1948 to 1957, the ethnic element in politics was more subdued than it was elsewhere in tropical Africa. Neither the UGCC nor the CPP was an ethnically based party. Only a relatively weak National Liberation Movement spoke for Asante separatism briefly in the mid-1950s, and independence was formally in achieved in 1957 on the basis of the British or Canadian system, where the executive was responsible to the elected members of Parliament. The Gold Coast was renamed Ghana, after the ancient African kingdom on the desert edge to the north. It had, at independence, the highest per capita national income in tropical Africa, and it was widely believed to have great promise as a future leader of democratic Africa.

That promise lasted less than a decade. In 1960, Nkrumah's CPP voted democratically, if unconstitutionally, to turn the country into a one-party state and a republic, which lasted till 1966. Some democratic elements remained within the CPP, but Nkrumah gradually expelled or dismissed the principal original leadership, moving the party to the left and simultaneously increasing his personal power. By the mid-1960s, the economic modernization promised at the time of independence had not only failed to appear, but some sectors of the economy began to decline. Shortages of food and other consumer goods became evident, and real wages were falling. The CPP government also alienated particular ethnic groups. By 1966, the situation had so far deteriorated that the army felt free to intervene. A military oligarchy removed Nkrumah from office and abolished the one-party government, but the new regime was no more democratic than its predecessor.

The coup of 1966 was the first of a sequence of coups and counter-coups dominated by the military, and the period of economic decline was to continue until the late 1980s. The fate of Ghana over these decades was neither markedly more favorable nor less favorable than that of other newly independent states in tropical Africa over the same period. The early promise of democracy was achieved only fitfully any-where. Authoritarian governments often ruled in their own interests, and many made serious mistakes in economic policy. It is hard to avoid the irony of Nkrumah's statement of 1957, already quoted in another context: "Seek ye first the political kingdom, and all things shall be added unto you." Insofar as all things included economic mod-ernization, leading to high production and consumption per capita, they were not forthcoming.

In spite of major differences between Ghana and Indonesia, some comparative generalizations stand out, the most significant being the unifying role of overrule by a single colonial state. The experience of the Gold Coast and the Netherlands Indies shows, however, that what happened within the framework of the colonial state was not entirely, or even mostly, what the Europeans directed. They set the framework, including such important features as a common language for inter-communication above the local level, a single educational system, and a political entity within which economic change took place. Once the framework was set, much of the initiative belonged to the local people, beginning with the intermediaries whom the authorities chose to rule in their name, and spreading in time to many and diverse segments of society.

The political entity that emerged in these two cases has lasted for some decades, but this was not always the case in the postcolonial world. Several of the former colonial states broke apart. Even Indonesian unity was occasionally maintained only by force, and future violence between regions remains a possibility. The interaction of the European rulers and local people was nevertheless a complex and intricate process over the decades, which worked toward the pro-duction of a more cohesive and viable society than could have been reliably predicted a century or so sooner.

Further Reading:

Ajayi, J. F. A., and Michael Crowder, *History of West Africa,* vol II, Second ed. (Harlow, U.K.: Longman, 1974).

Austin, Dennis, *Politics in Ghana, 1946–1960* (Oxford: Clarendon Press, 1964).

Hill, Polly, *The Migrant Cocoa-Farmers of Southern Ghana: A study in Rural Capitalism* (Cambridge, U.K.: Cambridge University Press, 1963).

Kimble, David, *A Political History of Ghana 1850–1928* (Oxford: Clarendon Press, 1963).

Mazrui, Ali A., (ed.), *UNESCO General History of Africa, Volume VIII. Africa Since 1935* (Berkeley: University of California Press, 1993).

Wilks, Ivor, *Asante in the Nineteenth Century* (Cambridge, U.K.: Cambridge University Press, 1975).

Afterword

The rise of the West to a position of dominance is one of the most important developments in world history in recent centuries. Many have dealt with it in some central framework, whether that of European history alone, that of economic history, or that of a world system. Everyone writing about the world beyond Europe has had to take the rise of the West into account, consciously or unconsciously.

For the world outside the West, the central fact in this period is the challenge of the West and the responses to it, and many historians have dealt with this subject in different ways. These essays represent a particular approach, with an emphasis on the non-Western responses seen through case studies of particular problems, rather than through broad themes and overall generalizations. The choice of cases may appear idiosyncratic, but it was not random. They were chosen in an effort to look at a wide a variety of responses within a brief scope. The sharp shift in subject matter from a discussion of administrative decisions and their outcomes in Southeast Asia to the affairs of Maya peasants in Yucatan was intentional. Both views represent only a part of the whole reality, but together they represent part of the variety of what actually took place. The essays seek to incorporate the perspective of world history, not by telling all the important things that happened anywhere – a clear impossibility – but by telling about a selection of different things that happened in different places within the framework of different human societies.

The essays also incorporate a strand of comparative history, with a particular attitude about which comparisons are valuable. Some compare situations that are similar; others look for common threads in dissimilar circumstance. Both approaches have their uses. The comparison of modernization in Japan and Turkey is familiar and has been dealt with by others from different points of view. The comparison of the Yaqui and the Maya has a common factor in Spanish and Mexican overrule. Other comparisons are intentionally distant – like the responses of the modernizing oligarchies in Japan and Buganda. Such comparisons of events in distant parts of the world can help to rise above the immediate cultural setting. The chapter about culture change in plural societies as distant and South Africa and Soviet Central Asia had that objective, and so did the pair of chapters about nation-building in Ghana and Indonesia.

Some common themes emerge in retrospect. One is a reflection on historical change in general; it is the gap between the intentions of the major actors and the actual outcomes. A second is the degree to which the European empires were actually run by non-Europeans. This is not merely a reflection of the fact that Europe conquered the world mainly with non-European soldiers, though this, too, was the case, but also of the fact that the actual rule over the conquered societies was far more in local hands than in those of European administrators. This theme merges with a third. Cultural borrowing from the West was rarely a matter of wholesale imitation. The borrowed cultural items were fitted into an existing cultural matrix. Nor was the globalization of world cultures a one-way street; Western borrowing from the non-West is less obvious to Westerners because it, too, was fitted into a familiar Western cultural matrix.

One final theme has been more explicit, though not emphasized because it is so obvious. Human cultures have been converging since the invention of agriculture, and the convergence has been more rapid than ever since the beginning of the industrial era. The controversial question is: What, if anything, should or could be done about it? The homogenization of human cultures is only one part of a broader pattern of change making the world a less varied place than it used to be. Biological species are disappearing at a faster rate than ever before, and the technology that has come with the industrial age is largely to blame. Biologists are alarmed and would like to preserve as many species as possible. It is hard to advocate a similar course of action for human cultures, especially regarding cultures other than one's own. Globalization has some benefits, but it also has costs. Perhaps the place to begin is to be conscious that they exist.

Index

BELMONT UNIVERSITY LIBRARY